T0246489

THE TIME WE HAVE

Also by Michele Weldon

I Closed My Eyes

Writing to Save Your Life

Everyman News

Just Me and My Three Sons

Escape Points

Act Like You're Having a Good Time

THE TIME WE HAVE

ESSAYS ON PANDEMIC LIVING

MICHELE WELDON

NORTHWESTERN UNIVERSITY PRESS

EVANSTON, ILLINOIS

Northwestern University Press
www.nupress.northwestern.edu

Copyright © 2024 by Northwestern University. Published 2024 by
Northwestern University Press. All rights reserved.

Printed in the United States of America

10   9   8   7   6   5   4   3   2   1

Library of Congress Cataloging-in-Publication Data

Names: Weldon, Michele, 1958– author.
Title: The time we have : essays on pandemic living / Michele Weldon.
Description: Evanston, Illinois : Northwestern University Press, 2024.
Identifiers: LCCN 2024003122 | ISBN 9780810147348 (paperback) |
    ISBN 9780810147355 (ebook)
Subjects: LCSH: Weldon, Michele, 1958– | Women journalists—
    United States—Biography. | COVID–19 Pandemic, 2020——Personal
    narratives. | LCGFT: Essays.
Classification: LCC PN4874.W396 A5 2024 | DDC 070.92—dc23/
    eng/20240212
LC record available at https://lccn.loc.gov/2024003122

To Paul
and my three sons,
Weldon, Brendan, and Colin

One's life has value so long as one attributes value to the life of others, by means of love, friendship, indignation and compassion.

—Simone de Beauvoir

CONTENTS

PART THREE. THINGS

INTRODUCTION

COVID TERRIFIED ME. MOSTLY BECAUSE I WAS AFRAID I would die.

Many declared fear of the virus was politicized and that they would not surrender to fear, even as common sense demanded otherwise. But I was afraid—to my trembling, immunocompromised core. The fear has subsided and never led to inertia, but it is still here, like a lump in my throat that I can ignore, though sometimes it scorches every swallow.

Breathe.

That simplistic directive is offered as a quick antidote to sudden panic. But COVID kidnapped breath.

As a writer, mother, sister, colleague, and friend, I knew it was necessary to take in all available information, sort through buzzwords of social distancing and contact tracing, mitigate the dangers as well as possible, try not to escalate emotions, keep the fears compartmentalized and addressed, and never become fully immobilized.

At first I was only afraid of microbes, their unpredictability, thinking that masks and rubber gloves, antibacterial wipes, and hand sanitizer were weapons in this war—weapons I could buy and replace. I was afraid of touching the mail; I let it sit on the counter a day or two. I was afraid of breathing unmasked in public spaces. I was afraid my grown sons would get sick, though their strength, good health, and youth made me somewhat secure they would survive.

I was afraid of other people—as potential carriers and contaminators, but also as unpredictable warriors against truth.

I was afraid for other people. I feared for the safety and survival of health-care workers, initially covered head to toe in hazmat suits, goggles, and full masks, who were unfathomably brave—nearly four thousand died in the first year of COVID—as the world thanked them with sandwiches and treats. An American Medical Association study of thirty-one thousand health-care workers—physicians, nurses, and staff—showed that half of all of them felt burned out by the pandemic in the first six months of its reign.

The searing uncertainty born of the pandemic secured my belief that life is not guaranteed. Obviously, of course, but I have routinely handled my fears—harm, death, rejection, illness, heartbreak, cruelty, my incompetence, and any brand of catastrophe—as they happen. I do not shrink or shirk my need to respond and protect. I have waded through life phases of crisis or chaos by solving problems—or trying to.

Yes, even the notion that avoiding danger is feasible is a result of privilege, as many can't rely on their own survival walking down the street or ringing the wrong doorbell.

I am risk averse. Having picked up the shards of heartbreak decades ago to raise a family alone and survived breast cancer twice, I'm cautious in choosing friends and possible partners, saying no one hundred times to the one time I say yes; benefit of the doubt has an expiration date for me. I don't waste time on mediocre, nor do I seek out extremes. My modus operandi is to work toward the goal of conflict-free survival (thrival if possible) each day—as far as my choices and actions can determine my fate. And I know that only goes so far.

Elective fear is not recreational to me. An adventure does not have to involve heart-pounding anticipation of a narrow escape. I would never blindly jump into a situation that could possibly result in pain or harm to me or anyone—just for the adrenaline rush. I aim to be safe, to protect myself and my family. Some may say that is aggravatingly dull. That's perhaps true; I advised my friend Lisa years ago not to move to Afghanistan for work and love; she ignored me, and it turned out the move changed her life immeasurably for the better and filled it with love.

My fear aversion goes way back. I was afraid of roller coasters as a child of five or six when my parents would take my two brothers, my three sisters, and me to Kiddieland, a few miles west on North Avenue in Melrose Park, a suburb of Chicago, or the handful of times they treated us to Riverview, a Northwest Side amusement park that had great popcorn and cotton candy, though my father complained about how hard it was to find a parking space in the crowded lot.

I imagine the delirium everyone says they feel after climbing off a roller coaster or emerging from a capsule that catapults into the air before suddenly plunging is the automatic relief they feel because they survived. Never could I be an astronaut.

COVID was a cultural rollercoaster none of us wanted to climb aboard as passengers.

Not since I watched the Wicked Witch of the West appear from a puff of smoke in *The Wizard of Oz* (or the flying monkeys, dear God, the flying monkeys!) have I sought a fictional movie to terrify me. No *Halloween* movies, *Get Out*, *Nope*, *Scream*, or the recent apocalyptic movies and series like *The Last of Us*, and never in a million years *Nanny*. Agatha Christie or Hercule Poirot—including the many series bearing her name as well as those starring the character Poirot—and their streaming episodes are about as scary as I care to watch. Those and the finely crafted episodes of *Murder, She Wrote*, with the well-paced wisdom of the late Angela Lansbury; even angry she is calm.

No voluntary scares since my family of eight saw *The Exorcist* at the Lake Theater in Oak Park, Illinois, in 1973, when

I was a sophomore in high school and assumed demonic possession was feasible if you didn't go to Mass every week.

Raising three daredevil sons who when they were little craved roller coasters and so many more reckless expressions presented challenges. My goal as a single mom was to keep them safe—particularly in the face of their very foolish choices that occurred many times a day.

"Do not feed your brother nickels as a dare."

I did take them on the Ferris wheel at Navy Pier in Chicago and locked them into the rocking egg cartons—seat-belted into a false sense of security. I pinched my eyes closed even as we soared into the sky, slowly and surely, but surely not slowly enough for me. I imagine it was a luscious view of Lake Michigan, but I didn't see it. I gripped Colin's hand and tried not to think about the news stories of Ferris wheels—and ski lifts—first trapping passengers in the air for hours, then hoisting them to their deaths as the bucket's guardrails broke, ejecting passengers like rag dolls. Did I mention I don't ski?

Sustaining a life without precaution in the throes of a deadly pandemic felt like jumping onto a roller coaster. I preferred to avoid danger, waiting on the sidelines for the whirring to stop and reliable information to be posted. I prayed for relief in the form of a cure, a dissipation of the emergency, or at least products I could order online for contactless delivery that would keep me—us—safe and alive.

I followed the advice to mask up, vaxx up, get boosters, stay home, and avoid other people. But not everyone felt this way as COVID infiltrated—infested—our lives and the lives of everyone across the globe, against our wills and regardless of how we voted. COVID changed me. And the world.

* * *

IT'S A CLICHÉ THAT YOU ALWAYS REMEMBER WHERE YOU WERE when. You file away the facts of your location when something of historic note happens. The announcement of COVID as a national emergency. George Floyd's murder. Sandra Bland's death in a Texas jail cell while in police custody after a traffic stop for failing to use a turn signal. Tyre Nichols's murder video. Ukrainian president Volodymyr Zelenskyy's pre-Christmas address to Congress in 2022. The Uvalde shooting at Robb Elementary School. Barack Obama's inauguration. Whitney Houston's Super Bowl anthem. September 11. For my generation, the deaths of John F. Kennedy, Robert Kennedy, and Rev. Martin Luther King Jr.

When you witness news of a high magnitude earthquake— Turkey and Syria in early 2023—or a catastrophe such as the Israeli/Hamas war that started in October 2023, you perhaps remember the physicality of the moment: the place, the time, what you were doing, how it smelled, the sounds or colors of the surroundings, what you wore, and who you were with as you learned of an event or a tarnished discovery that tipped your realization of the truth about a person, place, or thing.

You are transformed, shape-shifted into the person you are after; all your life was before this. For a time, the rest of your life is the after. You can be broken. You can also be broken open in a process that is energizing, revealing, reshaping, and illuminating, unburdened. Newly immunized against harm, you can rebound with compassion, empathy, and an altered sense of how you fit in the world and what you owe to it. You can learn how to breathe—differently.

COVID offered such a moment—weeks, months, years of those moments stapled together into a ragtag notebook expanding to offer confusing conundrums and a chance to reconfigure belief systems.

For me, the before and after moment was March 14, 2020, when I understood that COVID-19 was changing life—mine and everyone else's—perhaps forever, as we are still discovering.

That shift was preceded by befuddling announcements from the president about COVID-19 arriving in the United States in

January 2020: "We have it totally under control. It's one person coming in from China. It's going to be just fine."

Over the next several weeks, the accumulation of danger signs engulfed most every minute as we tried to harness some understanding of this unprecedented whatever it was torpedoing through our lives—even if it attacked us through lettuce we forgot to wash or droplets circulating in the air from strangers on a bus.

It is in the air.

I wasn't one of those people who washed everything they bought at the grocery store before putting it away. But I was one of those people who let the nonperishables sit on the counter for hours before putting them away, thinking the nasty microbes would disappear as mysteriously as they arrived.

I watched the local news each morning and evening for updates of cases, deaths, hospitalizations. Newscasters stood before blue screens of numbers as if they were describing the timing of a tornado's arrival; the language and the tone were the same, if not the message.

Get somewhere safe.

On television, Illinois governor J. B. Pritzker offered dispassionate daily updates from a podium standing near a sign-language interpreter, Michael Albert, whose kinetic hands and emotionally raw expressions captured the anxiety many of us felt. In April, Pritzker and Chicago mayor Lori Lightfoot announced the opening of an emergency hospital with three thousand beds inside McCormick Place.

Each morning before starting work from my first-floor home office, my fear-tinged daily Google search for COVID news revealed an onslaught of the latest statistics on cases and deaths for every state and country in the world. My approach was to proceed with caution against an unknown, invisible force.

On March 12 of that year I arrived in Dallas to facilitate a day and a half of training for the OpEd Project, where I have been a mentor and coach since 2011. The day before the World

Health Organization had declared COVID a global pandemic, but the sessions were not canceled.

The next day, nineteen nonprofit and civic leaders and advocates arrived nervously in a classroom at the Wilson Historic District for the first day of training. One person stayed home and joined us on Zoom. We considered her overly cautious, but she had young children.

On that day President Donald Trump declared a national emergency when there were just 2,175 cases of COVID in the United States. Ten days later there would be 46,481 cases. On the last day of the month there would be nearly 200,000, about the same as the populations of Des Moines, Iowa, or Spokane, Washington.

That day in March, Dallas County judge Clay Lewis Jenkins declared Dallas in a state of emergency because there were five confirmed cases of COVID.

Five sick people. You could count them on one hand. Fit them in one car.

"This confirms what I have been worried about for quite some time—the virus is in our community already and, due to limited available testing, we frankly do not know how many people are impacted. The state of emergency is in effect for one week and may be extended in the future," Jenkins said to a reporter.

One week. We didn't have any idea what was to come.

The Cambria Hotel in downtown Dallas where my colleagues and I were staying alone and afraid in our own rooms had sanitizing wipes available at the front desk. No room service. The bar on the first floor was closed. I thought about the five cases—not deaths, but infections.

I wiped down all the surfaces in my room I could think might be contaminated by this strange acronym virus and threw the comforter on a chair. I dabbed my hands with the sanitizer I carried in my purse. I tried not to touch anything, taking a washcloth from the bathroom to click the TV remote and a wet wipe to touch the door handle to open the door. I pressed the elevator button with my sleeved elbow. Be careful. Mask up. Sanitize. Don't touch anyone or anything without rubber gloves. No one told me you needed to throw the rubber gloves away and not reuse them.

The following day we greeted each other, smiling through paper masks and offering elbow bumps. All gatherings of more than 500 people had been prohibited, according to Dallas mayor Eric Johnson: gatherings needed to be of 250 or fewer. We were meeting in a classroom with twenty-two people, three of us from the OpEd Project in Chicago and Los Angeles, plus nineteen local participants. The training ended about 2:00 P.M.

Were we safe enough?

Worried that the flight back to Chicago late that Saturday afternoon would be canceled, we wondered if we should rent a car. My colleague needed to be back in town for her son.

"We can drive straight through if we need to," I offered. I knew what it was like to have a son you were responsible for waiting for you to return from a work trip. My three sons were all grown.

The flight was not canceled, though other travelers at the Dallas Fort Worth airport seemed exaggeratedly nervous and suspicious. When I got to my seat—on the aisle—I wiped down the armrest and tray table with sanitizing wipes from my purse and looked askance at the person two seats over. We wore masks. No one spoke. Staff did not serve beverages. Or snacks.

That day my work and daily life fully changed.

In the first few months of the pandemic, it would have been unfathomable that just two years later the United States would see eighty million cases and nearly one million deaths. Later, online lists for vaccinations and test results were easy to find in a search, and Dr. Anthony Fauci of the National Institutes of Health felt like a reassuring uncle trying to keep everyone calm. By the start of 2023, there had been nearly eight hundred million cases worldwide and seven million deaths in 228 countries. Officials were arguing about the cause—a raccoon or dog at a Wuhan market or a lab leak, also in Wuhan?

By June 2020, two of my three grown sons had moved back home because of COVID concerns; they had been working remotely, paying high rents in crowded buildings—with elevators—where all the amenities were closed. It seemed safer for all of us; I was now working remotely as well. Brendan was living in Ohio and working remotely. At my house, Weldon and Colin worked and slept upstairs in makeshift home offices; daily encounters were within our small pod of family. We shared updates on virtual backdrops.

But then they would go out and visit friends, spend the weekends with friends. I was afraid of a virus they might bring home; I was sometimes afraid of them. We stayed physically away from each other, taking turns eating meals so as not to collide in the kitchen, maintaining six feet of distance when we were in the same room. We spoke loudly to each other across the hall.

When I dared leave the house weekly—masked—for the grocery store, I felt afraid that someone would spontaneously erupt in fury if a store clerk or customer asked them to wear a mask or step away. I made no eye contact and hastily bought the rationed toilet paper and antibacterial wipes, my head down, not wanting to incite anyone's ire. Breathe.

Excuse me. Thank you. Sorry.

Every interaction seemed to offer an incendiary fuse; a man in my neighborhood was caught on a phone camera in a racist tirade about a woman in line at Starbucks not wearing a mask.

Then I was afraid of me, of what I carried, the invisible virus possibly inside of me that I could house unwittingly, that I could infect someone I loved with, or even strangers. My brother Paul was four years into his diagnosis of multiple myeloma, and beginning in July 2020, he was hospitalized several times following seizures. Visiting him weekly and then daily required strict protocols; I had to protect him from me, as he was too sick for a vaccine. I could be responsible for giving him COVID that would kill him, and I would never forgive myself. On my visits, I sat six feet from him in his family room, masked.

I didn't travel for more than two years; when I drove with someone else, we wore masks and kept the windows open, regardless of how cold it was outside. If I did socialize, I met with friends outside—in backyards, parks, or on porches; everyone brought their own food and ate it separately, seated three or four feet away, each drinking from their own cans, cups, or bottles of water. In the colder months, we sat on porches bundled in parkas with hats, gloves, and firm resolve. We Zoomed dance parties. Friends who defied the odds and went to weddings hosted by people who declared COVID was a hoax all came down with the virus.

COVID turned our homes into cocoons. But isolated, alone, and afraid, we knew our homes could also be cages.

Pandemic restrictions offered permission to be more selective about who I spent time with. Forced into prioritizing activities and relationships, I could decide whether to keep or discard time spent with people or performing distractions that no longer made sense. Obligations became optional.

As the next months and years somersaulted over each other, the pandemic incited a vicious culture war of believers and skeptics, not just some mildly needing to be reassured, but an alternate nation of doubters fervently denying and acting out aggressively in the face of mandates, closures, rules, and restrictions. Some violently attacked bystanders in stores, parking lots, churches, schools—over requests to wear a mask or not stand so close.

In July of the pandemic's first year, a black-and-white video showed a frail-looking woman in a Hackensack, New Jersey, Staples store who was wearing a mask as she walked slowly with her cane toward the copy machine. After she asked a woman standing near her with a mask slung below her chin to pull up her mask, the woman shoved her to the ground. The woman who had been shoved later explained she had liver cancer and was immunocompromised.

A security guard in a Flint, Michigan, Family Dollar store was killed when a father returned to the store to shoot him in the head after he had asked the man's wife to put a mask on their daughter, per the store rules.

For months, thousands of maskless people of all ages protested in cities across the world, carrying signs about tyranny, freedom, hoaxes, and evil—screaming about conspiracies and shouting that forcing vaccinations and masks was a threat to civil liberty. The bizarre "fifteen-minute cities" theory was born out of textbook paranoia, claiming that QR codes and digital surveillance were controlling the universe.

When the unvaccinated died, there was what many called "death shaming," or a condescending head-shaking "I told you so." See what happens when you don't listen to the warnings?

Still, some claimed the deaths were fake.

"Have you gotten both your vaccines?" I asked a woman I had been friends with since our sons were in kindergarten almost thirty years earlier. One year into the pandemic, we ran into each other in the parking lot of a grocery store a few miles from my house.

"People are not dying from COVID; they're dying from other causes. This is all a lie."

I am not proud that I shouted at her. "That's so foolish; you have grandchildren. What if you get sick?"

She shouted back that I was gullible. We didn't speak for two years.

COVID became polarizing, not just within friend and family groups, but around the country; it was measurable in data that residents in red counties were less vaccinated than those in blue counties and that entire swaths of the country had higher rates of hospitalizations and fewer vaccinations. Whataboutism ran wild: COVID minimizers tried to present the equivalence of other dangers with the presumption, I guess, that you would become so frustrated you would cave in to the denials because it was easier than dousing the screaming flames of inaccuracies.

Some buttressed themselves against the truth, barricading their worldviews in denial. Millions refused to ingest the reality of COVID—dismissing the hand sanitizers in stores, masks on buses, calls from the emergency room, stories from friends and family about infections and hospitalizations. And deaths. Funerals no one could attend. Fathers, brothers, sisters, mothers, spouses, and grandparents who died alone in hospital rooms with no one nearby, loved ones FaceTiming their final breaths.

It was almost impossible to cognitively absorb that the pandemic was an unprecedented sci-fi-movie takeover of real life. A horror film with a scary narrative arc and an unclear ending, one I would never have chosen to watch.

In the winter of 2022, the triple pandemic bloomed. COVID. The flu. RSV, or respiratory syncytial virus. The large get-togethers for the December holidays were canceled in my family, even though Thanksgiving, just a few weeks earlier, hadn't been. And then came the variants. There is no assurance the effects of long COVID will not last forever. Some suffer for years after an initial diagnosis.

Life changed much less for me than for so many others in this country and around the world; I am aware of the stark contrasts. Mostly I was safe because I am privileged to choose to work remotely, uninterrupted. COVID infected and killed more Black, brown, Asian, and Indigenous people than white people for many reasons. I had a vaccine and two boosters and still got a mild case of COVID in the summer of 2022; I was tired and didn't feel much like eating. I took over-the-counter drugs for congestion and isolated myself, napped between work meetings and deadlines, grateful for the insulation.

The virus did not choose its hosts; the systems blocked access to testing, vaccinations, treatment, and hospitalizations. Blockades were historic, socioeconomic, and geographic—upheld by a deserved mistrust. Multigenerational homes prohibited social distancing, safe isolation, and quarantining. Demands on essential workers in high-risk environments doomed thousands. Many kept working because they had to; some died because of that need.

Zip codes, ethnicity, and race determined who lived and who died from COVID: who had access to hospitalizations and treatment, who was trapped in a nursing home or a prison, and who was or was not believed when they described their symptoms. You could not quarantine safely in your home if you did not have a room or a home of your own to quarantine in safely. Or if you lived with multiple family members or roommates.

The Kaiser Family Foundation reported two years into the pandemic that "Black, Hispanic, and American Indian and Alaskan Native people have experienced higher rates of COVID-19 infection and death compared to white people, particularly when accounting for age across racial and ethnic groups. People of color are disproportionately impacted by surges caused by new variants, with disparities widening during these periods, particularly for infection rates."

The layered mental health impact was staggering. US Surgeon General Dr. Vivek H. Murthy wrote in a *New York Times* opinion piece in April 2023 that half of all Americans experience loneliness, and that is partially due to COVID. The country is in a crisis of social disconnection, he wrote, "an epidemic of loneliness" resulting in higher incidence of stroke, depression, heart disease, and more.

COVID, of course, impacted incomes, but some more than others. Opportunity Insights, an economic tracker powered by researchers from Harvard University, Brown University, and the Bill & Melinda Gates Foundation, found that by 2020, 35.3 percent of Americans earning less than $27,000 a year lost their jobs. For those earning more than $60,000 per year, the job loss rate was 12.8 percent. Two years later, those in the higher income bracket had a net gain of 10 percent in employment.

I obsessed in early 2021 about when and how to get vaccinated: I was a cancer survivor with preexisting conditions of asthma and high blood pressure. I spent hours online tabbing between different sites open trying to sign up for a vaccination at local government locations, drugstores, chain stores, hospitals, or park districts. Appointments filled up in seconds.

I was able to take the day off work, so I drove seven hours in one day—to Pekin, Illinois, and back from Chicago because no vaccines were available near me. Some had the means to fly their entire families on commercial flights to states where more vaccines were available. "Vaxx-cations," some called them; most did not have that luxury of money, childcare, or the time off work to take such trips. Until all my sons were fully vaccinated and boosted, I felt I could not sink into complacency.

Still, hope filtered through: Music washed the streets from balconies. The aroma of bread baking in ovens filled kitchens. Sketches drawn at on kitchen tables brought comfort. Neighbors put lawn chairs in their driveways and shouted greetings to each other.

I relished my Saturday art classes—the outdoor plein-air oil-painting classes I took in the summer of 2020, then the online classes in 2021 and 2022. On Saturdays I could escape, banish the worry, and complete something wholly separate from COVID thoughts for a few hours. I could pretend that finding the right shade of pink for the sky was the most important concern.

My 92nd Street Y figure-drawing instructor for the hybrid in-person and virtual class was amused that in my pastel drawing I did not put a mask on the model—who was indeed wearing one—as he posed in the classroom while I observed him on my laptop. I didn't want a sketch of someone in a mask; I gave him an imaginary smile.

The stretch of time since the dawn of the pandemic has, of course, been influenced by other news, declarations, warnings, starts, stops, horrors, wars, and tragedies that insert themselves into the consciousness of the world—unavoidably and permanently. COVID was the pall over it all.

We remember where we were when.

I was watching TV news in my bedroom at home on Tuesday, March 26, 2020—taking in the scene of protests in downtown

Chicago over the murder of George Floyd in Minneapolis the day before at the hands of four police officers. There was no justice rendered, even as the guilty verdicts and sentencings attempted to issue it. He could not breathe.

The news updates of thirteen-year-old Adam Toledo's murder by Chicago police scrolled across the bottom of the TV screen as I watched CNN from a bed in the ICU on April 17, 2021. I was admitted because I developed a pulmonary embolism unrelated to COVID. Less than one year later, the two police officers who killed Toledo and later another man, Anthony Alvarez, were not charged with any crimes.

I was scrolling through email trying to get a head start on my day when my niece Marirose called before 7:00 A.M. on May 24, 2021, to tell me that her father—my brother Paul—had died in his rented portable hospital bed in the den of their home. She was in the next room and had fallen asleep a few hours before. He stopped breathing. My closest friend in the world was gone. We all knew he was dying, and soon, but I was not fully prepared.

I was brushing my teeth in the upstairs bathroom with the pale gray tile when I stopped to witness photos from Kyiv, Ukraine, showing burned vehicles, explosions, fires, and billowing black clouds of smoke from shellings, as lines of Ukrainian refugees and their tears filled the TV screen on February 25, 2022.

In January 2023 I watched the video from police cameras of Tyre Nichols pleading for his mom feet from her home as Memphis police officers beat him after a simple traffic stop, his injuries so severe he died days later.

Sorting through email on the morning of April 4, 2023, I learned my good friend Lisa had died from stage 4 lung cancer. She had been diagnosed more than four years earlier. COVID had kept us apart since our last trip together in 2019.

Wherever we were, this is the time we have lived through; it is now the time we have to reflect upon it all.

Over a lifetime, certain words you hear and images you see embody so much irrefutable power they can never be erased. They can alter your life and your view of life. Thankfully—yes, dear God, thankfully—sometimes it is for the better: "I love you." "You won." "Yes." "Your test is negative." "They will recover."

Sometimes the words or images are unforeseen, sudden, inevitable, and the source of a wellspring of grief, pain, and loss that never fully evaporates but is only absorbed into something else: delayed, detained, condensed, hidden from view.

"He's gone." "I'm not coming back." "Your contract is not renewed."

Following this stretch of time the world experienced together unlike any in history, the reverberations continue; the long haul of COVID reaches into the future, disproportionately and unfairly affecting some communities and people in ways beyond their control.

It's still not fully known how the pandemic came to blossom and infect the planet, but by early 2023, there were fewer than two thousand deaths per week in the United States, a huge improvement. In April of that year President Joe Biden announced the end of the pandemic as a national emergency. The World Health Organization declared COVID no longer a public health emergency in May 2023, even as its reverberations may never end.

Some of the pandemic-forced changes in systems and for individuals are for the better—an editing of our overly complicated lives, a new vision of what is necessary and what is best, a reinvigorated closeness to family, friends, and partners. Resolutions to change the self and the world for the better, an appreciation of the value of social connection.

Will the pandemic scar us irrevocably? Perhaps. Some are forced to be branded by destruction, pain, and loss. Some choose to be tattooed by the truth and consoled by their resurrection from the disruption.

For many this phase in history brought about renewal, redemption, reinvention, and reincarnation. It reignited compassion and validated resilience, reteaching the value of each life and each breath. Many quit unfulfilling jobs—or were downsized, let go, fired—and found hobbies of passion that could be income producing. Some reconnected with partners, parents, and children who had been alienated by the busy circumstances of a life unslowed by pandemic halts. Without daily commutes to physical workplaces, many discovered ways to use their found hours for creating a life softened by imagination and creativity—and through those found sacred solace.

Breathe.

We are changed. It is prudent to examine the who, what, where, when, and why of those changes—even if that examination seems superficially incomplete.

The words that surround these moments, years quilted together with tattered episodes engorged in confusion, require us to tussle with them in a hunger for clear-eyed vision, begging to make these words into something we want to hear. Sometimes we are happy as a result, a welcome makeover.

Perhaps the yearning for truth is why Merriam-Webster's declared "authentic" the word of the year for 2023.

The words we assign these revelations matter. The investigation of our lives during those fragments of time—when truths reveal themselves naturally or the truth is forcibly dissected and made plain—can offer clarity, if not comfort or hope. Sometimes honoring the story is what we need. The stories bear the reassurance that yes, you remember it correctly, yes, yes, yes. And what's next? The stories nudge open the door to a fresh, untainted tomorrow. That was before. This is after. This is now.

Even if we were hand-tremblingly afraid, we remember where we were when because we want to respect the past as we scale the future to make it into something we dreamed possible.

COVID changed me. I am more sharply aware of my mortality. I am still risk averse, but I pause more frequently to observe, notice, witness, breathe. Life pushes you onto roller coasters you did not anticipate riding or choose as a willing passenger. But now I will buckle the seat belt, remain still in the moment, breathe deeply, and open my eyes to take in the view—unblinking, grateful for whatever and whomever I can see.

December 2023

PART ONE

PERSONS

1

CAPTION WRITER

THE TICKETS WERE SIXTY DOLLARS EACH, INCLUDING A bonus poster that we could choose from the gift shop after the exhibit; parking across the street was eighteen dollars for two hours.

The *Immersive Van Gogh* exhibit had been touted on social media since the pandemic started, and it was finally arriving in Chicago in 2021. I bought tickets several weeks ahead for Memorial Day weekend—the Sunday of the long weekend to be precise—for my three sons plus me, of course, since this was my idea. It would be safe; we would be masked and socially distanced. No worries.

I was eager to get out of the house and feel a semblance of joy. It had been a horrific week.

The visual and musical tribute to Vincent van Gogh, one of the greatest artists of the nineteenth century, spread its technical charms across the Germania Club, an unlikely venue but one I was familiar with. I went there in the '80s for parties or maybe just drinks, and my niece was married there in 2014.

In my niece Molly's wedding photos, I'm wearing a sleeveless black satiny dress with taupe swirls. I cannot zip the dress right now and, yes, I have articles of clothing in my closet that I use as barometers of how my body shape and physical health are doing. I try them on periodically. I do not believe I am the only person who does these things. No size shaming; I pay attention to the literal shape-shifting of my body and I try to stay healthy and aware. And also my doctors tell me to pay attention to my weight to minimize deeper health concerns.

The Germania Club was built in 1865, when Van Gogh was twelve, but there was no reference to him having any knowledge of the German Renaissance building, and he was Dutch, but these were only a few of the questions I had. That no one answered.

This Van Gogh immersive exhibit was playing in twenty-one cities—some of them predictable, New York, Los Angeles—but also in Columbus, Kansas City, Pittsburgh, and Nashville. I had been oohing and aahing Vincent's works at the Art Institute of Chicago since I was a child and remembered the Van Gogh exhibit a few years ago there that reproduced his bedroom, furniture and all, though you couldn't sit on anything, God forbid, or lie down in the bed with the four wooden posts. But you could see it close enough, and it pretty much looked like the painting. It was the reproduction of the room he lived in before, you know, before the end.

This exhibit was previously in Paris, so it must be good. "Pair-iss" some people pronounce it. I love the way National Public Radio reporter Eleanor Beardsley, who is based in France, pronounces it, and I respect her and want to be her a lot of the time, but I don't know if she is truly happy because I don't know her, I only know her voice. I do know that she's really good at what she does as a journalist, and I smile at the way she pronounces "President Emmanuel Macron." I like that about her. That and she has a soothing voice and she says "Pair-iss" in a way that does not come off snooty and condescending like some people I know who maybe went there for a week and came back French with the receipts to show for it. No one, it seems, goes to Paris without consulting Fodor's or googling "top Paris attractions." You need the informed instruction about where to go to see the main sites, otherwise you spend your days in cafés and bistros like an Instagram influencer, and you might as well have spent your time in a hotel by the airport without ever leaving your room.

I'm also a huge fan of *Emily in Paris* on Netflix, but I watch it for the clothes and the food scenes; I think the relationships are shallow, and no one has that much fun at work, no matter what continent they live on. I read that many Parisians are insulted by the tropes and stereotypes and the presentation of the city as majority white, majority elite, caring more about food and clothes than work and mission. I watch it because I feel validated for wearing old funky yellow blazers with flowered pants and striped tops because, well, because Emily does that.

The Van Gogh exhibit website said it has five hundred thousand cubic feet of projections, 60,600 frames of video, and ninety million pixels. I know as much about the size of pixels as I do about Bitcoin, so they may as well have said it had fifteen pixels and I would have nodded in agreement that it was indeed quite impressive. I looked up five hundred thousand cubic feet on Google, and that cubic footage translates to more than 3.7 million liquid gallons. I agree that's a lot but still don't really have a sense of half a million cubic feet.

Of course, five hundred thousand was the COVID death milestone in the United States that was hit in the spring of 2021. OK, so, a lot.

I'm trying not to think about the pandemic, give myself a brain break, a visual rest. I'm trying to think about Vincent. In his shortened life he created more than twenty-one hundred artistic works, including almost nine hundred oil paintings, many of which are iconic and not only the sunflowers or *Starry Night*, which has its own song by Don McLean who sang

"American Pie." That was perhaps a vapid song, but we all knew the words.

Drove my Chevy to the levy but the levy was dry.

And good ol' boys were drinking whiskey and rye, singing, "This will be the day that I die."

Vincent was thirty-seven when he died. When I was thirty-seven, I had filed for an emergency order of protection against my then-husband, had three sons ages seven, five, and two, and was about to begin an eighteen-year career teaching journalism at Northwestern University; I had a weekly column for the *Chicago Tribune*, where I was a freelance contributor, which means you have no benefits and meet your deadlines for monthly payments. The babysitter was the most important person in my universe. I did not have time to paint.

Some details about Vincent's life fascinated me—that he was close with his brother, Theo, whose wife, Johanna Gezina van Gogh-Bonger, was instrumental in getting his work noticed, that he was institutionalized for mental health concerns, and that his brushstrokes were thick, brilliant swipes of paint.

But I learn none of these facts at the lauded immersive exhibit that costs as much for one person as I would pay for a pair of shoes I do not deeply love or need on sale at DSW. I do not learn these details because there are no captions to tell me any of this. None.

I need captions.

Even without on-site captions, I wanted a Van Gogh booklet to read before; I would even have been OK with downloading it, and I would have printed it out at home, in black-and-white, of course, not color, because I use so many ink cartridges lately that it's probably my biggest work-from-home expense. The color cartridges cost more; the double cartridges cost more.

I miss working at the university, where I copied a whole lot of things (and a whole lot of things that had nothing to do with the university, I now confess), and paper, pens, and supplies were free. I bought maybe one ink cartridge a year for my home-office printer. Then I wonder if the copier is what I miss most about working there, and yes, it's up there, along with the Keurig machine in the faculty lounge. But I have one of those in my kitchen, so it's fine. I just got the new compostable cups, so I feel less bad about my coffee every morning. I miss laughing with my good friends David, Mango, and Jack down the hall, and Craig and Caryn upstairs, then Karen a few feet away, but we're still in touch. Oddly enough, I miss the IT guys. They were nice. They were really nice if I brought them doughnuts, brownies, or cookies.

Before the exhibit, I had also known and loved the fact that Van Gogh was good friends—and roommates for a time—with Paul Gauguin, and I don't know why that is so endearing to me, but it makes me think about what they must have talked about on, let's say, a Tuesday that was overcast.

"Want me to make some coffee, Vincent?"

"No, I'm in the middle of my painting of this bedroom; not going to be like those sunflowers, thanks. Are you still planning that trip to Tahiti that will leave your wife and children penniless?"

These are details of the artists' lives I learned from captions at other museums showing their exhibits, the exhibits where you can imagine a hundred art history majors were vying for the job of curator, and only a handful of people were given the honor and the privilege of writing those captions, which were likely edited by a whole lot of people, maybe even the donors. I imagine those people have fake accents—mostly British, and maybe some French.

You see, the captions are necessary. In exhibits and in life.

The Van Gogh immersive exhibit had none. Not one. Zero.

It did have wildly colorful projections of his paintings onto thirty-five-foot ceilings and probably over a hundred feet of walls, and we did go into the space all wide-eyed and in love, like when you're deciding you'll live happily ever after with the guy you met on Bumble before your first in-person meeting.

So today I'm here with my sons Weldon, Brendan, and Colin and we're settling into our marked circles on the floor, pandemically spaced, and the sitting is not so comfortable an activity. Colin leaves to retrieve a folding chair for me. Brendan says he needs to sit against a wall. He is six foot something and 200 plus pounds, and Weldon and Colin are each six foot something and also 180 to 200 something plus, and I'm not that tall or big, but I'm not going into specifics, and, yes, the black and taupe dress now zips all the way to the top.

I'm wondering how many cubic feet of space we take up, but then I stop thinking about that because the lights go dim and the music comes on and it's instrumental and very New Age and then it goes into the Edith Piaf song "Non, je ne regrette rien." I'm instantly disturbed that this isn't the proper alignment of eras, but I let it go. I also mix up Edith Piaf with Marlene Dietrich, not as people, but just visually. I hear the nothing song and Marlene's photo flashes by in my mind, but I think that's just because they are both mysterious, thin, strong-jawed, beautiful women, iconic in their strength and their mystery, and I am envious.

Then I wonder if the producers of this show that debuted in Paris think dumb, sheltered Americans only know this one Parisian song. And then I think, no, they figure dumb Americans might know a song or two from *Les Misérables*, which went from Broadway to PBS, and a lot of people could sing the songs. Including me. I have cried sometimes when I heard "I Dreamed a Dream" but not when Anne Hathaway sang it in the movie. Rather, I cried when I saw it performed on stage in Chicago at the Auditorium Theatre, and I'll likely cry again if I happen to hear the stage version someplace. There's a lot of death in that play. In between the songs.

Huge paintings are flashing above and around us, and I look at Weldon, who's on his phone, and ask him please to look at the exhibit. I almost remind him how much it cost, but then I think I have already spent a lifetime telling him how much things cost, so I refrain. But I'm thinking it: $240.

Some projections of Asian-inspired Vincent paintings float by, above and around us, and I want to know when Van Gogh was there and what countries he visited and then some of his paintings I have never ever seen before erupt on the walls and they are gorgeous and I am wanting, so wanting, to know what the names of the paintings are, where he painted them and when. Another ten thousand pixels flash by and I'm left there in the dark on the folding chair near Weldon flipping through his text messages.

I don't think I'm longing for context just because I'm a baby boomer, and that millennials love their immersions in experiences, because a whole lot of people my age with backpacks and sensible shoes are seemingly engrossed in the forty-five expensive minutes of Van Gogh. They don't look like they miss the captions: they're all smiling and pointing.

I think it's because I'm a writer and I believe life and people are complicated and we need to know backstories or a little bit of information to see our shared humanity. Captions provide verbal explanations, neat dives into history, and a place to focus attention, providing boundaries and anchors into the chaos. We need the story.

If I smoked pot, ate the chewables my friends keep telling me to try, or imbibed any other selection from the socially acceptable list of mind-alerting drugs, I imagine this immersive exhibit would be a grand holistic experience. But I'm not high, and the smell of pot irritates me (oh, that's a long, painful parenting story), so I'm left wondering about absent facts and the meaning behind each Vincent video blast; I even want to know who is singing or performing the songs. A close friend gave me the Indico chocolate bar for my birthday and told me to eat two squares before bed and I would have a great night's sleep. I'm afraid, so I don't.

I am desperate for a guidepost. I want the captions.

But I didn't get any, no, not for the sixty dollars per person and not for anything extra cost-wise because if I had bought a guidebook I would have rallied. I didn't get text explaining the history of any of these paintings, not even the history of the people who created this immersive hoopla that I'm quite certain by now is a gazillion-dollar gold mine. I'm certain of that because it was really hard to get tickets and friends of mine say they waited months to get in and there are maybe 150 people in this show now, and the same number the hour before, the hour after, and the many hours after we leave. A friend of Colin's from high school walks by; we're surprised to see him, and we meet his girlfriend, who is quiet, and he tells us he is in graduate school at University of Chicago. I tell him to say hello to his mom, who's nice. She was married to a man who was not.

We didn't get captions, we got a poster, and I'm in my early sixties, so I don't need or want posters or have anywhere to put them. I think you get to be a certain age and you have framed art by artists (I have my own framed artwork, of course), because I had posters in college and that was kind of the last time—well, a few years after college. I think at some point I even had the sunflowers poster. In my first postcollege apartment on Fullerton Parkway with Mariann, I had a framed poster in my bedroom, of what I cannot recall, but we also had a framed poster in the kitchen and threw it out when we moved. That apartment is super expensive now.

I love the captions in museum exhibits so much that I believe the best job in the universe is to write them. I don't know how you go about getting that as a full-time job, but if anyone knows someone hiring for that, I'm all about applying. I will do speed-writing of captions as a test. I worked with a woman once who said she wrote captions for the Field Museum in Chicago, and she said it wasn't a fun job at all and not that hard to get; she said someone in the communications department she knew called her and asked her to write them for an exhibit.

"The pay was not all that great," she said, and she seemed surprised I was so intrigued.

I forgot to ask her if the exhibit was about animals with tusks or maybe something more interesting like musical instruments over the centuries or birds in different habitats.

In 2021 I did get a chance to write captions for an exhibit for the Museum of Broadcast Communications on a hundred years of radio history because my good friend Susy was the head of the museum, and that job was challenging but enjoyable. It also was maybe the first time in my life when I may have actually manifested something out of thin air because I was working on this chapter when Susy emailed to ask me if I could write the captions for the project.

Let me reiterate that I am still not a card-carrying believer in writing things down and putting them out in the universe so you can make them happen because I have written a whole lot of dreams down, said them out loud, even lit candles and incense—and squat, nothing. I think those vision boards are kind of silly, but people swear by them, or maybe at them. The reason I don't believe in the manifesting magic is that sometimes just the opposite of what I imagined, wrote down, said aloud, and pictured happening did end up happening in real life. Maybe my writing is illegible to the universe; my sons tell me it is.

On this caption project on the history of radio for the past one hundred years, I learned more than I could include, such as many tidbits about Glenn Beck that were grotesque, but also more about Yvonne Daniels and Robin Quivers and how Eleanor Roosevelt had the nation in the palm of her hand because of her broadcasts. I also learned that podcasts have jillions of listeners all over the world. I tried my best to make them scintillating and captivating. I wrote about Joe Rogan before he was all over the news for his Spotify misinformation. And my name was there on the wall when the exhibit went up, and I drove to see it. No photo of me or anything, but there was my name and not in small type either. I smiled the whole ride home.

People need captions.

At national parks from Zion to Glacier, I read the captions engraved at the sites in stone or laminated on those stand-up podiums where people take photos, and sometimes random strangers will not move even a smidge to the right or left to get out of the frame. But I guess you can always crop them out. There is an app that removes the background, so I suppose people you don't know or like anymore can be zapped out instantly. Boy that would have saved a lot of time for a lot of divorced people I know who did not want to get rid of all those photos from the honeymoon in Hawaii, even though the marriage was doomed. It seemed so tacky and overly dramatic to cut people out, let alone rip them out of the edge of the picture. It's so Stephen King—like the 1990 movie *Misery* with Kathy Bates tying up her favorite author and keeping him captive. Oh, and if you're queasy at all about the safety and privacy of photos you post on social media, maybe don't watch *Clickbait* on Netflix because you will not sleep and the ending is really, really shocking. Right?

Neither caption connoisseur nor afficionado, I'm a caption appreciator, someone who wants to learn and can appreciate a solid, fact-filled sentence that is lyrically phrased. Just like when I read a great piece of journalism or a well-researched book, I value the knowledge behind every word of a caption, the hours spent reading documents or digging online to find the specifics and the exact dates, places, and people involved in a work.

At museums, the captions are placed into neatly packaged sentences and paragraphs that make you sigh because they are so exquisite. Sometimes the captions are painted on the wall—or printed on the wall—and are ten feet high and four feet wide, and they may or may not go with the audio tour. Mostly they stand on their own as works of word art.

The *Frida Kahlo: Timeless* exhibit I visited a few weeks later at the Cleve Carney Museum of Art with my friend Teresa and her mom, sister, and stepdaughter had exquisite captions. There was also a video you could watch before attending that was playing in the lobby, and there were room after room of captions for the paintings, the photographs, the reproductions of her dresses, and the reproduction of her bed, where she painted in pain lying on her back, her canvas suspended above her.

On one wall were Frida's definitions for eleven colors, extrapolated from her diary. "Yellow: Madness, sickness, fear. Part of the sun and of joy. Cobalt blue: Electricity and purity. Love. Dark green: Color of bad news and good business." I snap photos of the color captions on my phone. I had never read explanations like that before, and I was swooning.

From the captions placed around several rooms, I learned about Frida's lovers, visits to doctors, surgeries, paintings, and the name her mother had for her husband, Diego Rivera—Elephant. These are captions for all of posterity, and I'm profoundly grateful and have been wondering who wrote them.

I want to be just like them.

I insinuated my desire to be a caption writer to my beloved sketching instructor Mark at the Art Institute of Chicago and even mentioned it in passing when I did a profile on the new president of the School of the Art Institute, but I don't think either of them thought I was serious. I was. This is what I mean about me not being able to manifest my own destiny.

The Art Institute has exquisite captions for its exhibits, and the recent *Obama Portraits* exhibit had captions on the walls that were magical. Adjacent to Kehinde Wiley's 2018 *President Barack Obama* oil-on-canvas painting is this: "The lush background alludes to his presidency as a space of blooming possibility, and the flowers reflect important milestones in his life."

Heavenly.

And then there's Michelle Obama's commentary in white letters on a green wall: "The paintings are lovely, but what matters most is that they're there for young people to see—that our faces help dismantle the perception that in order to be enshrined in history, you have to look a certain way. If we belong, then so, too, can many others."

Upstairs at the Art Institute was the Bisa Butler exhibit of vivacious portraits in quilts, with captions artfully posed in narrative that is as surprisingly vivid as her work. "Although Butler's finished works are exclusively fabric, her methods remain interdisciplinary; photographs inform her compositions and figural choices, she layers fabrics as a painter might layer glazes and she uses thread to draw, adding detail and texture."

I went twice to see Butler's exhibit, and I'm going a third time. I have already devoured its charm, but I feel her work offers surprises and fulfillment each time.

Museums are to me what restaurants are to foodies; I go to the most famous museums in the city I live in and the cities I visit—Toronto, San Francisco, Washington, DC, New York, Tampa, Milwaukee, Minneapolis, Boulder, Paris, London, Barcelona, Los Angeles, Madrid. These are the ones that are comparable to the four-star restaurants, where it's hard to get a reservation, especially on a weekend. I also go to the small museums, the new ones, on side streets, not just the Smithsonian-level museums, but the ones dedicated to local art. They have good captions, too.

Captions for museum exhibits are the antithesis of Twitter (now X) and Instagram and Facebook because the factual explanations and the gracious wording are what is important: not condensed hashtag memes, but fleshed out, generous wording regardless of word count. I imagine there is a word-count limit because a caption can't go on and on forever, there's only so much room for them. But they never feel rushed, certainly not measured in characters. The wording always feels just so. Perfect. I take it in, then move on to the next.

Writing captions would be one of the greatest jobs—yes, my dream writing job—even though it has no byline. And I do love my byline; I'm very protective of it and want to have any words that go under my byline at least try to be my best work. I know that's not possible, and one former acquaintance who has only written one book in her life (and this is my seventh, not that it matters that much) once said that I was prolific because I wrote crap for money. She was talking about my newspaper and magazine columns; I gathered she was not a fan.

"I write for love and babysitting money, as well as mortgage payments," I told her. This was when my sons were little, and it was true. And later I wrote for their college tuition, their college rent, and the enormous food bills for three growing athletes, and I could go on and on, but we're no longer friends, so what's the point. Though I did see her at a party before the pandemic, and I wasn't mean—even asked how she was.

Yes, I also write for the love of writing.

Sure, the captions on the wall for a temporary museum exhibit would not be permanent, but maybe the captions would travel to the next city for the next museum, and maybe someone in some annual report would make sure I would be listed as the author of that exhibit's captions, and that would be enough.

Captions by Michele Weldon. I'll even take six-point type, but I don't think it's reasonable to think anyone can decipher text smaller than that. My friend Stacy has a printing business, and I'll ask her the smallest size people can actually read without those cheap magnifier glasses. For the record, Stacy's roller-derby name was Hell Vetica.

It would be enough just to see the writing on the wall—and I did mean that pun—but recognition is also nice. Maybe the curator of the museum would love my captions so much they would send me champagne or flowers, hopefully not a gift card to a restaurant that serves a charcuterie board because I hate those, not the restaurants, but the pretentiousness of the rolled meats and the cheeses, though I do like the olives and the mini pickles, the seasoned pecans and sun-dried tomatoes if they have them. Maybe they would hire me again to write more captions. I'm not certain whether this would be lucrative enough that I could quit all the other things I do to pay the bills, but maybe I would be so famous and so good at writing captions that I could make it profitable.

I could add "caption writer" to my social media profiles, my email signature, and my resume. What the heck, I'll order new business cards. Wait, no one wants those anymore; you just type your email address in their phones or tell them to go to your website. It's also the norm now to have a QR code and not a business card at all, and it goes straight to your LinkedIn profile or your website. Who knew?

I like captions because I think we all need captions for our lives. We all need a well-written, eloquent backstory that accompanies us on every encounter—maybe even one permanently outside our homes, apartments, or condos. A tombstone is the ultimate caption, and a brief one at that, but I think a caption that changes not on whim but when new things develop in our lives would be worth having.

Captions would not be excuses or apologies but just more insight.

You could have a closet full of different captions—not like closets filled with clothes that no longer fit and you use as weight barometers, black shoes lined up by heel height, or white shirts that need to be ironed. These would be captions that sum it all up: the who, what, when, where, why, and how of your life at any given period of time. Selectively, of course. Succinct. Poignant. You wouldn't have to include anything gruesome or shameful, or maybe you would. Your caption could put everything else into context. There might be varying captions for different audiences because some readers of your caption might not care at all about your preferred eyebrow-pencil shade—light taupe, by the way. Imagine!

"That explains it," people would say as they read the caption outside your home.

Because doesn't just living through the pandemic earn us some proper captions?

Captions could be the gracefully articulated and condensed descriptions of our work and our lives, crafted into a tidy box. If you could inject mission into your existence with carefully chosen words, then perhaps none of what we do is for naught. A caption might answer some of the burning questions, on display for anyone and everyone—not a jumble of posed photos and hasty selfies like a Facebook or Instagram profile or a Match bio but an authentic, composed reality captured in one hundred words or fewer.

You could delve into the trauma, the moments that changed you, and the years you bore a different persona: those truths would allow you to forgive yourself. How you got through the pandemic. How you came out on the other side a newly invented version of an enviable, well-put-together human being. Or you could keep those revelations private, skip over the horrors or maybe put them in parentheses or at the end with an asterisk. It would be your decision what parts of you to offer as a glimpse to anyone.

You could skip 1989 and 1995 because those years were bad. Do not even talk about 2016.

You would be the creator and the editor of your caption—the caption of your ship. Or maybe you could decide who would be your curator and caption writer. Be careful who you ask. Because I have also observed over the course of many decades that for 10,760 different reasons I am not as kind to myself or about myself as other people are about me—at least not on birthdays.

I recently ran into an old friend from grammar school and high school who lives near me and is a very successful dentist and a great husband and father—our children were in grammar school together. He threw into the conversation his recollection that I was the high school homecoming queen. I was absolutely not—no, not anywhere near—but I was sort of flattered that I had been elevated to superficial teenage royalty. I corrected him with a smile; his wife smiled back. Maybe people remember me wrong because they don't know as much as I do about me, but how could they? How could anyone? I have no caption.

May 2022

1

CHILDREN

I HAVE BORNE SAFE, DISTANT WITNESS IN MY LIFETIME TO the news of mass fatalities: the fallen soldiers in the Vietnam War, the first Gulf War, and the wars in Iraq and Afghanistan; the people we lost to the HIV and AIDS epidemic; those killed on 9/11; the massacres of kids in schools; the shootings by hate-mongering replacement theorists in synagogues, grocery stores, churches, dance studios, parades, city streets, and malls; the long scroll of missing and likely dead Indigenous women; and the slow and steady roll call of the murdered that is the ongoing reality of police shootings and killings in Black and brown communities.

Yet until COVID-19, I have not been updated hourly on the rising death tolls in my suburb, in my county, in my state, in this nation, and in the world.

Mortality feels imminent and pressing.

As a cancer survivor twice, each year I fear a recurrence. As more and more of my friends and colleagues deliver their own news of cancer, COVID-19 diagnoses, and other illnesses, that fear grows in me like I imagine the cancer did. Perhaps it is my age or my history, the pandemic or the unrelenting news of unjust killings at the hands of hate-mongers, but I think about dying often.

With the drumbeat of my own mortality—and that of so many other people's—thrumming incessantly around me, I reintroduce and resuscitate my fear that I will never be enough, that I have not done enough, that I have wasted my opportunities and ambition. Damn. This is it.

I think, mostly, about my children and what I did or did not do for them. About all my mistakes. If I was a good mother as I tried to be or thought I was. Or if I fell woefully short. What is my legacy as a parent?

I raised my three sons in the '90s, also known as the era of life-size participation trophies. The privileged parents I knew from their school and college years approached parenting with heaps of praise and opportunities—as well as rewards, gift cards, and—later—cars and trips.

I did the praising; I mastered the declaration "When you pick up your pants off the floor, then you can have a treat." But I was more wary of heaping an endless conveyor belt of treasures upon them and was, as a single working mother, less financially able to do so. Something about inculcating the expectation of a relentless stream of shiny trinkets and dollar bills, as advocated by my contemporaries, struck me as off. So I didn't applaud every bite of broccoli; I didn't give quarters for every flushed toilet. (Perhaps the latter is why toilet training proceeded more sporadically than I would have liked.)

I was less about forever applauding each baby step than about attempting to mold accountable boys into good men. But that applause—those rewards—were all in the name of building our children's self-esteem. Somehow, my generation had determined the key to success for our own offspring was to convince them to believe they were worthy.

We were surrounded by parents, teachers, and the authors of popular parenting books who advocated fervently for the belief system that you could best shape your children's future with positivity. We would be different, we said, to our children than our parents were to us. We would not pass on the indifference we believed we had endured. We could manifest their happiness—as well as good report cards, positive friendships, successful athletic pursuits, and fantastic destinies— through intentioned and well timed treats.

Still, in 1999, during an afternoon visit to my mother's house with my young boys, then eleven, eight, and five, she had finally endured enough unbridled little-boy confidence. "That child has too much self-esteem," she said, referring to my youngest, Colin. He had been racing through the first floor of her ranch house, screaming that he was the green Power Ranger while his two older brothers, Brendan and Weldon, ignored him.

Her clipped remark reminded me that her approach to parenting—stern words and a neck pinch—made it unthinkable that my five brothers or I would ever have dared run through our home untamed. (We all turned out fine.)

"I'm not sure that too much self-esteem is a thing, Mom," I responded.

My mother was a daughter of the Great Depression: born in 1922 and the oldest of eight children, she was raised in both frugality and faith—which included not thinking too much of yourself, while thinking often of others. Her parents, I also learned, were pretty strict.

She and my father raised the six of us much the same: "To whom much is given, much is required." Self-esteem for your children was not the goal of parenting when I was a kid but rather the byproduct of a productive life. We knew we were lucky, privileged, and blessed; we understood that much was required of us.

The pendulum, I realize now, had swung. Perhaps my generation, feeling bereft of productivity or purpose, or not quite up to the task of meeting that which was required of us, deliberately chose to decouple our children's sense of accomplishment from accomplishments, to try to allow them to find happiness in being themselves for themselves rather than simply in service to others.

So instead we committed the crime of trying too hard, despite knowing how awkward and insincere it looks. Yes, it worked out fine for many, but it also reduced parenting to an aphorism— "follow your bliss"—while assuming that there was a kind of purity in the constant enhancement of self-esteem, rather than that it potentially ignored teaching children basic decency.

I heard other parents—from the time my oldest son was born until my youngest son graduated from college—constantly say, "I just want my child to be happy." But that never felt like my primary mission as a single mother who was trying to be all things to all sons—as well as be the driving force of my own career.

I saw up close as a single working mom that what made one family member happy could ruin the entire family's existence in one ill-conceived event. I had to avoid that obsession with happiness and its potential for hedonism and instead rally my boys behind the idea, taken from my parents, of being responsible, grateful, and generous with others—as well as being themselves.

Then and now, I want my grown children to be good people, as my mom wanted her children to be good people and as I want to be a good person, and I want us all to be happy with the people we are, too.

Real happiness, like self-esteem—as opposed to self-regard— feels inextricable from purpose. And just as I wish it for my children, what I seek is not just to be happy but to be purposeful and to have that deliberate intention translated into meaning beyond this day, beyond this life, into something lasting. Happy is not the goal; it's the byproduct of a life well lived.

I still wonder if anyone can have too much self-esteem. But what I seek in this moment—for myself, for my children, and for others—is adequate self-esteem, or to know that we are enough.

Now, in my sixties—with more life behind me than ahead—my focus has reverted to my own considerations, and I've begun a closer scrutiny of myself, which was a luxury that felt inaccessible for many years.

The realities of COVID-19—as well as the inevitable illnesses and deaths of friends, acquaintances, colleagues, strangers, and role models—infuse urgency into that self-examination. I feel compelled to immerse myself in an honest accounting of my privilege, purpose, and effort—not just in what I do every day, but in what I have done every day as a parent, person, daughter, sister, partner, friend, teacher, and mentor.

Have I been enough? Have I done enough? Did I give enough? To whom much is given, much will be required. Did I give at least the required amount?

August 2020

3

POSITIVE PATIENTS

I OPEN THE WINDOWS UPSTAIRS—THE ONES THAT DO OPEN, more than a few of them do not—in the second bathroom (that I still call the boys' bathroom because it was, in this house we moved into twenty-five years ago when they were indeed boys), the three bedrooms, and my separate bathroom, which used to be called a master bathroom, but thankfully the world has gotten wiser about what that designation really means and has meant for four hundred years. I turn on the ceiling fan in the hall and shut the door to my room, as if it's that simple.

I am extraordinarily lucky that nearly two years into the pandemic—December 2021—this is the first positive result on a quick antigen test for COVID-19 in my immediate family. By this point, millions had died across the globe.

Two of my double-vaxxed and boosted adult sons moved back to live and work here in this house due to the pandemic. My oldest son, Weldon, races out the back door with a suitcase, saying he is headed for a hotel because he is positive. He is not calm on his exit. I had asked days earlier about the hot yoga class he attended three to four nights a week during the omicron surge.

"Does anyone wear a mask?" I ask.

"Of course not."

He gets a text that he is positive from the drive-through testing center a few miles away that he sought out the day before as he complained of a headache and fever. He did not take his temperature with the thermometer I said was in my room on my dresser in the jewelry box.

All the online home tests have been sold out for weeks; there've been no tests on store shelves in forever.

Positive is not a good thing. I'm not quite sure what deep clean means, but I know I am supposed to do that because I googled it, so I'm opening the windows first and will google how long the virus stays on surfaces.

"Up to five days on drinking glasses and ceramics. Up to five days on paper—newspapers and letters."

The two sons who moved back home, Weldon and Colin, keep their drinking glasses and cups in their rooms, so I will avoid the cups and the glasses. Not so sure they get up close and personal with any ceramics in the house.

I have so many receptacles of disinfecting wipes—in varying scents and proclaimed percentage of effectiveness—that I can swipe left and right and in circles on the kitchen areas. I will wait five days to go to the basement, where they do their own laundry; not a problem, mostly my laundry is underwear, and I can wash those items in my sink.

I'm not a helicopter or bulldozer mother who is enabling any sort of failure to launch or thrive—my sons are successfully working and are gone pretty much every weekend. They work hard (I know because I hear them all day long in Zoom meetings), pay rent, and do their laundry. I don't cook for them, which means that many days of the week they each have meals delivered separately to the front door from Uber Eats or DoorDash or whatever sumptuous deli, café, or brasserie offerings they have a fancy for that day—sometimes up to twice daily. Occasionally they offer me something because they are independent and grown working men, you know, though it has been thirty-five years since I have made a meal for one.

"Can I have an egg roll?"

"Wait, loaded fries have coleslaw on them?"

Colin occasionally orders enormous platters of Indian food delivered from our favorite spot, which we all devour. He orders palak paneer, tikka masala, and far too many different kinds of naan. I keep telling myself I don't eat carbs, but the naan with the herbs and the garlic is so devilishly good, I rip off six inches of the warm-pillow delicacy and eat them in two, maybe three bites.

I know dozens of friends whose grown children have returned—with their own children—to their parents' houses because they believe it's safer. I don't know what to believe is safe anymore.

Paper contamination is not a threat, as no one opens their mail because they are usually just credit card taunts.

"Sign here and we will send you $72,000!"

No one but me reads the Sunday ink-on-paper edition of the *New York Times*, which I get delivered to the front door wrapped in a blue plastic sheath, even though I have a digital subscription. I like to lie down with it on the couch in my home office with too many pillows and throw the sections I complete to the floor with a randy flourish (or maybe just turn the pages looking at the ads). Reading the Sunday *New York Times* reminds me of my twenties, when if I was not wiser, I was happier. Saturday night out turned into late Sunday afternoon in reading the paper, maybe running out once to Burger King or maybe never leaving the apartment at all.

After opening the windows upstairs and downstairs in the mudroom off the kitchen, the next thing to do (after I make soup for Weldon to have in his hotel room) is cancel Christmas Eve dinner. It is two days away, and unfortunately, because I am an unapologetic planner, for the festivities for twelve I have eight salmon steaks and an enormous eight-pound beef tenderloin (so *Downton Abbey*) that I acquired following a deep philosophical discussion with the butcher at the grocery store about expectations of rareness and au jus. The tenderloin was on sale—only expensive, not incredibly expensive. My meat queries were stupefying to the man shifting back and forth on his feet impatiently next to me, who went from a smile to a question that could be construed as steeped in annoyance: "Are you done?"

I do not eat red meat so I needed expert advice.

I had already purchased all the vegetables and the fresh herbs, butter, lemons, freshly grated parmesan, and many bottles of wine. The onions will keep the longest; the spinach can last a week or so, as I will sauté the shoebox-sized plastic container of fresh leaves and reduce its contents to the size of a fist. The asparagus will not last, nor will the twelve portobello mushrooms the size of powder compacts—remember those? I will later make soup with the asparagus and will stuff the portobello discs with artichokes, parmesan, mayo, and panko breadcrumbs because anything is good with panko on it, as my friend Deborah recently affirmed in a passionate phone discussion we had. Our talks often involve food, and in this chat she also included her discovery of lasagna soup; the surprise is there were no diced tomatoes involved. Imagine!

The parsley and cilantro are doomed, so I consider making a wreath of them and decide I don't have the time or energy for such an indulgent fluke, or maybe I do, because all I will be doing in the evenings for the next week or foreseeable future until I turn sixty-five or ninety is watching Netflix and talking to myself after typing all day in silence, except for the occasional expletive outbursts at people I email who can't hear me and will never know I can't stand them. Or maybe they do.

I text my nieces and tell them I can't host Christmas Eve, their first since the death of their father, my brother Paul, in May. His oldest daughter is ten weeks pregnant, and I can't guarantee there will be no lingering COVIDity in my house. I feel the worst about my nieces, as doing everything I could to make them feel joy on Christmas was a driving force behind every second of preparation—even if it was pretty expensive, but it is Christmas—and now I'm failing at that. Yes, I am. Is it a mistake to cancel? Not as big a mistake as I had made earlier this week reading texts in my phone from my late brother that I will never erase. They made me cry.

The Christmas before this one, I did not go to my brother Paul's house. It was 2020, and I wasn't vaccinated—no one was vaccinated yet, except maybe people who worked in nursing homes and health care. Paul was deep into the fatal dive that was the multiple myeloma that would claim him five months later. I wanted to see him, of course, and be with him on Christmas, and I was so pleased he asked, but I knew no one at the dinner would mask. There were no enforced mask rules in his house, even with Paul's severely compromised health. His second wife of a few years was inviting several people in her family and some of her friends for dinner, including one conspiracy theorist who was always on the guest list and whose habits included making loud claims about the "media" and igniting arguments with me and whichever son happened to be with me.

Whenever I responded to the bait, Paul gave me looks that I know meant, "Really? Rise above it." Paul was always a better person than I am.

Because this was the first Christmas without my brother, I was planning to give Paul's daughters Christmas ornaments that their late mother, Bernadette, had given me years ago. She died in 2004 of an undiagnosed brain tumor, and one of the ornaments is a little girl in a present-laden sleigh that their mother gave me while she was dating my brother in the '80s. The other is from the '90s, a white ceramic heart with green lettering. This is my nieces' first orphan Christmas. I have been an orphan since 2002, but the first one without parents is rocky; you're looking for them in the kitchen or in their favorite chair in the den, and you think you hear them laughing. You have phantom sensations and knee-jerk responses in which you catch yourself wanting to ask them if they care for another scoop of potatoes, and you feel foolish and desperately sad all at once.

I also bought beautiful ceramic flowers (one is pink, the other green) for them to hang on a wall or place on a table. They were made by my friend Melissa, a ceramic artist and potter I roller-skated with a few years ago in roller derby—amateur roller derby, that is. Her derby name is Smashius Clay, which I think may quite definitely be the best derby name of all the scores of derby names belonging to women I skated with for six years on Tuesdays. That and Pepper Spray Patty.

I text my sister Maureen and tell her and her daughters not to come either, even though I bought everyone small stocking stuffers (fuzzy socks and hand cream). The presents are under the fake tree that I suddenly despise as if it is a repulsive, poisonous, man-eating *Little Shop of Horrors* entity. I plan to dismantle it as soon as I am done texting them. Good riddance. Some of the Christmas lights have stopped turning on, and I know it's bad for the environment, but when that happens, I throw the whole ten-foot strand out because I don't believe it is reasonable to suggest someone go one by one replacing those eeny weeny lightbulbs (just two or three replacements are squeezed in a too-small plastic bag in the box) when the lights only cost $7.99 for the whole darn strand at Target or Walgreens. At Costco you have to buy a one-hundred-foot garland of lights, I think, but some people do.

Colin will not be coming for Christmas, as he is caring for his girlfriend, who has contracted COVID. I cook two servings of the vegetables and the sides and most of a pork tenderloin and drive it down to meet him outside her apartment. We stand six feet from each other and say, "Merry Christmas."

Weldon says on the phone from his hotel room he doesn't feel like eating, so he doesn't take me up on the offer of food. He is resting and starting to feel better.

Adam Grant wrote in one of the most-read *New York Times* articles of that year about the tsunami of "languishing" that many of us suffer as a result of the pandemic, this existential ennui of uncertainty and hopelessness, this straddling between despair and fatigue. I think I am languishing, yes, and I also feel way more negative than just blah and am angry about being trapped in my house where I live and work and put up holiday decorations no one will see, feeling I am going to die if I go out to dinner. I'm upset my son has COVID and that the others may get COVID and that because of them I may also get COVID because I think I may die soon anyway since no one knows their expiration date and mostly because my brother just died, and he did not deserve that and maybe I do.

I am languishing. Or maybe I'm just treading water. I'm not sure because this is my first pandemic. The polio outbreak was a few years before I was born.

The languishing perhaps comes because the shouts and whispers of people dying (even as my own family was spared COVID deaths) are now ordinary. What used to catapult me into tremors, shock, and orders of sympathy flowers delivered the next day now seems like a daily occurrence. Mothers, fathers, brothers, sisters, spouses, boyfriends, girlfriends, aunts, uncles, coworkers, bosses, long-lost mentors, long-lost college friends, high school friends, neighbors, in-laws, cousins, friends of friends, second cousins, third cousins, daughters, sons, former bosses, former employees, former lovers, former spouses, the woman who dropped her kids off at school in front of you in line, everyone, anyone; omicron has made it so ordinary to be positive that it erases the cataclysmic enormity. And it shouldn't.

The obituaries are never fully satisfying, though the obituary I wrote for my brother Paul, I felt, captured the majesty and kindness of him. The obituary I wrote for my friend Lisa made me cry.

One death is too many. There should not be a capacity limit on compassion. I am afraid I fall short because there may be one for me.

The global tragedy feels heavy because when I do focus on it and think about the catastrophic grief, I find it hard to put one foot in front of the other and maintain a full workday; my heart is sore, and my brain feels too swollen for my skull. My cheekbones hurt. I know that I am privileged to choose to look away. I'm not a frontline worker or an essential worker or in health care or eldercare or childcare or someone who has no other income options. I understand the haughtiness of my grief capacity is an abomination to many: I have a home big enough that we can open windows and quarantine with separate bathrooms, and I think perhaps I don't deserve to have what I do. At birth I automatically received the lottery ticket that spares me most of the anxiety. I have choices.

My homebound pandemic remote-work life unavoidably intersects with the reality of this horror from a safe distance; as a senior leader with The OpEd Project, I engage with leaders, experts, social justice activists, medical practitioners, academics, and health-care heroes around the country who write about it almost every day. I edit and mentor them, and I help them get published; I press Send and stay numb. In my capacity as a freelance contributing journalist, I write about business, popular culture, gender, and the economy on deadline each week and at will for many outlets.

I wash my hands, wear my mask, spray disinfectant, wipe down the carts at Target, and go to Costco for the raspberries, the $4.99 baked chickens, and the chicken salad that is so good on crackers. I head to the small grocery store two blocks away or the chain grocery store, where I go with embalmed trepidation if I need lots of items and toothpaste, saving myself a trip, protecting myself feebly and hoping no one I know is positive, really hoping that I don't get a positive.

Because I do not want to die. Not now. I realize I do not have a choice or control over when that will be; believing otherwise feels foolhardy.

My life is not hard, just changed. I bubble wrap myself in work and distractions, knowing it's like trying to hold off a stampede of angry buffalo with the handheld snow scraper that I keep in my car. Actually, I have two snow scrapers. I remind myself that I'm extraordinarily lucky, and I will be fine if I can get from Monday to Thursday because then soon it is Friday and Friday is almost Saturday and Saturday is bliss or as close to bliss as one can get in three hours while one is languishing. My bliss is my virtual art class.

The final straw of this damn pandemic (why not call it a pandamnic?) is that my beloved art instructor whom I have been taking virtual weekly Saturday pastel-drawing classes from since the start of 2021 has decided she is burned out and not going to give any more Saturday classes online because she works all week and is tired. It has been the best part of my week for almost a full year.

"But I love you and can't go one week without you!" I want to screech on the Saturday morning Zoom call when she informs us—her gaggle of devoted, sycophantic Zoom followers—of her decision.

Even the gentle mansplainer who talks about himself too much (but is admittedly very talented) and name-drops his famous old friends too often is speechless.

But I do not say what I'm really feeling and thinking, so I express altruism and compassion and say of course she needs to take care of herself and that the hybrid classes she runs back-to-back on Saturdays after teaching Monday through Friday all week are too much. I unmute and pretend I'm not seething like a poisonous snake.

"Please take care of yourself. Of course I understand." I smile because I need her.

And then I want to cry because no one in the nearly ten years since I have been taking art classes as an amateur has been as directly instructive and patiently helpful as she has. Yes, I've had some wonderful instructors I admire and appreciate (and some not so wonderful ones), but she's different. She is the only one ever in the history of the universe who told me never to use black—in pastels or oils—because layering on different colors will always make the art more interesting.

"Never use black?"

I was incredulous, wondering how I had never heard of such a pronouncement. I didn't go to art school, but I did take a painting class in high school and another in college that I loved and also an art history class, the introductory one, where we looked at slides for an hour in a dark auditorium twice a week and were supposed to memorize them all. A lot of people cheated on the tests; that was common knowledge. I think everyone but the professor knew.

I typed the assigned papers for my boyfriend's friends in the class, and they paid me twenty-five dollars for each paper because I sometimes edited what they wrote; they always got As. That was a lot of money in 1976; my monthly allowance in college was sixty dollars from my parents (in addition to the monthly stipend from the campus newspaper). With sixty dollars I could get a few nights a month of beer and pizza plus pay the phone bill and buy a pack of cigarettes. I smoked Salem menthols back then before switching to Merits, but it was so long ago and only at parties to look cool or in the library lounge to look smart and cool; the packs cost sixty cents at Hoos Drug Store down the street. A pack could last a month in the freezer, and I haven't smoked since the '70s.

But yes, never using black was a revelation.

"Well, I wouldn't know if you did ever use black, but there are more interesting choices," my instructor cooed, suggesting layers of dark purple, red, green, and cobalt blue. I imagined the colors all piled neatly on top of each other like logs trucked away from the rainforest headed to a destiny as smart standing desks sold at IKEA.

I am soothing myself about my pastels-class loss at the same time my holidays evaporate. I had carefully assigned appetizers and desserts to others, so one very sore truth about my canceled Christmas Eve is that I have no creamy or gooey chocolaty bakery goods in the house to indulgently assuage my disappointment. I did buy a jar of caramel sauce and a jar of hot fudge in anticipation of marrying them to the cookies and the pie that others were assigned, so I take to gorging myself on large tablespoons dipped into their caloric promise late at night. There are no dishes to wash, only spoons.

What I do have are those everything pretzel chips (that are supposed to mimic bagels) and two tubs of cheddar pub cheese (one with horseradish) because I have learned you must have an alternative appetizer planned even after assigning several hors d'oeuvres because sometimes people forget to bring their dish or come very late, and then you have guests who arrive at the designated time and think—God forbid—that you have no idea how to entertain with abundance. In two nights, I consume one tub of orange pub cheese the color of iridescent pumpkins on the porches of people who pretend they like giving away candy to strangers. My stomach is so upset that I google COVID symptoms.

"Fever or chills; Cough; Shortness of breath or difficulty breathing; Fatigue; Muscle or body aches; Headache; New loss of taste or smell; Sore throat; Congestion or runny nose; Nausea or vomiting; Diarrhea."

OK, so I have the last one plus fatigue.

"You're lactose intolerant," my sister Madeleine reminds me, but I worry anyway.

I am waiting on the PCR test seventy-two hours after the rapid test that never arrived.

"We'll text you in twenty-five minutes if you're positive," says the handsome thirtysomething young man who looks like Rob Lowe in 1995 (who still looks like Rob Lowe in 2022) and who shoves a chopstick up my nose and twirls it after I sign in at a card table outside a former CVS store near the Dunkin' Donuts where the parking lot is always full, across the street from the Harlem Avenue stop on the Green Line. "No news is good news." He smiles.

How odd that he's so cheerful. I see someone I know in line, and she looks upset and is on her phone having a rapid-fire, agitated conversation with someone. Hopefully it is a wrong number or the robot people who ask you if you want to up your car warranty or stay at a hotel (really, a hotel?) and it's not her telling someone she loves she is positive. I pretend I don't recognize her in her mask, and I think she pretends back because we lock eyes for a second and I pretty much have looked the same as long as she has known me—at least my eyes do, I think—which is a very long time since our kids were in grammar school together.

I feel like I do this a lot lately—pretend I don't recognize people. And sometimes when I'm walking in the neighborhood and not in the mood for empty chatter, I take out my cell phone and pretend in an Oscar-worthy fashion that I'm deep in conversation and can't hang up to say hello. I motion and wave that I have to take a call and walk past, hoping they can't see that the face of my phone is not lit up the way it is when you're actually on a call. I don't intend to be the crabby old lady of the block, but then we're not totally in control of how others perceive us, right? Masks are a free pass to eliminate undesired social connection and fallow talk. Sometimes I just don't feel up to what my late father would call "silly talk."

I wonder if the young man is a volunteer or if he is part of the Great Resignation. He is dressed very well and wearing shiny brown leather oxford shoes that tie, the kind of shoes that I know from my youngest son cost a few hundred dollars. This is the son who doesn't shop at DSW and, instead, gets his shoes delivered, and they arrive in fancy boxes in their own cloth pouches as if they were baby rabbits you need to pamper and keep out of the sun. He has eight pairs of white, what I would call, gym shoes, but he gets upset when I say that, and when I say, "Another pair of white gym shoes?" At least I don't call

36

them sneakers, as my late mother would have, and it sets me off on a worry tangent trying to decide if they called them sneakers because the rubber soles made the shoes silent and wearers could sneak up on you. I wonder why I always have to shift to nefarious intent. I also don't call them running shoes, athletic shoes, or walking shoes, as if you have to assign an adjective to all your articles of clothing, like eating shoes and flirting hat, or working blazer and seducing skirt.

I drive home from the rapid testing site and wait, wondering when the twenty-five-minute countdown started: Was it as soon as he swabbed my brain, or was it when they got around to testing it, however that happens? So two hours after I arrive home, I figure I am not positive because no one texted. Again, the positive thing.

Positive in this case is not good, not good at all; it can kill you. It's not like when the pregnancy test comes back positive when you were planning it twenty-eight years ago and wanting it deliriously, illogically hopeful as if the nine years of couples therapy were working. So you're rubbing the genie's magic lamp, and it's your third wish, knowing you're married to the wrong man yet still believing this final baby wish will come true because your heart craves children to love and you somewhere consumed the delusion that this will magically transform the person you're married to into someone he's not, even though you know it didn't work the two times before this. You believe you're powerful enough to change anything and anyone, and if you do all the right things with the right intention, it will miraculously all be fine.

Not so much.

April 2023

4

OLD LADIES

I REFUSED TO GOOGLE IT. I HAD A BOOK YEARS AGO, THE *Flip Dictionary*, that was enormously helpful because you could reverse engineer the names and titles for objects you absolutely could not remember or never knew, but that was in the years before Google made us all know-it-all fools. I forget where I put it; it's here somewhere, possibly under something.

Instead it became a challenge for me to see how long it would take me—it was six days, to be exact—to naturally come up with the word for the beneath-the-skin infection, no, not acne or pimple, but that word that was lost to me, the one that disappeared like the earring I lost on the dance floor but don't regret losing because, well, I was dancing.

I was reflecting on the images I had seen online and the stories friends had told me of having this thing lanced on a back or a leg or—shriek—a face. But I couldn't remember what it was called.

Not obsessive about it exactly, I would spend a few minutes here or there in the day, take a break from my work and try to retrieve it, and it felt like I was sifting for it blindfolded in a muddy, burbling creek—a bear grasping for salmon, frustrated and so sure it was just beyond my reach. Of course it is there.

What is a writer without words at her disposal?

I would lie in bed at night and think, just try to remember where I heard it last, and I could recall someone's recitation of a dermatologist's diagnosis and the treatment. I thought about how I never ever could stomach that reality show *Dr. Pimple Popper*, though I've heard that it's oddly and wildly satisfying. Like discarding evil in one premeditated, medicated swoop. Control.

Cyst.

I couldn't remember the word *cyst*. And then I forgot why I wanted the word to begin with: Was I writing about it as a metaphor? Was I telling a story about someone inundated with them and inconvenienced by their protrusion? I no longer know.

I'm older—early sixties—maybe oldish or just old, and I forget things now and then and am not nearly as witty as I used to be, or perhaps it's that I am only now realistic about how witty I ever was. Nothing of what I'm experiencing as a mature woman is earth-shatteringly new, but you might think so the way women of a certain age are supposedly erased or made invisible in every corner of our culture.

Or are we?

I was watching a Zoom interview with Meryl Streep, Dianne Wiest, and Candice Bergen on CBS recently (Meryl had the best lighting, though Candice had the best hair and Dianne the best backdrop) about their movie *Let Them All Talk* and about how refreshing it is for women of their age and mindset to be the stars of a major movie.

And while I am a fangirl of all three of these glorious women and spent a portion of my twenties believing I resembled Candice (it was the hair, I believe, and the long nose), I do not agree that we haven't been treated to a lineage of gorgeously complicated older women on screens large and small. I know because I remember most all of them—fondly.

40

I watched *The Loretta Young Show* as a very young girl (must have been reruns, as I was born in 1958 and the show ran 165 episodes from 1953 to 1961) and dreamed of descending a winding staircase with a knowing smile and half-moon cheekbones and those twin eyebrows that made her look forever surprised. She was in her forties at the time, and I knew she wasn't young, even though that was her name. I don't believe I saw her in any other movies; she died at eighty-seven, still regally beautiful.

Doris Day was also a glistening vision on TV, her camera close-ups in the '60s famously smudged with Vaseline on the camera lens. But she was smiling and smart and wore hats. I watched Angela Lansbury solve every problem there ever was without losing her temper on *Murder, She Wrote*. Lucille Ball was no spring chicken, but she was funny and I adored her, appreciating Ethel as much as she did. Eva Gabor was older and not American and delicious looking, like a goblet of Grand Marnier, a better version of her sister Zsa Zsa.

Yes, Aunt Bee from Mayberry was always in the kitchen, but she was wise and had good Sunday churchgoing hats and her elderliness was a virtue, not something to dismiss her for, even if Andy kept repeating, "Oh, Aunt Bee." I wanted an apron like hers, if not the waistline.

Agnes Moorehead, oh Mother, she was truly a witch on *Bewitched* and immensely powerful, none of that odd nose twitching; her magic was performed with a swoop and grand gestures. I am a believer in grand gestures. Angie Dickinson, for goodness sake, she was on the good-cop side, and she was fast and smart and carried a *gun*.

I grew up loving these older sisters, mothers, aunties, and grandmothers, not thinking they were less than, but knowing they were more than I was, women who were capable and held their own. Why, Barbara Stanwyck held all those sons and that whole ranch together—and even had a teeny-tiny waist.

The older women on the big screen, too, were worth learning from and longing to be. Of course, they were not as plentiful as the old men because this is a country for old men. But if we fail to salute the grandeur of the women who have gone before—even if there were not as many of them—then aren't we guilty of erasing them too?

In "Frail, Frumpy and Forgotten: A Report on the Movie Roles of Women of Age" by the Geena Davis Institute on Gender in Media, researchers analyzed how women over fifty were depicted in thirty top-grossing films from the United States, the United Kingdom, France, and Germany in 2019.

It's not pretty.

None of the leads are women. Only 25.3% of the characters over fifty are played by women. Nearly half, or 46.8 %, of the female characters are depicted in stereotypes as senile, home-bound, feeble, or frumpy, the report shows.

The Davis Institute report continues, "Older women are particularly erased in entertainment media. Older male characters outnumber older female characters two-to-one, and only 11% of male characters on television between ages 50 and 64 are perceived as 'old' compared to 22% of female characters."

Still, I remember the older screen ladies, for they offered me not only their talents but a vision of what I could become—not the granny of *The Beverly Hillbillies* or the *Grey Gardens* freaks, but Catherine Deneuve and Cher as the grandmother in that unfortunate remake, *Mama Mia! Here We Go Again*, or Helen Mirren in, well, absolutely anything.

We have Jane Fonda, Sheryl Lee Ralph, Rita Moreno, Gloria Estefan, Lily Tomlin, and Helena Bonham Carter, who looks the same as she did in 1990, and a constellation of older stars who are not decrepit or age-defying but are age embracing in their daring and their shine.

I loved Julianne Moore in *Gloria Bell*, Angela Bassett in *Otherhood*, Alfre Woodard in *Juanita*. Woodard looks better at sixty-eight than I did at twenty-eight. Diane Keaton, well, it's enough to just say her name.

In her 2019 book *Elderhood*, Louise Aronson writes, "Often people's worst nightmare about old age looks like this: a bent old woman with wild hair, missing teeth, a hooked nose, and bulging unfocused eyes—a crone, a hag, a witch. This is the stuff of the original fairy tales collected in the cold north by the Brothers Grimm, considered on their first printing to be unsuitable for women."

I am more selective about what old age looks like. With the help of chosen memories of older women who have danced across a screen, my best view of old age looks like this: a competent, attractive, powerful woman with wild hair, vibrant eyes, and a love of life—and herself.

December 2020

5

FEMINISTS

IT WAS THE EARLY AUGHTS, AND MY FRIEND WAS HAVING A late June *Sex and the City*–themed party at her house. (And yes, she asked me not to name her. You'll see why in a bit.) Since we were mothers in the same suburban neighborhood, our children were together from preschool to middle school, and we were fans of the cable show that started airing in 1998 and ran until 2004.

I didn't have cable (because I couldn't afford it), so I rented the VCR tapes from Blockbuster—yes, the big, black, clunky tapes no one watches anymore and that I still have somewhere in the basement. I think. I bought all the seasons and watched them in my room alone, when my sons were asleep in their rooms, guffawing and toasting the friendships and the unapologetic candor in every scene. I did wonder, however, exactly how there were so many men available for the taking. Every single episode. But that was New York.

Her girlfriends-only party was at her house just a few blocks from me, and the instructions were to come dressed as your favorite *Sex and the City* character. I was, of course, Carrie Bradshaw, loving shoes and clothes and all that fashion hysteria. I wore a short leopard-print skirt, a sequined tank, and one of my favorite hats. But I was similar to her only in her reverence for friends and fashion. As a single mother of three sons, the youngest born in 1994, I could mimic her wardrobe maybe, but I wasn't having her nightlife and love life, at all. *At all.*

One friend was dressed as Charlotte in tennis whites; a few arrived as Miranda in lawyer-leaning suits. Several were Samantha Jones. Many of us were Carrie. We thought we were cool, or as cool as suburban mothers could be on a Friday night in June with babysitters watching our kids at home.

My host friend was also costumed as Samantha, having walked down the day before to the local fire department a few blocks from her house to borrow a pair of fireproof firemen's pants, explaining she needed them for her costume and would return them promptly after the party. Anyone who watched the show may remember a scene in an episode with Samantha and a fireman fresh from an alarm; Samantha is topless in the fireman pants with the suspenders. My friend, however, veered from authentic reproduction of the outfit and wore a T-shirt.

She told the firemen when the party was and the address where it was taking place—Friday night starting at seven, and yes, the firetruck showed up with a few of the firemen walking up the driveway, apparently to make sure the house and all of us were not on fire. They didn't put on the sirens to announce their arrival or departure. They didn't accept our invitation to come inside, even though we had wine and cake.

Fast-forward to late 2021, and the star engines of the incredibly popular and lucrative *Sex and the City* franchise, Sarah Jessica Parker, Cynthia Nixon, and Kristin Davis (minus Kim Cattrall at first), jumped full on into an updated remake with *And Just Like That . . .* for HBO Max. The midpandemic reboot was surrounded by more positive hype and breathy, anticipatory headlines than any show I had ever seen, except maybe *Game of*

Thrones or any installment of the *Star Wars* saga. Leaving aside the racial blind spots and the dumbing down about aging, the newly revamped series appeared to be just what spice-craving, pandemic-isolating fans needed: close friends unmasked and boldly moving through an imaginary, glamorous life with the best wardrobes imaginable.

But only days after the airing of the first episode, the *Hollywood Reporter* ran stories of reported accusations of sexual assaults by actor Chris Noth—Mr. Big, Carrie's on-screen fictional love interest then husband—from three separate young women over a span of nearly two decades.

Big?

I expected outrage emanating from the feminist icons, my personal feminist heroes. Not so much. For women who have reputations as role models of forward-thinking feminism, actors Parker, Nixon, and Davis merely wrote a mild and lame disclaimer: "We are deeply saddened to hear the allegations against Chris Noth. We support the women who have come forward and shared their painful experiences. We know it must be a very difficult thing to do and we commend them for it."

Their reaction was the equivalent of offering victims "thoughts and prayers" or breaking up with a lover on a Post-it, which is what Carrie had done to her by an unrepentant lover in one *Sex and the City* episode. I know; I watched it maybe twenty times.

Shared on their Instagram and Twitter (now X) accounts, their only public accounting suggested that what made them sad was hearing the news, not the physical harm and trauma the first three women say they endured when they were eighteen, twenty-two, and twenty-five years old.

Even as an unattributed source leaked later that Parker—Carrie—was "livid" and "heartbroken" by the news of the sexual assaults, the modest public nod from the cast of women so many wanted to be, then and now, was several days after initial reports of the first three assaults went public. There was no official peep in the weeks or months after, even as a fourth and fifth woman came forward.

To be clear, Noth denied the claims and said the sex was consensual in the first three incidences. He remained silent on the two more recent accusations.

As a journalist, I have read the research that only 2 to 10 percent of sexual assault allegations are false. What is more common is for victims not to report, as only approximately three in ten women do so. Seriously, are there no takeaways from #MeToo and #TimesUp?

This is not about these superstars not wanting to dive into cancel culture or the knee-jerk response from many who say accused men have their lives ruined when women make specious claims about a sexual encounter that can have two sides. But the two sides of sexual crimes are victim and perpetrator, and one side is usually lying. That side is not often the victim's. Ask E. Jean Carroll. Or Amber Heard.

Cancel is the wrong word for an activity that is nowhere near as minor as running a red light or as major as committing murder or heading a pharmaceutical company that contributes to many deaths. Cancel is what needs to happen to someone who commits intimate violence against a real person, not a place or a thing. The better word may be accountability.

And then all the mentions of Noth's assaults disappeared. Like it was all a bad dream. Does outrage ever really go away? I guess you can ask Harvey Weinstein.

Months after the Noth eruption, Evan Rachel Wood, the *Westworld* actress who publicly accused her partner Marilyn Manson (whose real name is Brian Warner) of sexual assault and sexual abuse, was sued by Manson for defamation. She was not backing down, she was not canceling, she was telling the truth.

"This is what pretty much every survivor that tries to expose someone in a position of power goes through," Wood told the ladies on *The View*, which I don't watch because of all the hosts screaming at each other when they get upset, but I followed the news online.

Wood talked about the abuse in 2016 but only named Warner in 2021. It took the HBO two-part documentary she created, *Phoenix Rising*, about Warner's rape and sexual abuse of Wood for him to sue. She turned her assault into advocacy. It's what is possible when you have a public platform.

The same month, in Sweden, journalist Cissi Wallin was facing prison time for defamation after she posted in 2017 the name of the businessman who sexually assaulted her eleven years earlier. A dozen other women in Sweden who accused men of sexual assault were also facing charges of defamation.

British journalist Nick Cohen, a columnist for the *Guardian News & Media*, resigned in 2023 amid a flurry of investigations about sexual harassment and misconduct of colleagues, but not before *Financial Times* editor Roula Khalaf spiked the investigation by Madison Marriage, refusing to run the story.

That '70s Show star Danny Masterson was found guilty of two counts of rape in 2023, on assaults between 2001 and 2003. His famous costars Ashton Kutcher and Mila Kunis were silent on the conviction.

Just after the 2023 holidays, fifty-six actors signed a letter published in the French newspaper *Le Figaro* defending actor Gerard Depardieu who was accused—and charged—for rape by more than a dozen women. His defenders declared the attacks on him were a "lynching" and pleaded not to "erase" him because he is a good actor.

This is not new; it is ancient.

Rape was defined as "forced sex against a boy, woman or anyone" as early as the third century B.C.E. It was considered a crime by 50 B.C.E., and one without a statute of limitations. The passage of time has not lessened the harm of sexual assault, even if current norms attempt to minimize it, blaming women for what they wore or whether they had been drinking. Assault traumatizes the mind and body. Anyone who has experienced trauma knows it lives forever inside you. Anyone who has watched the NBC series *Law and Order: Special Victims Unit* with Mariska Hargitay over the past twenty-three years knows what I mean.

While some assert it is an unfair expectation for all those identifying as women to bear the burden of support and apology for the egregious behaviors of their male colleagues and acquaintances, as a feminist and domestic-violence survivor, I contend it is the least these card-carrying, high-profile feminists can do: speak up, speak out loudly, and work for awareness of sexual assault.

No, these celebrities are not responsible for another's actions. Yes, they are responsible for what they do with information. And yes, if they say they are feminists, they can make public declarations about fairness. You don't get to be a part-time feminist. Maybe that's why so many roll their eyes and sigh "white feminist" with such disdain. Because it's true?

No spokesperson for the *Sex and the City* franchise officially responded to the news of two later separate accusers. Cattrall, who did not appear in the updated series initially but did come back for appearances in subsequent seasons, said little publicly about Noth's reported actions.

Perhaps the stars avoided damnation of his behavior so as not to contaminate the new franchise that debuted as the most-viewed series premiere on HBO or HBO Max. The first episode was ranked in the top ten of all its movie and series debuts. HBO triumphantly jumped into a second season of *And Just Like That.*

The first season's ten episodes were HBO's "most popular original offerings of all time," prompting Casey Bloys, the chief content officer of HBO Max, to tell a reporter: "It's been phenomenal. I couldn't be happier with how it's doing in terms of reception."

In terms of its stars speaking out against sexual abuse, I couldn't be more unhappy.

Even as he denied culpability, Noth was severed swiftly from his other endeavors in the time after the allegations surfaced. He was suddenly no longer costarring in the CBS series *The Equalizer*, his talent agency A3 Artists Agency dropped him, and his tequila brand, Ambhar, was done with him, losing $12 million in the process. Peloton wanted nothing to do with him either, even though earlier it had been a key factor in his fictional demise and offered a humorous ad rebuttal.

Noth's accusers say the incidents were on set and in private. Heather Kristin said Noth's behavior was "toxic" and sexist on the *Sex and the City* set. Lisa Gentile said Noth groped her without her consent two decades earlier. That's in addition to Noth's public record of a 1995 restraining order against him for physical violence and threats filed by his then-girlfriend, model Beverly Johnson.

Yes, it is possible Noth's *Sex and the City* and *And Just Like That* costars were agnostic concerning his treatment of women. We can't know everything about everyone we think we know well. But the feminist costars were on sets with him for the series from 1998 to 2004 and then for the two feature films that hit theaters in 2008 and 2010.

Women reported that Noth assaulted them in Los Angeles in 2004 and in New York in 2002, 2010, and 2015. The restraining order filed by Johnson against him made headlines in New York in 1995. Kristin wrote about the behavior in February 2021 for the *Independent*.

The silence of the feminist *Sex and the City* stars did not interrupt the media bubble bath surrounding *And Just Like That*. The content glow featured mostly Parker in favorable interviews, magazine covers, and photo shoots, all with a positive spin on her ideas, creativity, favorite necklace, collaborations, wardrobes, idyllic family life, enviable marriage, proclamations of antimisogyny, professional acumen, even her shoe line.

But what bothered me was the notion that you could stay quiet when someone you considered a close friend and work colleague for decades was accused of a crime. Friends don't let friends assault women.

With their media influence and power, it's not outrageous to expect a more direct response from the trio of strong women who entertained millions across generations as the aspirational epitomes of supportive female friendships. They could have used their enormous platforms to speak out on sexual assault, definitions of consent, the paths to healing for victims, and accountability.

They could have called attention to the pattern of manipulative "fragmentation" of behaviors by the accused as part of a strategic plan; it's why historically so many get away with their crimes and so many are silenced by the imbalanced power dynamic. They could have talked about how easy it is not to know but also how easy it would be to inquire when something seemed "off"—either about his behavior or that of the people around him. Assuredly there were hints.

The paper trails of Andrew Cuomo, Bill Cosby, Harvey Weinstein, Jeffrey Epstein, Donald Trump and Prince Andrew demonstrated that in the cases of charismatic public figures, the buck may eventually stop, but it can take many, many, many depositions and loud outcries. Sometimes the accused—and convicted—still walk free.

The apparent agnosticism of the *Sex and the City* stars also feels oddly similar to Ghislaine Maxwell's claims that she had no idea what Jeffrey Epstein was up to with all those young women and Elizabeth Holmes's declarations that she was completely unaware that her statements about Theranos were untrue. They both landed in prison.

Instead of a brief acknowledgement and months of silence, these *Sex and the City* feminists could have launched a counternarrative about what they didn't know and why and demonstrated how anyone can move forward with accountability and compassion for victims. Speaking out could have educated the public and perhaps assuaged the mea culpa regrets of so many in parallel scenarios who also missed the dangers of a nefarious elephant in a darkened room.

But instead more and more time passed and the accusations about Noth became just a blip to be forgotten, like a bumpy Uber ride home after a bad date. What I wanted them to do, what I still want them to do, is show us what you do when you didn't know.

In his book *Apology, Forgiveness, and Reconciliation for Good Attorneys and Other Peacemakers*, author Peter Robinson asserts there are five types of apologies. The remorse apology acknowledges fault and assumes accountability, while the regret apology (a milder version) asserts the behavior was wrong but does not acknowledge that the action hurt someone.

The empathy apology exerts compassion but does not assume wrongdoing, while the social harmony apology shows empathy but is just intending to avoid conflict or save face. The harmless error apology admits a wrong but knows it did not cause harm. This situation caused harm.

Parker and her colleagues extended a social harmony apology; they could have gone in for remorse. Now they need to go in for education about how everyone can be mindful of safe workplaces and unsafe behaviors exhibited by coworkers, friends, and family. And when there is a breach of safety with sexual assault or harassment, people need to know how to support the accuser on the way to recovery.

Just to compare levels of indignity, Parker went further in her response about a lack of apology in 2014 on Twitter of author Sarah J. Symonds, who said Parker's twins didn't look like her. "I'm certain there isn't a woman on this planet who would support your specific kind of cruelty. No apology, no explanation," Parker wrote.

Cruelty.

Perhaps Parker and colleagues could apply that level of strong language to Noth and the physical and emotional harm he reportedly caused five separate women. He may actually deserve the kind of intense reaction Carrie and her bridesmaids dealt Noth's character in the 2008 *Sex and the City* movie when he stood her up at their wedding.

That was pretend, but this is real.

Instead, their banal response is comparable to the indifference and lack of humanity that Parker's character, Carrie, endured when her fictional lover, Berger, ended their relationship in a terse Post-it note that became a meme for cruel indifference.

I watched only two episodes of *And Just Like That*. I loved the banter among the friends, and I especially loved everything they wore. I couldn't bring myself to align with women who claimed to be feminists yet didn't do enough when sexual assault was in their backyard. Or in the hotel down the street. I was disappointed. I stopped watching.

No, every actor or celebrity with a large public profile does not have a moral responsibility to be an advocate. They can just be famous, and that's that. And those who have committed crimes against trust and intimacy, crimes of violence, can apologize and make restitution on their own. Someone is not automatically damned with guilt by association. But apology for association needs to be deeper than a social media post.

When the charismatic actor William Hurt died in March 2022, the accusations against him for sexual and domestic abuse resurfaced in news stories but were outnumbered by tributes. Marlee Matlin spoke publicly in 2009 about Hurt's rape of her. But he reportedly made amends. "My own recollection is that we both apologized and both did a great deal to heal our lives. Of course, I did and do apologize for any pain I caused. And I know we have both grown. I wish Marlee and her family nothing but good," Hurt wrote in 2009 when the accusation was new.

A former girlfriend, Sandra Jennings, accused Hurt of domestic violence in court in 1989, but she made no statements after his 2022 death from cancer.

It was Donna Kaz, Hurt's partner from 1977 to 1980 and author of the 2016 memoir *UN/MASKED: Memoirs of a Guerrilla Girl on Tour*, who wrote about Hurt in terms of the truth of their relationship, which was marred by violence. "You have to understand something about surviving violence," Kaz wrote in *Vanity Fair* shortly after Hurt's death. "It is always with you. It is something you will never get over. And just as you are never going to get over it you incorporate the experience into the fabric of your life. It becomes a part of you."

Hurt never contested the validity of her story, attempted to stop the book's publication, or interfered with her public advocacy for those who have endured personal violence, sexual assault, and harassment.

Bizarre testimonies and cruelty characterized the trial for the $50 million defamation suit actor Johnny Depp brought against his ex-wife Amber Heard for writing an op-ed in 2018 for the *Washington Post* about her role as a representative of victims of domestic violence—the article didn't name Depp. The grotesque claims and the persistent horror alleged on both sides only served to confuse and muddle the case and the broader landscape of intimate-partner violence, making the trial a popularity game of celebrity power and control. Heard's countersuit of $100 million literally upped the ante. More than fifteen billion Johnny Depp fans roared their approval on Instagram with #JusticeForJohnny, compared to fifty-one million rallying with #JusticeForAmber.

At the height of the maelstrom that was this carnival trial, I read that the case was the embodiment of "himpathy," the automatic siding with males accused of wrongdoing, an aggressively forceful pushback to #MeToo. The takeaway was a loss of credibility for survivors of sexual assault, intimate partner violence, sexual harassment, and workplace harassment. Will anyone's truth be believed? Depp got a seven-minute standing ovation at the 2023 Cannes Film Festival, even as #CannesYouNot swelled on social media.

In May 2023, E. Jean Carroll won a $5 million settlement in a civil lawsuit about sexual abuse and defamation by Donald Trump. She told the world about an assault in a dressing room in the '90s, and his attorney blamed her for not screaming during it. She did not apologize for not screaming.

What is the crime—committing the act or telling? And who is canceled? This also leads to the question of responsibility that women hold for each other: to warn, to support, to honor, to believe.

As a survivor of domestic violence, I have neither forgotten nor forgiven my former husband, but I have let the anger go. I simply want to be free of him. He does not have the power to contaminate my life for five more seconds. The physical and emotional violence that ended for me in 1995 with an emergency order of protection I sought is forever housed in me; it is just no longer an active thought, nor is he. I know who he is, and he apologized many years ago, never denying what he did and the harm it caused the family. Perhaps forgiveness is possible far into the future. Forgetting is off the table. Domestic violence and sexual assault, though different in specific circumstance, are linked in the longevity—an eternity—of consequence for the person who is harmed. It is their choice to tell or not to tell the truth of that harm as loudly and to as broad an audience as feels right. It is also a choice to support those who do tell their truth—even if the accused is a friend and colleague. Even if you don't want the inconvenient story to decrease your fan base.

There is a burden of truth. There is accountability for causing harm.

Anita Hill, in her book *Believing: Our Thirty-Year Journey to End Gender Violence*, writes that addressing the enormity of gender violence and all its forms is like "boiling the ocean." It is possible, though, to change the story by treating the stories differently.

UN Women called gender violence a "shadow pandemic." We are all affected by its presence.

In the case of the four *Sex and the City* and *And Just Like That* feminists whom millions of women adore and have pretended to be—even if just for one night at a costume party—the least they can do is vocalize strongly the need for truth and how to move past the harm into healing and safety. That requires more than two sentences on Instagram.

In the bestselling book *The Body Keeps the Score: Brain, Mind, and Body in the Healing of Trauma,* Dr. Bessel van der Kolk writes: "We have learned that trauma isn't just an event that takes place sometimes in the past; it is also the imprint left by that experience on mind, brain, and body. This imprint has ongoing consequences for how the human organism manages to survive in the present." The book has been on the *New York Times* bestseller list for more than five years.

The trauma remains. And in the time of COVID, it is one more trauma to add to the Jenga game of life: trying to determine what pieces of wood you can remove from the tower of carefully stacked blocks so you don't crumble to the floor.

Yes, I would have loved to spend my homebound, sequestered COVID nights laughing at the delicious banter about work, love, family, children, and dreams between marvelous fictional friends wearing amazing outfits. But I just couldn't.

I want to remind my former feminist idols that as a high-profile feminist, you don't just ignore a crime and distance yourself from the accused so the stain doesn't spill on your amazing Met Gala–ready clothes—especially if you proudly put "feminist" on your nametag. You do what it takes to make reparations. You not only help the women and men harmed by someone you were closely affiliated with, but you speak up and out against sexual assault as a crime that is too often silenced and excused. You explain how easy it is not to know what is happening around you, and you offer resources and possibilities for help. You speak up loudly and often.

December 2023

6

PARTNERS

"I CAN'T BELIEVE NO ONE WANTS YOU!"

As if I am a ten-year-old German shepherd at the rescue shelter or the lone vegan cupcake still available come closing time in a bakery display case.

She shouts this to me at a pre-COVID cocktail gathering at her tidy house, where the pillows are placed just so; some still have tags. The cashmere throw was not tossed on a couch in haste but placed with such deliberation you would think a life was in danger if a fold was off.

I am here because she is dating someone I'm close to; I'm here for him. I believe she means it as a compliment, and I also believe she had had many glasses of rosé prior to her declaration. Wearing a spotless apron and flitting about, she arranges a charcuterie board with folded meats and wedges of expensive cheeses; no putting out chips and salsa and calling it a day. I believe the bright-yellow cheese spread I love would make her faint.

"You're so pretty and smart and such a good cook!"

Apparently this is the reason my unaccompaniedness is a stunner. She is pointing to the tray of bruschetta that I brought and artfully arranged, complete with flowers on the tray. The toasted asiago bread points were rapidly disappearing; guests were smiling. As if bruschetta prowess could earn a MacArthur Genius Grant or a podcast deal.

I assume she is trying to be supportive of me, as her partner—my friend—has no doubt shared my single status, just for background. But, unlike my friend's new partner, my relationship status is not in the top three factors of my identity. And it's also no one's business, unless of course I'm writing about it—like now—or telling a live story about it onstage. It comes after author, journalist, and mother, definitely after friend and sister. Artist is up there, but I'm an amateur. Good dancer even comes before relationship status. Dancer is not on my résumé.

Who I am with does not define who I am.

If I'm alone at a party it could mean my partner was working, receiving the Nobel Prize, saving lives on top of a mountain, had a prior dinner engagement, had a cold, did not like the host, refused to attend, or did not exist. Or he is tied up in the trunk of my car or in a soundproof glass cage in my rented storage unit. And yes, I believe that comes to mind because I watched too many episodes of *You*. (And if you're not familiar with that show, then check it out on Netflix and see how many bodies piled up over the seasons; most of them he professed to love.)

The fact that I'm alone does not mean no one wants me. Maybe I don't want them. I'm not saying I'm better than any of the potential partners I've encountered, but I do think I'm a middle-aged, oldish rank of seven out of ten (in candlelight), and I do think I can offer a lot to someone who also has a lot to offer.

The notion that a decision about my coupling is outside of my volition is very rose ceremony and ancient, as if a single person holds the power. Like a prearranged marriage, a royal coupling between England and Germany to stave off a war a thousand years ago or at the turn of the century. Maybe there is no one who has yet crossed my path that I want? I am of the mind and heart that these choices are mutual. I get to pick a partner who gets to pick me back. I am discerning. I hope my partner is as well.

The woman who screeched her shock that no one wants me— and yes, friends who were within earshot still repeat that line in greetings to me—did eventually marry my dear friend. And, for the record, it absolutely did not turn out well—at all.

Note that this party was before COVID, when people went to parties indoors and did not stay home to watch TV for fun.

I have not always been alone, even though during my marriage, I was officially and legally not alone but felt decidedly alone most of the time.

Once divorced, I dated a nice, kind man for more than six years, who deliberately bought a ninety-inch TV and put it in his wood-paneled den. It was the size of an elk, and he wanted me to sit in front of it with him often. This was years before the pandemic made sitting in front of an enormous TV for uninterrupted hours a prescriptive national sport along with yeast rising and yoga pants. Big-screen TVs saved a lot of relationships during the pandemic. Or ended them. One friend got divorced during COVID because her then-husband retired and she could not bear that much idle proximity.

We watched what we considered a lot of TV when I was a child in the '60s in the tawny brick house with the center entrance on Clinton Place, across the street from where they filmed *Planes, Trains and Automobiles*, starring John Candy, who died too young.

Back then there were only network TV options, and we watched perhaps an hour a day, more on the weekends. I remember all eight of us—my parents and my five siblings— gathered in my parents' metallic blue wallpapered bedroom in July 1969 during what felt like the middle of the night to watch the astronauts walk on the moon.

"This is history," my father sighed, awestruck, as the six of us sat quietly cross-legged on the floor.

I was eleven and thought what Neil Armstrong said was dumb and missing a word: "One small step for man, one giant leap for mankind."

My son Weldon bought me a Fire Stick for my TV the Christmas before COVID; he installed it and allowed me to be a parasite on his subscriptions so now I get everything I ever wanted—and a lot that I don't—on the TV in my bedroom. Brendan added me to his subscriptions, and I couldn't leave my room for seven years if I wanted to absorb all the channel possibilities. I do not. But I'm starting to understand why that man I no longer date wanted to sit in front of his TV all the time. I still don't consider reaching out. He saw everything he wanted to see on that screen; he was nice and all, but he didn't really see me. He also didn't have a passport and didn't like to travel.

In the first two years of the pandemic, I became obsessed with reality shows that have to do with dating, romance, and, of course, breakups. There were many to choose from: *Too Hot to Handle*, *Love Island*, *Are You the One?*, and *Love Is Blind*, where those folks get married in three weeks after not seeing one another before getting engaged.

Pursuing the perfect partner is an international pandemic obsession. And time waster.

There are also the tried and untrue decades of *The Bachelor*, *The Bachelorette*, or *Bachelor in Paradise*. Most of the time I'm shaking my head and wondering who the parents of these young people are and whether those parents are thoroughly ashamed, particularly for not expanding their children's vocabularies so all of them don't say "amazing" dozens of times in an hour.

"It's an amazing journey."

"You are amazing."

"This tastes so amazing."

"Our one-on-one date was so amazing."

They also say "um" too much. Did no one ever teach them how to avoid saying "um" or "like"? (For the record, the cure is to say the sentence over in your head before blurting it out.)

But then some of the participants do go on hometown dates, and the parents never seem to reprimand their offspring for such vapid vocabulary. I also wonder if those parents ever gave their children context about what a struggle is and what constitutes "so hard," as those are the words the romantic contestants use repeatedly when describing time spent on an island dilly-dallying for free, working out, dancing, dating, drinking, eating, and thinking about what they will eat and drink next and with whom. I also wonder if the parents are embarrassed watching their sons or daughters do those deep kisses while sliding on top of each other in hammocks wearing bathing suits. I have three grown sons, and I could not stand it.

I spend a little bit of time thinking about the *Bachelorette* and *Bachelor* wardrobes and whether the show contestants packed all those great outfits themselves or if the network provides a lot of the fancy clothes. I worry about this because the ones who get sent home—roseless—only have one small suitcase and yet they never repeat outfits. Also, none of the women has a purse. Ever. Where do they put their room keys and lip balm?

On a reality level, the racism permeating the franchise was disturbing, but the deserved judgment and expulsions were swift, with forever host Chris Harrison deleted in early 2021 after his inexcusable comments defending a white *Bachelor* contestant's complicit attendance at an Old South plantation party. And this was the season to be anti-racist, with the first Black bachelor, Matt James. Maybe the network's DEI training was not so well attended? Or affirmed?

Later that year, the racist-tinged attacks on *Bachelor in Paradise* participant Natasha Parker caused a spate of more shallow apologies, if not a loss of Instagram followers. So the unbearable whiteness of being single on reality TV is still rampant, as the bystander impulses to watch these shows to garner a speck of insight into how relationships work—and don't—continues.

And then there is *90 Day Fiancé*, a show that completely wipes out all rationality and makes me scream at the TV. I guess to channel my incensed fury I could live tweet during it and find camaraderie across the globe with thousands of others who think the people who make these rash romance choices are stupefyingly naive just as I do. Really, you gave Evelin $40,000 for her bar in Peru, and she's still seeing her old boyfriend?

What I find these partner-seeking shows all have in common is unfiltered hope, a blind belief that you can manifest romantic happiness by saying the right thing, making the right first impression, and declaring your intention. They adhere to the conviction that the driving piece of the puzzle is that someone chose you—not that you have much to do with it. It is a passive acceptance of another's whim. I'm sorry; that feels medieval.

Of course love is a fast and easy process and can be decided before the commercial break, as if people really do make life partner choices that quickly. Me? I think ninety days is not so long a time. I may take ninety days to answer someone about whether I want to go out with them again. I believe choosing a partner should account for more factors than choosing a wine to pair with a specific dish at dinner.

"I have to think about it."

If I'm interested in dating someone, I search for them on LinkedIn and Whitepages to see if they exist. You may be surprised to learn that some of them do not.

"Oh, no, that's not my real name. Is that a problem?"

And for sure some are not the age they report to be. Sometimes the age lie is fifteen years long. No, fifty-five is not seventy. No, forty-five is not sixty-two.

And while it may seem sort of sweet to delete rational discernment from the love equation, I find it dangerous to ignore the cautionary tales—these grim fairy tales with mythic-level red-flag tropes—that are lurking behind every twenty-one-dollar glass of wine or flirty glance. Armored with incredulity, I watch these shows because I want someone to at some point sometime say this is hopeless. Few seem to. Well, the ones sent home crying in the back seat of the black SUV sometimes do, and then I feel bad, especially if it's a woman I was rooting for who says this always happens to her, all the good men are taken. I hear you, sister.

And yes, I watched *The Tinder Swindler*. Note to self: it is probably not his private jet, so don't lend him $25,000, even if you somehow have $25,000 to lend.

I'm cautious because it appears to me that for every random happy ending to vicariously enjoy on the small screen and IRL there are the same number of horrible pairings dragged from the beginning to the middle and onward to the end. Cumulatively I know perhaps an equal amount of unhappy partnerings as blissful ones. I'm related to a few happy couples. So it's possible! But under the shadow of some of the unfathomably cruel and heartless dissolutions of marriages and relationships, I applaud the marriages that last thirty, forty, or fifty happy years with exclamation points and a tinge of distrust.

In my dating world, there is also a lot of gray area to cover: miles and miles of vague disinterest and people who get insulted when I ask them to please spell my name correctly (one *l* not two), have multiple cats I am deathly allergic to, live two hundred miles away, or bristle when I suggest that such a staunch opinion about transgender individuals is lacking in empathy or humanity.

Some of my best friends and relatives are in very happy and successful quarter- to half-century marriages. (I see you!) Some of my closest friends are also in glorious recent marriages; I can upload the photos of second- and third-time brides and grooms dancing euphorically down the aisle with grown children and stepchildren to "Happy," of vows exchanged in gardens, of black-tie weddings at glorious hotels, of ceremonies that make everyone cry—and laugh.

In the past five years or so I have been to many second weddings of close friends. Some of them are low-key and cautious, others are way over the top with indulgence, as if they are a warning shot that life is short, might as well risk it all and dress alike in a choreographed TikTok dance routine at the wedding in an exotic locale, like a scene from *Bling Empire*.

The fifty-, sixty-, and seventy-something brides and grooms do not take this trip down the aisle or straight to the five-tiered wedding cake lightly—no, they do not.

But being the skeptical once-married, once-divorced person I am, I'm always waiting for the phone call or the text that would prompt a lesser person to say, "I told you so."

Of course, for many of these partnerings, the call never arrives, thank goodness. But at times it certainly does; I have not done a spreadsheet to see what the actual numbers and percentages are, but I think it's about half-and-half. Thankfully, those databases are available, so I don't have to work on my Excel skills.

The World Population Review holds up my belief: in the United States 50 percent of all married couples divorce, the sixth-highest divorce rate in the world; Russia is at the top with 4.8 divorces per one thousand citizens, as if that would not seem obvious. Sri Lanka has the lowest, with a rate of .15 per one thousand.

In the United States, 60 percent of second marriages end in divorce, and 73 percent of all third marriages end in divorce, putting an end forever to the meme that the third time is the charm. I wonder if that will make any of my friends who suffered their second- and third-time-around fails feel any better. I doubt it; heartbreak is heartbreak, no matter how old you are or how blindsided you were. There is also this new pandemic-inspired trend of committed couples living apart peacefully and joyfully. Yeah.

I hold in my memory vault and not-so-distant hippocampus the wrenching tales of good people—men and women—who have been touched by deceit, greed, and aggression in their pairings. The collapses of some of these second marriages were so horrific and unimaginably cruel, not just to the partner but sometimes to the partner's children and siblings, that it's enough to make me swear off the remote possibility of a successful second marriage for anyone. I am one and done, and you can hold me to that.

It's kind of like getting food poisoning from one batch of bad portobello mushrooms. You will never eat portobello mushrooms again, even though millions of people do and they are delicious. It is sort of like me and tequila after the pitcher of margaritas in 1981 in New York on a business trip. I have not had a sip of one since.

It makes one hesitant to go out on a limb, or maybe just to go out.

And then there are the benign stalemates, the blandly coexisting partnerships that are neither euphoric nor horrific, as in the couples I see out to dinner at a nearby table who never say a word to each other for a polite two-hour meal. They both seem nice and also look like they're enjoying their food, but they only speak to the waiter, not each other, and chew carefully their forkfuls of Caesar salad or the salmon steak; very few of them have dessert. And if they do have dessert, particularly if a candled delicacy is brought out with a song by the waitstaff celebrating a birthday or—heavens!—an anniversary, I want to weep or join them. "I'm sorry," comes to mind.

* * *

I WAS LIVING IN A STUDIO ON WRIGHTWOOD AVENUE IN Chicago and working as a regional editor at *Adweek* magazine, when I set my alarm on July 29, 1981, to watch the middle of the night royal wedding of Lady Diana Spencer and Prince Charles, complete with her poufy dress and shy smile. It seemed so magical.

Royal wedding watching is another kind of reality show binge, as I also watched Fergie marry Prince Andrew (I even went as Fergie for Halloween later that year). Years later and not any less bedazzled by the pomp, circumstance, and extravagant hopefulness, I marveled at Kate Middleton and Prince William's 2011 nuptials. Seven years later it seemed as if the palace would finally embrace diversity with Harry's choice of Meghan Markle, but that rosy after-party didn't go as planned. Harry tells everything about all of that in his book, *Spare*, and they both talk about a lot of things on TV shows. And then, wow, the Andrew formerly known as a prince was called out and dethroned for his sexual assault and abuse allegations. Fergie probably knew. And to think people thought Fergie was the bad egg way back when.

Perhaps we are willing voyeurs in other people's courtship rituals and marriage vows to try to further define what romance, partnering, and love really look like—or not. It also reveals strategies, game plans, and goals that you could mimic or abhor. We have a dream of what romance translates to for us, what kind of partner is the ultimate touchdown, perhaps taking in all these images and scenarios to build a framework for happy ever after. At the very least we might learn what to avoid.

I had my parents to look to for a role model of what solid marriage meant; their marriage of forty-four years ended only because my father passed away. I remember them as empty nesters holding hands in the grocery store and working together every day at my father's manufacturing business, then spending their free time traveling. My house is filled with photographs of them smiling together from boats and in front of iconic destinations, the legacy of their relationship unbroken still.

Of course it was not all perfect, as they were not perfect, but I grew up knowing what it looked like to be seen as you were authentically. I bore witness to parents who saw, knew, and understood each other, for better and for worse. And I was the recipient of knowing what it felt like to be seen. They also saw me. So I expected—and likely demanded—to be seen for who I was, am, and will be. That has not happened.

While I do know I am lucky to have lived as a child and teen under a roof held up by equal partners, I acknowledge that such positive role modeling can backfire—the expectation is that every partner (that I encounter at least) behaves with integrity and the best intentions. So I watch these absurdly unrealistic reality TV shows—and not just because COVID has crimped my social life outside the house—to see what to avoid and remind myself that caution is required because people are not always as they seem, especially when they're trying to earn the first-impression rose.

* * *

WHEN I SETTLE IN FOR THE NIGHT, I CAN SCROLL THROUGH my on-demand choices of real-life romance and partner picking and its fails, or the new niche of old people falling deeply in love movies that always seem to star Sharon Stone and Julia Roberts; these have implausibly happy endings.

If I am in one of my online dating phases (I log off for many, many months at a time), I can also choose to meet for coffee or cocktails any of the dozens of online matches who are waiting for me to like them back. On principle, I *x* out all the men who take photos of themselves in mirrors in public bathrooms with urinals behind them, as if they don't know where the selfie button is. I also will not chat with someone who declares he is conservative in his leanings, is unvaxxed, aligns with conspiracy theories, or voted for the man who shall not be named. I dismiss the ones who say "polyamory," the ones who swear they are in an "open relationship" and their wives think their dating is fine, the ones who want "something casual," and the ones who are vague about where they live and are in the airport, waiting. Are we meeting in the cell phone parking lot? The man whose profile photo was of him in a hospital gown did not get a swipe from me.

I wrongfully x-ed out all those who listed they were "sapio-sexual" until I googled it to see they liked smart people. I will not click on the person who is lying on his rumpled bed with his shirt off, giving a longing look implying that he wants whom-ever checks him to join him in that spot as soon as possible, because, well, ew.

My discernment plan has led to a few wonderful, if short-lived, encounters with smart, kind men. I am cautious. I have trust issues. Like a lighthouse flashing danger to ships at sea, I am perpetually wary of the signals I'm receiving and also the signals I'm sending.

I once went on a first date with a man who wore a fanny pack—and not cross-chest ironically—talked with his mouth full of food, and spent about thirty-five minutes in the bath-room. I was worried he'd had an episode with irritable bowel syndrome or, God forbid, had died in there.

Before he returned to the table, the waitress came over to me and said, "If you want to go, I'll split the check now so you can leave, and I'll cover for you."

I stayed—much to the server's surprise—but it was our only date.

Then for five months in 2022, still in the throes of COVID habits, I ventured into a relationship with a man who was kind, attractive, funny, smart, and intensely devoted to telling me how much he loved me, wanted me, desired me, and was amazed by me. He lived a mile and a half away, and if I had gone along with every one of his requests for my company, I would have seen him every night of every week. Plus a few mornings and afternoons.

"It's a school night," I would remind him. "I have meetings starting at 8:00 A.M."

In the summer months—we met in July—we went to out-door concerts, ate dinner on my patio, and drank wine on my back porch. When the weather grew cold, it was good to be alone with him; he made me laugh in a way I had not laughed in years. He was doting and helpful with anything I needed to be fixed—caulked all my windows and cut down dead tree limbs in my backyard—but ultimately didn't care enough to change old habits.

The last time I saw him, he drank more glasses of whiskey on ice than I had ever seen one person consume in one night, or maybe a month—and that includes my late Irish uncles and college fraternity friends before they passed out. He behaved unfathomably aggressively toward me, my sister, my brother-in-law, my nieces, and even my environmentalist poet-friend at an important event where I was telling a live story on stage. He picked a fight with Colin and heckled the other storytellers. I asked him to stop drinking and shouting. When he told me to shut up, my sister Madeleine almost burst into flames. I did drive him home, though my friends told me to leave him there; it was raining and he didn't have his wallet. I am certain many would say I should have stayed in the relationship and consider the benefits of being with a good man—however flawed—who loved me. Some would criticize me and assert I could be helpful to him, sign on for assistance in what he called "work I need to do," bargaining that his love was worth the mistakes made in between.

I ended the relationship the next day in a phone call because this was his second chance and I was not willing to be with a partner who was a distinct Jekyll and Hyde. I have terrible memories from when I was married to someone who was two different people and I could not be sure who would show up when—even with the reassurances that it would never happen again. *Never*, I have learned, is a big word that many have a hard time living up to. I am not willing to excuse mistreatment, however infrequent. Pandemic or not.

*   *   *

IN HER INSIGHTFUL AND WITTY BOOK *LOVE IN THE TIME OF Contagion*, Laura Kipnis writes, "Could the pandemic turn out to be a reset, a chance to wipe the bogeyman and -woman from the social imagination, invent wilder, more magnanimous ways of living and loving as we go forward into whatever comes next?"

Well, perhaps. For me the pandemic has made me even more wary, cautious, and suspicious. It has raised the urgency for partner-testing to a whole new level of mandatory requirements. And I mean this literally and as a metaphor.

"You were just on a plane; please get a COVID test before we meet for coffee."

"I don't have time."

"Well, then, we can meet next week."

I am not inclined to get COVID from a random partner I will never see again. I am not inclined to overcompromise with someone I may need to quarantine with. Maybe I should take the leap and endure the risk. Maybe not.

Sometimes—for the sake of sanity and perhaps productivity—you just need to press pause. As Miley Cyrus sings, "I can buy myself flowers."

I am, after all, very good company for myself. We don't disagree all that often.

March 2023

1

CLASSMATES

I WAS NOT A NO-SHOW BECAUSE I AM A CONSCIENTIOUS objector to my forty-fifth high school reunion from Oak Park–River Forest High School, class of 1975. The fall 2020 reunion, scheduled at a bar on the Madison Street strip in Forest Park, Illinois, where as teenagers we snuck into bars with fake IDs, was cancelled due to COVID-19 concerns.

I wanted to go.

Not because I was craving conversation with other sixty-somethings who look vaguely familiar, but because I bought the most amazing one-shoulder black top from my designer-friend Takara and an off-white pleather jacket on super sale at Kohl's with military zippers and a floppy collar that I was planning to wear with high-rise black skinny pants that have some kind of elastic or spandex built in that give me a body I do not see in the shower.

I wanted to go because my fortieth college reunion was marvelous the year before, in October 2019. Months before the pandemic turned millions of us into WFH recluses who never wear shoes while tweeting about snacking preferences and Netflix obsessions, I jubilantly attended my Northwestern University reunion with my very best friend in the whole wide world and roommate all throughout college, Dana.

She flew in from Los Angeles, where she lives with her two sons and works as a therapist. And if you're wondering what it is like to have a bestie who is a therapist, it is beyond my wildest dreams. We Facetime when texting or calling doesn't cut it and the current dilemma or trauma needs closer attention. She does not charge me, of course, and she's always right.

"Is that a negative intention?" she purrs.

Though I had meticulously planned multiple days of outfits—for the college reunion lunch and campus tour, newspaper staff reunion, cocktail party, post–cocktail party, breakfast, football game, dinner, post–dinner party, final campus tour, and breakfast—all with different audiences, requirements, moods, goals, and expected outcomes, Dana shuffled and reworked every one of my wardrobe choices.

Yes to the zebra-print silk double-breasted fitted blazer with gold buttons. Yes to the long purple skirt and the purple coat and can she please borrow my coat for the football game?

The shallow and tired phrase "It is better to look good than feel good" was playing in my head on repeat. I believe for reunions that is true. I confess it is absurd.

I have long had a gendered theory of reunions. Those who identify as women and attend reunions almost always look spectacular. And those who identify as male, maybe not so much. Having attended every five-year incremental college reunion and many of my high school reunions (the last few inconveniently scheduled when I was out of town on business), I have formed my opinion that this theory is true partially because women take better care of themselves. But the other part may be that women attend only if they feel great about themselves. The men think it will be fun and do not question whether they look good. They all believe they do.

I've surmised from casual research that centers totally on my own personal anecdotes that most people subscribe to the theory that it is better to be judged well—or not at all. I know.

Smiling in forty-year-old sweaters, many of the men pose for every picture and grin broadly, assuming they look the same as they did in 1976 when they were shirtless in running shorts on South Campus Beach, where we went instead of going to class in spring quarter because someone else was taking notes.

The women seem more self-consciously careful with the photos, and many do that sorority-scripted hand on waist arm forward bend, chin lift and (facial) cheek suck that gives everyone the same look. I am not a fan of the girl pose, deep forward lean plus hands on knees squishing because I think diminishment of yourself is not optimal.

No, looks are not everything, but if you only see people from your very distant past every five or ten years, you understand that looks are pretty much almost everything in the first hour or two of those superficial encounters. Not that you have to go for fake eyelashes, but at least do your eyebrows. Why that matters so much now I don't know, but I know from billboards and Instagram that brows matter. A lot. Especially during COVID, because everyone can see your eyebrows even when you are wearing a mask.

Yes, what a person looks like then and now all starts to come back to you in waves of intermittent memories, and then you think to yourself, "Wait, you look nothing at all as you did when we dated," and all of that readjustment is contained in the seemingly innocuous "I didn't recognize you!" announcement.

Women get it more often than men. Some say it's because they perhaps bore children, and others attribute it to added stress. But then there are the celebrity goddesses who blow all those theories out of the water, and I am talking about you, Christie Brinkley, Angela Bassett, and Michelle Yeoh.

I care what I look like, though I do not body-shame and age-shame anyone. I dye my gray roots every two weeks with

L'Oreal Preference No. 9 and go into a slight panic when they are out of it at CVS because the other brands are not exactly the same color. Still, I know Walgreens a few blocks away will accommodate me, and I'll drive through many zip codes until I find it. I always do. I wear concealer, eyeliner, and lipstick most every day (mascara only on very special occasions) and believe that in my new work life of Zoom conferences and webinars, lipstick is the new SPANX.

I ordered this amazing concealer online because I just couldn't stop watching the Facebook ads where I saw so many age spots disappear. I was overcharged (not a mistake, it is overpriced) for a tube and it arrived maybe three weeks later. I was so giddy when the text announcing its arrival at my doorstep pinged. I stopped typing (I was on deadline), raced to the door, ripped open the box, and went to the bathroom mirror to put it on.

Well, it was a miracle. My flawed skin was now spotless and glowing from just a few dots of concealer. I went back to typing, thinking I would indeed make my own Facebook video about it. An hour later, I looked in the mirror and it had completed evaporated; I was no longer flawless. And then I read the directions: it said you need to apply every two hours.

I am a staunch objector to volunteer plastic surgery and Botox injections because I have seen what overdoing it can do to a face, and I also cannot fathom why anyone would purposefully inject poison that paralyzes the facial muscles in your lips and eye area. I want my face to move. I firmly (see what I did there?) believe that the older I get, the more important the lighting I surround myself with is. Whenever possible, I surround myself with candles. Scented candles. They take the sting out of most everything.

Linda Evangelista, the supermodel many know from the '80s and '90s because she was on more than seven hundred fashion magazine covers (so how could you miss her), maybe should have been on my bandwagon. Linda went the fat-freezing route, and it didn't go so well. Even though I think she looks OK, or like most of the fifty-six-year-old women I know, she sued the parent company of CoolSculpting for $50 million in damages in 2021, claiming she contracted paradoxical adipose hyperplasia from the fat freezing. Her fat expanded instead of shrunk. I'm sorry she suffered.

And then Madonna at the 2023 Grammy Awards picked up her award looking only vaguely familiar. Her face was distorted or injection skewed, and the mean comments flooded in on social media, causing an ageism typhoon that it is not about Madonna choosing to have cheek injections but rather a culture that demands she have cheek injections. Madonna fans rallied around to support her; if she wants to treat herself, it is her choice, and it is because society damns old ladies. Yes, it does.

A month or so later actor, director, and author Justine Bateman told *60 Minutes* that she would never do Botox or plastic surgery. "I feel like I would erase, not only all my authority that I have now, but also, I like feeling that I am a different person now than I was when I was twenty. I like looking in the mirror and seeing that evidence."

Amen.

And then Martha Stewart at eighty-one was on the cover of *Sports Illustrated* as the swimsuit pinup. She was photoshopped. Still, it was refreshing.

I believe ageism is very real, yes, but I do not believe any of us are forced to have surgery that will distort our faces beyond recognition. I am afraid of injections. I am afraid of having muscles in my face paralyzed. I am afraid of getting "that face."

Maybe the concealer will help? Reapply often.

Though I am not what you may classify as a natural woman, it is true that I deplore what years of multiple cosmetic surgeries do to women—they all end up looking alike, as if they are cousins who share the same DNA propensity for feline eyes, permanently pouty mouth now deflated in areas, and misplaced, overinflated cheeks, like they stayed on steroids for muscle aches too long. Plus I understand it hurts, and I do not elect to have procedures that I need to recover from—unless of course it is to stay alive. Having survived cancer and having been through a few surgeries—appendectomy, lumpectomy, oophorectomy (say that ten times in a row), and others that you don't really need to know about but were medically necessary—I don't do surgery that is optional: that fear and risk aversion thing I have.

Romy and Michele's High School Reunion came out in 1997, when I was twenty-two years out of high school and just two years past the twenty-year reunion, where I wore a gold sequin sweater and was diving into a brutal divorce and trying desperately to look happy, as if working and raising three sons ages seven, five, and two by myself was just a walk in the park. Besides, my former husband was in the same high school class. He didn't go to the reunion. Thank. God.

I loved that movie because Michele was a one-*l* Michele like myself, and I assume her mother told her the same thing as mine did about my name spelling that was not the norm: "Why would I give you a name with hell in it?"

I was familiar with all of the elements of the movie's arc of insecurities: plotting, planning, lying, mean girls, and proving yourself. Except, of course, I would never claim to have invented Post-its, though I likely fabricated a few minor things about how well I was doing—and didn't I look it?

I was prepared to go to the forty-fifth high school reunion alone; I prepped for what I would say and how I would shape the narrative of my last decade. I would most definitely rehearse. I'd talk about my books and trainings, university teaching career, bylines, and travel (pre-COVID) and skip over the part that I have not been in a serious, lasting relationship for years.

I would buff and shine up some of the realities and say I am doing what I always wanted to do with my life, and that would of course be a lie—not a huge lie, but more than a little one. It is mostly true professionally, not completely true personally. I would for sure omit the part about feeling as if everything I said I would accomplish by now has not happened and that every time I go to a funeral I cry really hard because the people who are dying now are not just old. The friends and relatives in the caskets who suffered from COVID or cancer or a disease they didn't learn about until it was too late. The people shot by racists when they stop into a grocery store for milk or ring the wrong doorbell. The sons and daughters who are beaten to death by police after a traffic stop. The children killed in their classrooms as their teachers try to shield them and the police are afraid to go in and save them. I mourn when I watch a brutal murder by police on video because I not only mourn that young man—mostly it is young men, but women are killed, too—I think of the mother and father of that victim, and I cannot swallow. Maybe that wouldn't come up.

I was prepared to put on a show, as my friend Mariann (who also went to the Northwestern reunion with me) says, "When you start doing all that stuff you do about your work and your life and all of that," gesturing with a circle around my face. I wanted one night where I felt good about myself—even if it was just a little bit augmented.

The visuals and the optimism of this high school reunion were crucial because I am no longer automatically included in the tight group of six friends I was a part of since we were thirteen and freshmen in high school. The group of us—all neighbors— had been besties (that term was not yet invented, nor was *posse*) from 1971 through all the marriages, children, and more.

I am the only one no longer part of the close-knit tribe; it's been that way for about a decade.

They mostly still travel together to really great places— Greece was one—and go to each others' children's weddings. I see the photos on Facebook, and though I am still a holdover on a few of their holiday card lists and invitation lists and did go to a wedding a few years back, I am no longer a permanent resident in the group. They deleted me.

This group of friends is, of course, the committee to organize the whole reunion shebang, so they are official; I would be just a person with a nametag. Extra. Sidelined. The unpopular girl on the outs, booted from the inner circle. Not that it would remind me of fifth grade or anything.

"Are you all still best friends?"

I would be the only one of six to say no.

I was anticipating those questions. I was planning to smile in all the photos, chin up, and hear about everyone's sons and daughters-in-law and grandchildren, though that is not a conversation I can participate in. My three sons are grown, one in a serious relationship. But I contend their personal lives have little to do with me. I am happy—not jealous—for all these friends' successes and yes, I am a little hurt I got deleted. So I was planning to be cordial and ebullient and what my friend Amy calls "Teflon." I was planning to take an Uber both ways so I could drink more than two glasses of wine.

The one-shoulder Takara black top I bought specifically for the forty-fifth high school reunion is exquisite, so I hope there is eventually a post-COVID event I can go to so I can wear it and feel amazing. It is not really suitable for a work call on Zoom. Maybe I will wear it to the 50th.

Superficially speaking, the pandemic has canceled a lot more of our lives than a high school reunion, and I am mostly adjusting to it all. No more work travel—I loved room service and binge-watching chef shows—no more in-person encounters, no more holiday parties, no more indoor dining for the most part, no more hugging friends.

Millions of people in this country have had COVID, and millions around the world have died. Millions are unemployed, and millions are homeschooling their children while working remotely. I am grateful my sons are grown men so I don't have to quiz them on math skills or geography because I can guarantee that would not end well.

"What did you say was the capital of Wyoming?"

Blessed, yes, I am blessed and privileged because I am working and I do not have very close friends or relatives who have succumbed to COVID and died. They have died of other causes. I have not died from COVID. I am lucky. I am cautious. I am masked when I go to the small grocery store three blocks away where aisles are one way, hand sanitizer is a no-contact spritz at every aisle, and everyone is careful. They have amazing curry chicken salad with cashews and this lemon-dill hummus I have never seen anywhere else, and the marinated beets with the white wine balsamic vinegar are otherworldly.

So what that this one reunion got COVID-canceled. Big deal. It was to me.

November 2020

8

LIARS

THE WEIGHT I LIST ON MY DRIVER'S LICENSE IS A LIE.

It is a weight goal, not what actually appears at my feet when I step onto the bathroom scale; Lord knows, it is not the one at the doctor's office when I am fully dressed after a full breakfast. Or lunch, or both. It gets closer to that number at home if I hold one hand on the towel rack, but it does not get to that number precisely, so no, it is not accurate; it is wishful.

I understand doctors get it about this weight fear because now the weighing part is sometimes elective.

I do not endorse such a harmful, judgmental shaming practice on anyone else ever. It's a choice to be whatever shape or size works for you and makes you feel comfortable and powerful in your own skin. My fabrication affects no one else. I do have Scarlett Johansson goals—that is, my goal is to someday look like her healthy and fit older cousin, alright, alright, maybe her mom. I believe I will live longer if I am a healthier weight, and yes, I will likely feel better about myself if I am more fit.

But no matter what, the number listed after the word *weight* on my driver's license is a lie, a falsehood, a fabrication, an untruth. I'm good with the height. I am five feet six inches, at least I was last time I checked. I may or may not be shrinking: I understand a lot of women are at my age.

I do tell the truth in what I write, publish, and profess publicly. I tell what I know and believe is true; as a journalist and author, I know I am only as good as my research or my sourcing. And I also rely heavily on my memory when writing about my life, double-checking with the documents, data, and interviews that calibrate the evidence of my life and work. I do not tell the secret truths of other people, unless I am interviewing them on the record and that is the point.

I tell the truth in my personal life and fall back on omission as a self-protection tool when truths are impossibly difficult to express. I tell the truth to myself about who I am, what I do, and what has happened in my life. And some of it is not so good; some of it is awful.

The standards I hold myself to, the accountability I attempt to maintain in my life, are beyond the harmless untruths I say about myself on superficial details. But there is a broader category with a larger cultural nonchalance for untruth that comes at a time when lies are destructive. When the firewall between fact and fiction is burned down, the danger of lies moves past an inconvenient truth to a loss of moral integrity. And that is what I see happening now.

In the COVID era, it seems lying about reality is a national—and at times global—pastime, and for someone who has been participating in, practicing, and teaching journalism for more than four decades, it isn't just an amusing fudging of numbers on a government-issued ID. It is a crisis of truth and discernment.

* * *

secretary of state Hillary Rodham Clinton told an eager audience about her fears in the present and for the future. "It is open season on truth, decency, and civility," said the former New York senator and first lady of the United States.

"We are in a post-truth era where truth, facts, expertise—none of it matters. You try to change the narrative of what people accept as real versus what is happening."

Perhaps due to our fear and anger about a deadly virus, the facts of the pandemic turned into a war of credibility that spread into so many arenas of American culture that it poisoned us. Much of the lying started at the top in 2020 and spread into a treacherous web of untruths, fables fabricated to make the world seem not at all as it really is. Protests and violence over mask wearing, denials that the virus was even real—some confessing their misleading beliefs from the ICU.

At the 2023 World Economic Forum Annual Meeting in Davos, Arthur Gregg Sulzberger, chairman of the New York Times Company and publisher of the *New York Times*, declared in a feisty panel called "The Clear and Present Danger of Disinformation" that such fakery "attacks trust." And when "you see trust decline, society starts to fracture."

After the 2022 midterm elections, Republican New York congressman George Santos appeared to be a lie made flesh after his claims about identity, background, career, family, education, and religion were all proven false. His grandiose declarations about every aspect of his life were not just wishful thinking, like a weight on a driver's license, but evidence of how lies are accepted not just as impropriety but as a way of life, a way of being in a world completely manufactured.

His was not a benign résumé refresh; he made up from whole cloth where he went to school, that his grandparents were Holocaust survivors, his jobs, his nonprofit, his campaign contributions, even his name. It seems his alias, Anthony Devolder, didn't graduate from Baruch College, found a nonprofit, bury his mother after 9/11 (it was 2016), or work at Goldman Sachs or Citi either.

Then—alas—in May 2023 Santos pleaded not guilty to thirteen charges of fraud, including seven counts of wire fraud, three counts of money laundering, two counts of making false statements to the House of Representatives, and one count of theft of public funds. And because of all that, he was expelled from Congress in late 2023.

Convicted murderer Alex Murdaugh showed the world at his trial just how easy it is to lie about almost everything—a reprehensible range of stealing from clients to the gruesome murders of his wife, Maggie, and son, Paul.

An aversion to truth is not new; throughout mythology and history lies have been propagated intentionally. Even the anecdote that the first US president George Washington confessed to his father as a child that he chopped down a cherry tree with the unforgettable mantra "I cannot tell a lie" is false.

Washington biographer Parson Weems could tell a lie, and in the 1806 updated edition of his book *The Life and Memorable Actions of George Washington* he invented the story to make Washington seem more accessible and admirable.

Perhaps others have the same impetus lurking in their false histories.

"Misinformation is a defining issue of our time," Timothy Caulfield, author and University of Alberta professor, told Canadian Broadcasting Corporation. "I think it's good news that more and more people, including governments, are taking this battle against misinformation really seriously, because that's what's required."

I would agree that the United States in particular has become disfigured by disinformation and splintered by partisan attacks claiming media conspiracies, when actually the ones claiming the news is filled with lies are often filling the news with lies. You cannot simply stake a claim and call it a day. Something is true or it is not. Multiple views can be true at the same time, but only when backed up by facts. Injecting bleach or disinfectant does not cure COVID. Declaring COVID a hoax will keep no one alive longer.

As the highest-ranking health official advising the president on COVID, Dr. Anthony Fauci, who served at the National Institute of Allergy and Infectious Diseases for fifty-four years before retiring, sparked controversies when delivering scientific facts on the unprecedented pandemic. He was revered. He was hated. Many balked at the facts he presented, and as a result, some speculate that the resistance to masking and precautions in the early years of the pandemic caused at least two hundred thousand deaths. These were lives that could have been spared if adherence to precautions was in place.

Fauci was committed to science, and science is assuredly not opinion-based. Interpretations of scientific facts can be, but $e=mc^2$ and the periodic tables are facts, indisputable, as slam-dunk true as saying water is wet and the number one is followed by the number two.

Yes, there are versions of truth, and there are misrepresentations, which are misinformation and disinformation, the two separated by intention. Misinformation is the presentation of facts that are misleading and out of context; I have done that unintentionally, by reporting larger numbers or simply getting a quote wrong. This is why media sites run corrections. Journalists are fallible.

But disinformation is purposeful; it is intentionally propagating nontruths to achieve a goal. You can't label a tennis racket a cactus and it will suddenly sprout needles. You can't claim a pandemic is fraudulent and people will not get infected.

Such propagation of lies has led to a parallel pandemic of untruths and an urgency for people committed to telling the actual truth as is.

Then in February 2023 ChatGPT, an AI content generator, created as an experiment a fake digital news outlet, the Suncoast

Sentinel, complete with a fake staff with fake bios and photos and fake news. I don't find this amusing. I asked ChatGPT to produce my résumé, and it was only 70 percent accurate. Some of it was just made up out of thin air. No, I have not written nine books.

A National Institutes of Health study published in early 2023 with research from a team at University of Texas at Austin and Stanford University found a distinct correlation between misinformation and vaccine hesitancy and COVID denial. With six categories of misinformation listed as "medical, scientific, political, media, religious, and technological," participants reported that the misinformation gave birth to six themes of vaccine hesitancy. Those included "concerns about the vaccines' future effects, doubts about the vaccines' effectiveness, commercial profiteering, preference for natural immunity, personal freedom, and COVID-19 denial."

COVID happened at a time in history when more people than ever before were gathering their news and information from social media and digital sites—some with clear agendas and some propagating mistruths. A Pew Research study shows that 31 percent of all US adults get their news from Facebook, 25 percent get their news from YouTube, and 14 percent get their news on Twitter, now X.

Yet among the nearly four hundred million Twitter/X users, 53 percent say the app is where they get their news. Less than half, or 44 percent, of Facebook users get their news from that platform, and 30 percent of YouTube users say they gather their news from YouTube. Truth Social, an app founded by Trump in February 2022 when he was kicked off Twitter (before Elon Musk reinstated him in November 2022), has two million users.

"Those who are intent on spreading lies will do so somewhere, as evidenced by the dramatic rise in users on non-mainstream platforms," William Pelfrey Jr., professor in the Wilder School of Government and Public Affairs at Virginia Commonwealth University, told *Forbes* in 2022.

Still, there were objective entities hell-bent on correcting the falsehoods, including sites such as FactCheck.org, PolitiFact, and ProPublica, among others.

"Misinformation safety nets are meant to unbiasedly fact-check harmful, illegal, or incorrect information to protect platform users," Jeni Stolow, assistant professor of public health at the Tulane University School of Public Health and Tropical Medicine, told *Forbes*. "Even though these interventions aren't perfect, we know that they can positively impact health, wellness, and safety."

Nobel Prize–winning journalist Maria Ressa said in her 2021 acceptance speech: "Without facts, you can't have truth. Without truth, you can't have trust. Without trust, we have no shared reality, no democracy, and it becomes impossible to deal with our world's existential problems: climate, coronavirus, the battle for truth."

Former *New York Times* public editor, *Washington Post* columnist, and author Margaret Sullivan quotes this Ressa speech in her book *Newsroom Confidential: Lessons (and Worries) from an Ink-Stained Life*. Sullivan, who overlapped with me as students in the Medill School of Journalism master's program, writes of journalism: "The industry itself is in turmoil, and the changes brought about by the pandemic—working remotely for example—are adding to that. All these changes will shape the next decade and beyond of journalism, of its role in society and its relationship to the public it serves."

Yes, the media landscape is wholly different than what it was even ten years ago, but many of the foundational ethics are still in place.

Fact-checking in journalism and media sites has been a mainstay in responsible media for more than a century, with staff copy editors and independent editors hired for projects. Only now has the need for fact-checking ballooned into an emergency and become strained over what seems a professional disregarded commitment to telling the truth.

*   *   *

IN STORIES AND COLUMNS I WRITE FOR NEWSPAPERS, magazines, and digital sites, I provide my editors the sources' contact information for my stories; a fact-checker independently verifies with the source that all the information I report is correct.

Yes, sometimes sources I quote say they did not say a certain sentence. But I offer proof of the quote in notes or transcription of tape, and then their response can be, "I know I said that. But what I wanted to say was . . ." That is not a factual error on my part. That someone regrets what they say is not my problem. When I say the interview is on the record, ask questions, and record responses, it is a fair exchange.

As I write weekly business columns for Take the Lead, a women's leadership nonprofit, I often interview entrepreneurs, founders, CEOs, and organization leaders for profiles. As a practice, I do not offer previews of my work before publication. Nine times out of ten, the profile subjects are grateful for the published piece. But sometimes, they or their publicist requests changes after publication.

"Can you change the quote in the third paragraph to this?"

What follows is often an unnaturally wordy and stiff quotation that invariably makes the source look very, very good.

"But that's not what you said," I reply.

"I don't like how it sounds."

"But what's in the story is what you said," I reply. "Was any of it incorrect or not factual?"

"No. I just don't like how it sounds."

I only make changes to my work when something is factually wrong—I got the years or title wrong, the name of a company, a process I misunderstood. I am not an investigative journalist. I do not write exposés and uncover misdeeds, crimes, injustice, or outrageous behavior; I lack the tenacity to do that type of journalism. I am a feature writer and columnist. I tell stories in commentary, op-eds, essays, and profiles—those are of people who generally want me to write profiles of them. Though I am not paid by my subjects, I am paid by the site where my stories appear. Pay to play from sources is unethical in journalism.

In forty-four years as a journalist I have yet to meet someone who has nothing to say. As a feature writer, I rarely encounter a cryptic "No comment." Most people I approach for a story want me to interview them. They want their story told, and I want to tell it factually.

✴ ✴ ✴

REBECCA SOLNIT ARTFULLY SUMMED THIS UP IN HER BOOK *Orwell's Roses*: "I've always considered it a challenge as well as an obligation to work within the facts and believe a nonfiction writer can find the necessary latitude without twisting and distorting them."

Reality can be portrayed artfully and truthfully.

I graduated from journalism school in 1979, the year before Janet Cooke wrote her Pulitzer Prize–winning story for the *Washington Post* about a young boy addicted to heroin who did not exist. She ultimately confessed that her article was fiction and returned the Pulitzer.

In 1998, Patricia Smith admitted she fabricated a story for the *Boston Globe,* and her journalism career ended. That same year, Stephen Glass was exposed for imaginary stories he concocted for the *New Republic.*

In 2003, Rick Bragg left the *New York Times* in shame because he failed to acknowledge in his bylined stories that other freelance reporters did the legwork he took credit—full credit—for. Also at the *New York Times* that same year, Jayson Blair was fired for plagiarizing the work of Macarena Hernandez (a talented journalist and a friend of mine as well as a colleague for a time at The OpEd Project). Jack Kelley left *USA Today* in shame the following year for hundreds of stories he made up and passed off as journalism.

In 2004, freelance foreign correspondent Uli Schmetzer stopped writing for the *Chicago Tribune* when more than three hundred stories he wrote over sixteen years at the paper were called into question for fabrication.

In 2015 Brian Williams was fired as anchor at *NBC Nightly News* for lying about a helicopter he was in being shot down in Iraq while he was covering a story. "This came from clearly a bad place, a bad urge inside me," Williams told his former colleague Matt Lauer in an interview. Ironically that exchange was before Lauer himself was fired from NBC for sexual misconduct and harassment of female employees.

But Williams's career did not end with his lie. He was cohost of *11th Hour* at MSNBC from 2016 to 2021 before voluntarily retiring. It was only in January of 2023 that he conceded in an interview with the *Buffalo News* that he did indeed tell a lie.

Lies told in the media are not new. But claiming the media is all lies is a newly robust phenomenon, and it's one that is not true. Lying to the media as a common practice among sources is also spiking. What is befuddling and disturbing is that more public figures are telling lies to the media, in Congress, and to their constituents and pointing blame at the truthtellers for getting it wrong. They erase factual history, deny realities of slavery and historic, systemic oppression.

Just as DNA profiling has made solving crimes infinitely easier, digital evidence and footprints left in videos, texts, emails, and phone messages have made corroboration of facts and the elimination of lies much easier. Lie detection is faster now, but so is manipulating the truth into lies.

Truthtellers often have the necessary indisputable evidence that is hard to deny.

In their book about the crimes of Harvey Weinstein, *She Said: Breaking the Sexual Harassment Story That Helped Ignite a Movement*, *New York Times* journalists and authors

Jodi Kantor and Megan Twohey write, "This is also a story about investigative journalism, beginning with the first uncertain days of our reporting, when we knew very little and almost no one would speak to us. We describe how we coaxed out secrets, pinned down information, and pursued the truth about a powerful man even as he used underhanded tactics to try to sabotage our work."

The authors continue, "Our Weinstein reporting took place at a time of accusations of 'fake news' as the very notion of a national consensus on truth seemed to be fracturing."

The indefatigable *Miami Herald* reporter Julie K. Brown almost single-handedly brought down Jeffrey Epstein. Her 2016 exposé series about Epstein's sex trafficking led to his arrest and conviction. Epstein died, reportedly by suicide, in his jail cell.

In her book *Perversion of Justice: The Jeffrey Epstein Story*, Brown writes what can be considered a manifesto for truth tellers: "I believe that at this moment in history, when world events test our resilience, and when propaganda, conspiracies and lies threaten to undermine all that our nation holds dear, it will be journalists who hold the corrupt and powerful to account. As journalists, we cannot put aside this important mission even if we think the story has already been told."

Certainly mid- and postpandemic, sometimes the media stories delivered with screaming headlines and uniformed conclusions with only occasional shades of gray incited a viewpoint that was inaccurately negative, doomscrolling fodder with a political creep that had no basis in fact.

In early 2023, I interviewed Emma Varvaloucas, executive director of the Progress Network, for a business column. Founded by author and columnist Zachary Karabell in 2019, with a launch in 2020, the company has a mission statement that reads: "We live in a time marked by pessimism. Battered daily by negative headlines and facing a post-COVID world whose problems seem manifold and everlasting, it's easy to assume we are heading for disaster. It may be that the story of chaos and collapse will prove to be true. If so, the information and analysis undergirding that view are readily available. We need little help making those arguments. But what if it's not true?"

Concentrating content to report on what works and is contributing to progress shifts the mindset and counters the onslaught of negativity—and lies—Varvaloucas says. "Fundamentally it changes your mindset. There are so many hard, intractable problems we have made traction on, like poverty, vaccines, and more, but all you see are more and more problems, so you become apathetic and don't want to engage as a citizen or a voter."

What COVID has taught the world is that regardless of denials and parallel fabrications inspiring pronouncements of untruths, the facts and truths are unavoidable in the risks, dangers, and threats they present. Whether or not someone believes in the verity of COVID, if they are exposed and succumb to the virus, they can die.

It is that serious. And that simple.

What spread across the country and the world simultaneous to COVID was the proliferation of untruths, denials, and lies about most everything from history to gender identity, harassment, racial hate, bias, discrimination, antisemitism, a stolen election, and climate change.

In this parallel pandemic crisis of misinformation, it is critical for each person to adhere to truth telling—and not just journalists who define themselves as professional truth tellers—to promise to tell the truth, the whole truth, and nothing but the truth to ourselves and the world.

That, I believe, would make the world a better place.

"Lies gradually erode the capacity to know and connect," Solnit writes in *Orwell's Roses*. "In withholding or distorting knowledge or imparting falsehood, a liar deprives others of the information they need to participate in public and political life, to avoid dangers, to understand the world around them, to act on principle, to know themselves and others and the situation, to make good choices and ultimately to be free."

In a TEDx talk I gave in 2023, "Truth Is a Dare," I drew a line of logic between the courage it takes to own up to a personal truth and the intolerance for lies in the larger world. If you demand truth of yourself, it becomes much more difficult to be indifferent to untruths from family, colleagues, community, representatives, leaders, and media content creators. You cannot abide a world that worships lies and false facts. During the talk I said, "The collective impact of these lies is that when we consider truth optional, we as a species are doomed."

I have taken the risk to tell some personal, painful truths in public. I do not tell every secret of my life. I feel I can only tell my truth, not the truths of my sons, siblings, late parents, friends, or acquaintances. I hold myself to a standard of accountability and have an inherent expectation that others hold themselves accountable to their own truths. I'm not perfect, and I'm not taking this stance to be noble; I want to wake up each day not needing to wonder about the veracity of everything I read, hear, and watch.

Yes, I can tell a lie, and the weight listed on my driver's license proves that. But there is a galaxy of distinction between a lie that causes no one harm and the lies that can harm us all.

December 2023

PART TWO

PLACES

9

LATIN CLASS

"SEMPER UBI SUB UBI."

For anyone who was forced to take Latin in high school as my five older brothers and sisters and I were ("It will help you get into a good college," my mother claimed), that phrase is an unforgivably nerdy play on words.

"Always wear underwear" is the English translation of that mangled, illogical, potty humor Latin phrase, and it cracks up a thirteen-year-old who is forced by their parents to take Latin.

For those whose parents did not ascribe to this mandatory course of curricular action or whose more modern, progressive schools did not deliver courses in dead languages, in Latin, *semper* means "always." *Ubi* means "where." And *sub* means "under." Never mind that it is defined as "where" not "wear." We didn't know the Latin verb for "wear," so we improvised.

Semper ubi sub ubi. Always wear underwear.

I loved Latin class. Mr. Farrand Baker taught me and my classmates Latin my freshman and sophomore years at Oak

Park–River Forest High School in the early '70s, followed by etymology class my junior year. Etymology class, my friend Dean remembers, was one of the best classes at the high school. Mr. Baker's was a small classroom at the end of the hallway up a wooden ramp in the ancient part of the high school built in 1907, two years before Mr. Baker was born.

Mr. Baker seemed ancient at the time he was my teacher starting in 1971, but he was just sixty-two, younger than I am now. He rumbled along the hallways with a prolonged shuffle wearing gray suits and thin, bland ties, all of which were crumpled. He was as endearing as he was informative. His classroom featured a bust of Julius Caesar on a pedestal near the front by the chalkboard; he put funny T-shirts on Julius, mixing it up every few months, wondering which one of his students would notice. I did.

It was not a full class, maybe fifteen students (in 1970s terms, that is very small), and Dan Castellaneta sat behind me in most classes where seats were not assigned. You likely know who he is, an accomplished actor and the voice of Homer Simpson, among many other achievements. I wonder if Dan remembers the underwear joke.

Of course, they say Latin is a dead language, Mr. Baker would explain, but it is the core driver of several Romance languages—Italian, French, Spanish, Portuguese—and if you could learn the Latin basics, then your vocabulary might improve. It's like chicken broth as the base for a host of delicious soups from many different cultures (my analogy, not Mr. Baker's). I saw Latin as the starting point of understanding so many other words in other languages—foreplay if you will, or maybe not. You would see the roots of words in these languages beyond English and know how to define them. Latin was alive in your mind.

No, in school there was no mention of other ancient languages, the hundreds of different Indigenous tongues spoken and shared across the world that were not related to Caesar or European Romance languages.

SOME OF THE MOST POPULAR SAT TEST WORDS HAD LATIN roots, this of course before the creators of these tests had an inkling about diversity, equity, or inclusion, and all the tests were based on white middle-class experience. This was a part of the legacy of US testing and curricula intentionally whitewashing history—erasing truths and realities to exclude inconvenient facts. It was grossly rampant in 2022 and 2023, with schools and states banning not just fundamental books and literature but any critical race theory or hint at an America that was not just less than perfect but proud host to unspeakable injustices.

For the standardized tests over many years, Latin was the origin of the top, most frequently included words. For instance, "abate," meaning "become less intense or widespread," comes from the Latin prefix *ad* meaning "to" and *battere* meaning "to beat." "Bovine," meaning "related to cattle," comes from the Latin word for cow, *bos*. Through the years I could look at a word without knowing what it meant and try to decipher it to understand its possible meaning. Many times I could and only because I took Latin.

That's what my mom was talking about, I guess; you might score better on the SAT and ACT knowing the basics of Latin root words, which was one of the main purposes of high school, she said. Because that meant you could get into a good college and your wonderful life would begin; Latin was insurance for the journey. Never mind all the other life ingredients.

My mother came from a long line of Latin aficionados: she and her seven younger brothers and sisters were required—it wasn't a request—to take Latin classes in high school by her father. My grandfather, John James "JJ" Butler, died November 18, 1966, when I was eight years old. He was sixty-seven, born in 1899. I have his book, what is likely a more than one-hundred-year-old copy of *Cassell's Latin-English and English-Latin Dictionary*, on a bookshelf in my home office; the hard cover is worn at the edges, and the pages are tan and speckled with pink. There is no publication date for the book. It was revised by J. R. V. Merchant, MA, formerly scholar of Wadham College, Oxford, and Joseph F. Charles, BA, late assistant master at the City of London School. The publisher is Funk & Wagnalls Company, London and New York. On the first page at the very top in the far right-hand corner is the neatly penned autograph of my late grandfather: John Butler. My father and mother also signed their books, the ones I am lucky enough to have in my possession. I consider this book a prize.

The preface reads:

> In preparing a Revised Edition of the Latin-English part of this Dictionary, the aim has been to adapt this work that it may be suited for the middle forms of public schools. It is above all intended to be a Dictionary of Classical Latin, and thus a large number of archaic, or post-Augustan words, have been omitted, while nearly all the important articles have been entirely rewritten, chiefly with the view of introducing a greater number of quotations to illustrate constructions and usage. Etymologies have been added, but mainly those of an unambitious kind. It is hoped that the considerable changes that have been made in type and classification will make the work more intelligible, and so more useful.

The reverence expressed for the words inside its pages resonates deeply and across the generations for me. I am a continuation of this wish to sustain Latin's luster.

For my mother, and I gather all the other parents who advised or required their children to take Latin, the language was an expression of hope, the parental hope that you will aspire, achieve, and make a life for yourself that is abundant in possibilities. All you need to do is plan. And for the Depression-era generation—my parents were both born in 1922—that meant getting into a good college, or really any college at all. The goal of high school is to get into a good college. I believed my mother, in part, even though the dances and proms were way more fun than the Latin classes.

I did OK on the standardized tests, applied to three colleges (my sons applied to twenty each, I think), and was accepted by Middlebury College and Northwestern University (early decision). Princeton said no; clearly I was not Ivy material.

Mr. Baker was a congenial soul who smirked and chuckled when sharing his puns and got a far-off look in his eye when he would recite long passages of Latin text. He would ask us to memorize them and recite back to him. He sometimes talked fondly about his wife, Helen, and, more rarely, his daughter Marilyn. More often he talked about ancient Rome.

"Gallia est omnis divisa in partes tres," meaning "All Gaul is divided into three parts," is the line Julius Caesar wrote around 50 B.C.E. in *De Bello Gallico*. I still remember it fifty years later.

I got As—and some Bs—in Latin, and I memorized what he told us to memorize. Surprisingly, I did not find it tedious because I could hear the Latin definitions in my head when listening to someone pontificate on television, or when I was reading an assigned literature text. A few times a year Mr. Baker had us play a word game where we would stand up in two lines along opposite sides of the classroom facing each other, and he would give us a Latin word to define. You stayed standing if you got the word right, a spelling bee brand of elimination. You sat down if you missed it. A smart boy named Chad, who was in all the advanced classes I was in, usually got them all correct. I tried my best; I don't remember being the last one standing. But I sure wanted to be.

Fifteen years after graduation, I read in the local paper that Mr. Baker died in 1990, and that the Illinois Latin Teacher of the Year Award was renamed after him that year. Teachers across the state are still winning the honor, so I guess he was right—Latin is not really dead. I did not require Latin courses of my sons in high school; they all took Spanish, until Brendan decided to take Japanese because there was a field trip to Japan at the end of the year. He dropped the class way, way before that.

Mr. Baker's lessons did not incite in me a love for language, they enhanced it, along with the literature courses in high school, including my favorite, College English, taught by Helen Barclay my senior year: we read William Shakespeare's *Merchant of Venice* and James Joyce's *Portrait of the Artist as a Young Man*. Joyce chose an Ovid quote in Latin as an epigraph to that book: "Et ignotas animum dimittit in artes." Because of Mr. Baker I knew what it meant: "And he turned his mind to unknown arts."

I took as many literature classes as I could in college while still finishing all my other course requirements. I would have gladly done without the required math and science courses, so I got them out of the way. I was in a Perception 201 course for only one class because in that first meeting we dissected a bovine eye. I nearly threw up after touching the one glistening eye the size of a softball handed to me on a tray; but yes, I knew what bovine meant from its Latin root.

Early on I wanted to have a life that was based on the creation and transaction of written words, hopefully artfully written words, as a journalist, as an author, as a truth teller. From the time I was thirteen writing "teen features" for the local weekly, *Oak Leaves*, until now, whether I was writing down the words spoken to me in an interview or conjuring up descriptions and explanations about what I observed or researched, that is how I wanted to spend my life. Luckily, that's mostly how it has worked out—building a life on words.

If you could extract words and manipulate them in cogent ways, they were the vehicle of transportation, bridging the space between the past and the present and also shifting from the unseen into the seen, the read, the heard, and the remembered.

Words were inside me—inside everyone—and I could imagine them darting and swimming around like millions of minuscule cells inside a body. They were always there, waiting to get out; but these were not nefarious, like bacteria. Though omnipresent, the words were powerful and just waiting to be released, organized into stories and declarations. An abundance of possibility waiting for you to breathe them into life. You had to revere their power, claim them, and arrange them with intention, and that began with understanding their origins.

In her celebrated 2023 book *The Power of Language: How the Codes We Use to Think, Speak, and Live Transform Our Minds*, Viorica Marian—my friend, a Northwestern professor and the director of NU's Bilingualism and Psycholinguistics Research Lab—writes: "Although language does not fully determine thought, it is one of the key factors that meaningfully contribute to and influence how you think and who you are."

There are more than 350 languages and dialects spoken in the United States, Marian writes, with seven thousand natural languages used by people in the world today. The study of languages and etymology teaches us that "no language is static," she writes.

"If language is a colander that strains the input around us to interpret reality, then new languages poke more holes, or poke bigger holes to allow us to see and learn more about the universe," she writes. "When you learn another language, an entire world opens up to you in how you connect with people who speak that language and how you travel and experience the world."

Though I admittedly did not speak Latin outside Mr. Baker's classroom, and I studied French in high school and college to become modestly fluent for a time, it was Latin that injected in me a sense of word worship, of honoring the integrity of each word that I wrote, read, spoke, and referred to in trying to connect any new word to its origin.

I built a professional life on that love of words.

As an early career journalist learning how to use my words was how I got access to newsmakers to write about them, whether it was Dave Thomas, the founder of Wendy's in 1980 for *Adweek*, Jane Fonda for a freelance piece in 1981 for the *Chicago Sun-Times*, or Arianna Stassinopoulos in 1989, before she married and became Arianna Huffington. I wrote a profile of her for the *Dallas Times Herald*, where I was a columnist and feature writer, on the release of her book *Picasso: Creator and Destroyer*. She was pregnant at the time, as was I with my first son, and we talked a bit about that in her room at the Adolphus Hotel, where the public relations person ordered us coffee and I took notes in my reporter's pad. She was one of the smartest people I ever met and was gracious, cool, and intelligent. She looked directly at me as she spoke. I reminded her of that meeting years later in 2005 when she was at a conference I was covering following the launch of *Huffington Post*, and she said she remembered. I'm not sure she did; I think she was being nice.

I was paid to report truth, so I took to heart and mind the responsibility of recording other people's words accurately and felt it was not only an honor to be the scribe of some minute fraction of history—OK, so maybe the annual shoe fair and the travel stories about Santa Fe weren't historic—but I wanted my words to matter. I wanted to matter. Words literally could take me there. They could make me immortal.

Over the years I was able to interview and write about my author idols such as Joyce Carol Oates, Tom Wolfe, Isabel Allende, Kurt Vonnegut, Erma Bombeck, Anna Quindlen, Joseph Heller, and Anne Lamott. Interviewing Anne Lamott for a piece for the *Chicago Tribune*, I told her I was so overjoyed to meet her, it felt like meeting a Beatle.

"Well, which one? It better be John or Paul, not George, and for sure not Ringo."

Like every journalist everywhere, I took notes in restaurants, conference rooms, offices, and hotel rooms, like the one in New York where I interviewed the Texas-born supermodel Jerry Hall in 1985, then in a relationship with Mick Jagger and pregnant with their second child, a son, James.

"So what is your secret with Mick? Why has he chosen you?" I asked her.

"I put a lot of butter on my corn," she drawled slowly in a thick Texas accent with a cheeky smile.

My editor would not let me use that as the opening sentence of the profile ("This is a family newspaper," Ron said). Instead I got the same point across with the words she told me her mother used to advise her on men: "Be a maid in the living room, a cook in the kitchen, and a whore in the bedroom." After four children and twelve years with Jagger ending in 1999, Hall went on to marry billionaire Rupert Murdoch in 2016. I wonder if her mother's advice still applies. I started to watch a 2020 three-part documentary called *The Rise of the Murdoch Dynasty*, in which Jerry makes a few appearances, but I got bored halfway through the first episode.

For the Dallas newspaper, I wrote about a bank president who fussed about the color of his socks before the interview for perhaps ten minutes. He did not say it was off the record.

"Which look better?" he asked me. "The black or the blue socks?"

He then left the room to change his socks. He was not pleased I included the sock scene in my profile of him.

Over the decades, I wrote about newsmakers and celebrities of the age and of the moment for newspapers, magazines, and digital sites: I profiled Phyllis Schlafly, Ann Richards, Gloria Steinem, Morgan Fairchild, Tom Cruise, Baron Guy de Rothschild, Andie MacDowell, James Brown, Wolfgang Puck, and hundreds more, trying to have my words be insightful, revealing something little known about the well known.

I was six months pregnant with my first son, Weldon, when I interviewed Rod Stewart in 1988 at the Mansion on Turtle Creek in Dallas; he was in town for a concert.

"Are you married, love?" he asked, pointing to my pregnant belly.

"Yes," I answered.

"Good girl, that's how you do it," he replied. A morality lesson from Rod Stewart.

I have spent decades writing thousands of features, profiles, columns, and essays; I do not deal in hard news. I never craved the danger of covering wars, conflicts, fires, places where there was a possibility of harm; I am afraid, risk averse. Instead I write business stories, columns on popular culture, and insights on the news in op-eds and essays.

It is a satisfying way to make a living and a life—using my words as entertainment, distraction, distillation, explanation. Mostly I am a writer because I cannot imagine not being a writer; I am of course not alone in this.

In *Let Me Tell You What I Mean*, a book of her essays, the late Joan Didion writes, "I knew that I was no legitimate resident in any world of ideas. I knew I couldn't think. All I knew then was what I couldn't do. All I knew then was what I wasn't and it took me years to discover what I was. Which was a writer. By which I mean not a 'good' writer or a 'bad' writer but simply a writer whose most absorbed and passionate hours are spent arranging words on pieces of paper."

Though now most words are more often arranged not on paper, but on screen, I know I am a writer, too. There are many things I enjoy doing alone almost as much as writing—painting, sketching, cooking, creating—but nothing I enjoy more. It is a gift to produce and manifest something from nothing, to turn ideas bouncing in your head into something that lasts—hopefully—longer than the time it takes to read a sentence. For me, perhaps the best part is the power of doing it by yourself. Of course, you have friends who read and critique your work (thank you to my amazing writing group of more than twenty years) and editors who change sentences around and demand more of you, but the joy comes from knowing I am the sole proprietor of my words.

Sometimes the words you write catch you off guard, make you laugh, or change what you believe in that moment. Sometimes the words you write prove so satisfying that they fill you.

In her book *A Life in Light*, Mary Pipher writes, "Writing brought a new kind of light into my life. It was the light of living life twice, once in real time and once in reflective time. It allowed me to grow into my true self."

I feel the same.

During the pandemic words held new meanings and were used to injure, divide, soothe, and inform. Words on social media, protest signs, testimonies in trials, confessions—they all seemed to have heightened urgency, a deeper impact.

Pandemic-weary, people also wanted to play with words, escape, dabble with words on the side, and find a boundaryless escapade that connected them to others.

Almost two years into the pandemic, Josh Wardle, a Welsh-born engineer and developer out of California, posted a free, public online word game that is a play on words with his own name: Wordle. This crossword puzzle type of endeavor allows you six tries to guess the five-letter mystery word. And COVID is not one of them—yet.

Pundits claimed that this word game was a "drug" for many, helping them survive the despair of the pandemic. It brought couples closer together; friends competed on times every morning.

Wardle's Wordle had ninety players a month later in November 2021. By February 2022, when he sold his game to the *New York Times* for an undisclosed seven figures, there were 2.7 million players in 350 variations and ninety-one languages. Some of those languages are rooted in Latin. By the close of 2023, Wordle lovers had played more than half a billion games.

I know many people so obsessed with Wordle that their score blesses or ruins their day.

The effects of the pandemic on the world will be a source of commentary and wordsmithing perhaps for generations, even centuries; this book is one extremely narrow attempt. There will be many; some will succeed much more grandly than I will at articulating what needs deeper understanding.

What I have learned is that writing for me is an attempt to force order: to take back control of the narrative at a time when control is not possible. The pandemic wrenched control from our lives, from my life. The pandemic was also just the time capsule housing the death of my brother; his death was not COVID-related.

So I write from pain, loss, and confusion, trying to find rationale and validation, to see events and phases in a way that gathers the broken pieces back into a shape that is recognizable. The sharp corners of shards are still visible, but when you force and glue them back together, they can maintain their shape as a whole and uphold what is inside, even if they had been broken. The gaps between can offer sunlight.

"It is OK to hate the container, but love what is inside," my friend Deborah says.

Yes, it is logical to mourn and despise the pandemic and also look to the possibilities of what was gained and learned inside its grip.

Words sprang anew from the pandemic specifically to describe and define what the world was confronting, the novelty of a twenty-first-century scourge. It was a vocabulary wrestling with what was previously unnamed. Medical and science terms are most often rooted in Latin.

Coronavirus comes from the Latin: *Corona* meaning "crown," as the virus itself is crown shaped. *Virus* in Latin means "poison." The world had to literally learn the words specific to COVID: community spread, variant, subvariant, super-spreader, booster, and the difference between shelter in place, isolation, quarantine, and lockdown, all in hopes of getting to the time when we flatten the curve. Omicron. There was the language assigned to describing the pandemic—relentless, exhausting, chaotic—and the search for those words was called "doomscrolling." We dared to jump from the Great Resignation to the Great Reshuffle and the Great Reckoning, sidelined by the Big Lie.

We needed the words to make this time we have in our lives make sense, to allow us to be hopeful, to recover.

The Latin word *pandemus* was first recorded apparently in the seventeenth century; it comes from the Latin prefix *pan,* meaning "all" or "whole," and *demos,* meaning "people." This pandemic affects all people.

Latin is at the root of words assigned to modern timekeeping, a critical element of this stretch of COVID time. William J. H. Andrews, author, museum curator, professor, and maker of sundial clocks, wrote in *Scientific American* that the word *clock* is derived from the Latin word "clocca"and *minute* is taken from the Latin phrase "prima minuta."

Of the scores of Latin phrases I learned from Mr. Baker—or the silly ones we learned because of him—I latch onto one in particular that speaks to this moment: "Ad astra per aspera."

"To the stars through hardships" is the translation, and it's also the name of a 1991 Soviet-made science-fiction film. It's on the NASA plaque commemorating the Apollo 1 crew, who perished in the command module capsule fire in a prelaunch test at Cape Canaveral, Florida, on January 27, 1967. Astronauts Gus Grissom, Ed White, and Roger Chaffee reportedly died within the first thirty seconds.

The phrase is the motto of dozens of nonprofits, even states—Kansas—as well as governments and aviation entities from the South African Air Force to Thailand's Department of Civil Aviation.

Perhaps this is also a fitting motto for life during and after the pandemic. Though simplistic, it speaks to restoration and elevation following the struggles.

They are words at the center of hope. There is another phrase Mr. Baker taught us that fits well with how we move forward, through and out of the pandemic.

"Dum vita est, spes est."

While there is life, there is hope.

June 2022

10

LAKEFRONT

"BEACH OR MOUNTAINS?"

It's a fairly common question on the fairly tedious portion of a Zoom call referred to as Waterfall Questions. Those were apparently created by organizers and facilitators to waste time and make you feel as if you are not wasting time waiting for people who are not on time—because they likely wasted time.

I'm a water person, so beaches.

That is not to say I was born under one of the water signs in the zodiac—Cancer, Scorpio, or Pisces—because I am a Gemini, the twin, and I am an air sign, which makes sense, I guess. Supposedly an air sign is about intellectual stimulation and communication, so yes, if you believe in those things. I used to believe in it all infinitely more, but I grew skeptical and weary when on the worst days of my life I had good horoscopes about love and acceptance and finding new sources of money. The reverse was also true: best days of my life and the horoscopes were just meh. Sometimes I call them horrorscopes.

I grew up in the mostly white middle-class western suburbs of Chicago, where going to the beach downtown in the summer was a given, along with sand in your bathing suit and tan lines. As a teenager, you could get to Oak Street Beach by a quick Lake Street L ride (now it's the Green Line), or you went with your whole family in a station wagon filled with snacks and drinks and sandwiches—ours were on rye bread with salami or pimento loaf, American or Swiss cheese, and mustard. My mother lectured us on the dangers of mayonnaise in the sun and heat. Of course we believed her, though not everyone had a mother who was keen on temperature regulations; over the years, many friends succumbed to the perils of sun-heated potato salad at family picnics. I was not one of them.

Most people I knew and was related to took vacations to places with beaches because lying on a beach and doing nothing—other than reading a book and eating sandwiches with sand on them—was the sign of a life well lived. The good life.

Because I am white, every summer the goal was to be less white, to be tan. My mother did not subscribe to this, but the rest of us did, and the girls in my family and all the white girls I knew on my block and in my classes at school smeared baby oil mixed with iodine all over ourselves and checked our June, July, and August progress on tan lines as if tanning were an accomplishment, not a passive result of sitting in sunshine doing nothing with true purpose.

The best place to tan was at a beach, of course, though you could also accomplish it poolside, but lying on plastic lounges in the backyard did not cut it. Even if you had a stack of *Glamour* and *Seventeen* magazines to pass the time and if the quizzes were not already filled in by your older sisters.

Beaches were glamorous destinations where celebrities like Sophia Loren and Jackie Onassis and princesses like Grace of Monaco and Princess Margaret traipsed to—the south of France, the Caribbean, resorts in Mexico, Rio de Janeiro—all of the places you dared to aspire to visit seemed affixed to large bodies of crystalline blue water. Faraway oceans epitomized luxury and exclusivity. You had to navigate them in enormous yachts the size of football fields, where I was certain they served champagne in fluted glasses around the clock. But what does time matter to them?

The Bain de Soleil commercials were aspirational—you could get the "Saint-Tropez tan." Never mind I did not know where Saint-Tropez was, but I could get a tan as if I were there. And I could get that kind of tan if I bought the tube.

The Love Boat democratized the water dream; Aaron Spelling made the yachting and cruising life accessible for a stretch from 1977 to 1986, even though plenty of the cruise guests were has-been character celebrities. I imagined that in real life a guest appearance on an episode likely signaled you were at the end of your acting career. What's next, insurance commercials? *Hollywood Squares*?

I didn't think it odd that most every character on *The Love Boat* was white except for Isaac Washington, the bartender, and often he was the smartest of them all. Most every character on every television show was white.

Simultaneously, from 1977 to 1986, *Fantasy Island* sold hopes, dreams, and life fantasies to island guests; the arrival of "da plane" over sparkling tropical waters fooled us all into thinking that the exotic island setting was the only way such fantasies could be realized. No wonder most white people I knew loved beaches; they were the prelude to adventures, extravagant leisure, love affairs, and tans.

My family didn't ski, and my family didn't hike mountains, but we had Coppertone lotion—no one called it sunscreen then—beach towels in bright colors, and the will to spend a day staring at the water or splashing in it. Whether we were on vacation or just driving to the northern suburbs, every late afternoon we went back to the hotel or home to spread Noxzema on our inevitably sunburned skin because for us very pale Irish

Americans with a smattering of English and German, the tan was the phase after the red had healed.

We needed to get tan; being pale was one of the worst failures imaginable for a white teen in the summer. It meant you did not partake of the glorious water-soaked possibilities of the sunny outdoor beachside and poolside. It meant you were not privileged enough to have luxury time to spend charging your melanin. It meant you might have a part-time job that didn't afford you the beach time to get the deep tan that was the goal. But then there was always the self-tanner, which was even more Orangina toned back then.

My father drove us up to Winnetka for weekend beach days because my mother said the beaches were smaller up north and less noisy than the ones in the city; there was a parking lot with available spaces, and my mother liked that. It was an hour drive there and back, but she said it was easier to keep an eye on the six of us, and I'm sure it was. We had our family tokens that we pinned to our bathing suits with huge safety pins that looked cartoonishly large, like hummingbirds.

My mother sat in a beach chair with a sun umbrella fully clothed and never went in the water. She wore skirts and nylons with heeled pumps, thumbing through her latest book from the library. Thankfully my dad did go in the water with us, and there were lifeguards.

In the summers we also took vacations, to beachy places usually—California, Florida, Alabama, or up to smaller lakes in Wisconsin, beyond Lake Michigan, like Lake Geneva and Lake Lawn. Until we saw the smaller lakes, we hadn't realized we took Lake Michigan for granted, thinking every lake everywhere looked like the Atlantic or Pacific Oceans.

The lakefront to me is more than geographic eye candy; it stands for accessible luxury, for nature-made frivolity and beauty you can observe up close and personal. It resonates privilege. I understand this is true in many other beachside communities. Years later I watched *Jersey Shore* with both horror and appreciation, knowing these gym-tan-laundry experts were definitely going to be shocked when they grew old enough to be responsible and the cameras were long gone. Because you can't put gym-tan-laundry expert on your resume, unless of course it is to try out for another reality show spin-off.

My family had a beach house off Lake Michigan in Long Beach, Indiana; my parents bought it when I was in high school. It came fully furnished and sat on two lots, with a seawall and a deck accessible from the garage, one story above the beach with cement steps to the water.

Never given an option to stay home unsupervised as a teen when my parents drove to Long Beach every Friday after my father came home from work, I was sullen and resistant to missing the summer parties and the backyard BBQs of my friends. That is until I accrued a whole new Indiana set of friends beachside.

Thanks to my next-door neighbor, I was an add-on to the local party scene. My parents had no idea that inclusion involved driving to New Buffalo, Michigan, to drink beer at a local bar procured with fake IDs, sitting on someone's boat drinking beer, smoking cigarettes, and swimming under the moonlight. My neighbor was polite and my parents knew his parents, so they assumed everything was strictly under control. It was not.

I tried to water ski (I learned to briefly stand on the skis before falling) and watched the drama of local Long Beach and Michigan City high school couples play out over the course of a few summers before we all went to separate colleges and came back together a little more distanced and a little less interested in the same old talk. Some of the couples got engaged, and I wondered why there was a much more accelerated fast track to marriage in Indiana than in Chicago. I didn't know anyone getting married right out of college, let alone during college.

My parents seemed different in Long Beach; my dad was more relaxed, walked on the beach a few times a day, and then took over the Weber grill for dinner, freeing up my mom to only deliver the stream of appetizers—celery sticks with cheese spread and maybe devilled eggs—along with dinner sides of salad with ranch or Thousand Island, plus grilled corn. There was always dessert, thanks to a local bakery where we stopped first thing Saturday morning for the apple crullers for the ride home and a pie or two for after dinner.

My mom was all about the guests; she invited her brothers and sisters, my aunts, uncles, and cousins for weekends, as well as her group of friends that they called "The Group." It was where my brothers and sisters and I were allowed to have sleepover guests. My dad bragged that with couches, sleeping bags, floor space and twin beds in every bedroom, we could sleep twenty guests in the house; every room had double beds and the basement had four twin beds neatly placed next to each other side by side like books on a table.

I never once thought about my mom having to wash all those sheets, which she did every week.

The upstairs deck had maybe eight lounges and chairs with yellow and green flowered mats. My parents had turned the garage into a family room with couches and chairs and a color TV; no view was as great as the view of the lake, vast and limitless with the beach as backyard.

It was where during a summer in my high school years I overheard one of my parents' friends declare while sipping a cocktail before the sunset that the Holocaust was a hoax.

"I am ashamed to know you and have you at our home," I shot back before walking inside.

My mother scolded me immediately for being disrespectful to my elders, even though she announced she completely disagreed with him. My father walked into the house after me, silently seething. My father had been in Germany as a US soldier during World War II; it was not a hoax, and for him that comment was an affront and a disgrace. That guest did not return after that night.

"He can never come here again," he told my mother.

As a student at Northwestern University, I took jaunts to South Beach in Evanston—which was nothing like South Beach in Miami—and spread out a sheet and textbooks. I smeared Hawaiian Tropic on my legs, arms, and stomach because of course I wore a bikini, as did every other woman I knew. I loved to swim and flirt during spring quarter, but I also loved to walk a path near the rocks that I thought were just places to sit and read or stare, not working structures to keep the water in its place.

"Cooler by the lake" meant more than temperature to me; it meant that life was enhanced, more serene, augmented by the proximity to a large body of water that was predictable in its surprises. The feeling of being put in my place, the context of comparison, solidified my lack of importance and complexity, reinforced my humility—I was small compared to the depth and breadth of the liquid horizon. My problems were smaller, my feelings were soothed as the lake lapped a rhythm of assurance that whatever shifts in me threatened, the lake was forever.

Considering water only in terms of recreation and relaxation is a stance steeped in privilege, ignoring the realities of access blocked by zip codes, skin color, economic status, and riparian rights. Those rights bestowed upon the landowner with access to water on their property date back to English common law—as far back as the Middle Ages.

The Chicago lakefront has a cruel history of segregation and violence, punctuated by the Red Summer of 1919 when a seventeen-year-old Black boy, Eugene Williams, blissfully floated on his raft in the lake over the invisible line separating whites from Blacks on the Twenty-Ninth Street beach. He was killed when a white swimmer threw a rock at him; it hit him and he drowned. A week of violence followed, resulting in twenty-three Black residents killed, fifteen whites killed, and more than five hundred people injured. The murder of Williams was never prosecuted.

We never learned about any of this in school, nor was I taught that water as a source of recreation wasn't granted to everyone.

I didn't know that the lake swallowed up to fifty-six people a year—the highest number was recorded in 2021—from drownings and suicides.

In 2017, Tonika Lewis Johnson, a social justice artist and activist in Chicago, created the *Folded Map Project*, a photographic history that expanded during the pandemic into a storytelling project and then in 2020 into a documentary. From the start, Johnson chronicled two of the same numbered addresses in Chicago, from the South and the North Sides on the same streets, displaying the "disparity and inequity" immediately apparent.

With the goal of "reframing the narrative of South Side communities and mobilizing people and resources for positive change," Johnson displays the photos and the stories of these "map twins" in museums and exhibitions around Chicago and the world. In the midst of the pandemic, she turned Folded Map into a nonprofit, for which she is chief creative officer.

Her globally lauded creative work of photography and video shows the historic and ongoing segregation of a place where the lakefront rimmed the edges of both the North and the South Sides, with the east side of Lake Michigan only at times a neutral force.

In September of 2019, Chicago Mayor Lori Lightfoot closed 22 Chicago public beaches—North and South— for public safety concerns due to the pandemic. No one had access. Beaches reopened in May 2021.

Growing up middle-class, I presumed water was clean in the lake, as well as from the fountains and faucets in our houses and schools. The summers when dead alewives washed ashore, municipal crews worked to take them away and rake the sand, though the stench lingered. I didn't worry about failing infrastructures, lead in the pipes, or contamination from sewage. Like most every blessing I was given, it was automatic, not earned. I took for granted the insulation the lake afforded me.

And of course, I never considered that the beach or mountains question is indeed a historically triggering, loaded question. Most people do not get a preference. Most people do not take vacations. Most people do not have the luxury of lying motionless on a lounge or a beach with the goal of the sun's rays changing their skin tone.

Most people find it absurd to aspire to the Saint-Tropez tan.

April 2022

11

KITCHENS

THE COMMERCIAL FOR THE DESIGN CENTER THAT ERUPTS after one of the PBS cooking shows I devour (*America's Test Kitchen, Cook's Country, A Chef's Life*, or *Simply Ming*) insists it can help me build a dream kitchen. That is the assumption—that I dream of a kitchen at all—and a specific, perfect, well-applianced kitchen at that.

Dream kitchen: I hear the phrase often when people talk about their homes—houses, apartments, lofts, condos. It is the phrase repeated in *House Beautiful*, the glossy decorating magazine I have been subscribing to for thirty years but have liked much less since they stopped running exquisite personal essays in the front of the book in the "Thoughts of Home" column. There is a magazine called *Dream Kitchens & Baths*. I am not a subscriber; I dream of neither.

The Dream Kitchen is the center of many private conversations I am privy to but hope to avoid. I am mildly irked by Dream Kitchen talk: perhaps someone has recently fulfilled their Dream Kitchen aspirations, someone is replaying arguments with contractors about achieving one, or possibly someone is requesting emergency group input on granite choices.

Some of these intense back-and-forths where I stay mum revolve around shiny steel appliances that can be customized to order with colored accents to match the sink; I understand blue is this year's top color, a pandemic favorite. Some fridges have drawers that switch from chill to freezer mode with a click! And they offer not just water and ice but whatever else you may desire. The lighting is important, as are storage and seating. Apparently the wrong fixture can be catastrophic, not just for the individual whose dream this is, but for a marriage, a family, maybe the entire neighborhood.

I know this is judgmental and dismissive; I just cannot relate.

When months turned into more than two years of pandemic sheltering at home making sourdough bread or lavender biscuits, many expressed that the creation of a Dream Kitchen became a priority. I was focused on staying untouched by the virus, so I kept my mind set on working as hard as I could remotely so I would not be downsized or erased. I stayed home, washed my hands, and bought more masks so I would not get infected. I stockpiled at-home tests when they were made available. I also got vaccinated as soon as I could.

For those who can afford it, a Dream Kitchen is an accessory of the American dream. I understand that being in a kitchen for more hours a day than ever before because of COVID has forced scrutiny and faultfinding with a kitchen's shortcomings. I can imagine it's the same feeling as when you get a magnifier makeup mirror for the first time and can see your pores a thousand times their actual size. But these kitchen flaws escape my radar; if it works, why replace it? I regularly use a mixer that was a wedding present in 1986 for a marriage that ended in 1995. For many years I held on to a dishwasher that was older than my youngest son; it was not quiet and took more than an hour for the cycle to complete. But it worked.

"Mom, get a new dishwasher."

"I have to get new garage doors first. Can't do both."

Am I the only one who is proud of inanimate objects that seem to live forever? Look how this still performs! It's fifty years old!

I must be completely detached from the imaginings of kitchen dreams because I was befuddled to read Caity Weaver's *New York Times* piece in early 2022 about the need ultrawealthy homeowners have to make their kitchen appliances invisible. "The kitchens of the wealthy in the United States today are capable of providing a humbling experience to the uninitiated. Attempts to procure ice cubes can transform the most dignified guest into a hapless burglar rummaging through drawers for loose gems."

Maybe it is simply that I am not ultrawealthy so I cannot relate.

But for those who are, perhaps it is urgent to prove you are so morally and financially superior that you don't even really need to see a working fridge? Upgrade to inscrutability.

Upgrade Culture is about the next best thing in perpetuity—the next dream kitchen, dream car, dream vacation, dream spouse. I am not in line for any of these dreams. I would not buy an expensive car because Matthew McConaughey mumbles in his Lincoln. I would not fly to Aruba just because the couple in the commercial look happy on the beach. Because I know it is a commercial. And I know from friends who have gone on these exotic, Instagrammable vacations that sometimes someone gets stomach issues or severe sunburn, and that being together alone for an extended period of time is not always the best thing. Think *Nine Perfect Strangers* or *The White Lotus*.

It is not that I consider myself above pride of place or that I don't appreciate beautiful things; I love my home and work at it being clean, stylish, colorful, artistic, and welcoming. I rotate pillows by season and whim. I spend days on holiday decorations; even the guest towels in the bathroom are themed.

I recently paid dearly to have the peeling ceiling (wouldn't that make a good band name?) in the front hallway replastered and repainted (after the plumbers replaced the pipes from the shower and resealed the tub because they were the cause). The ceiling makes me happier just glancing at it as I walk up the stairs or go to collect the mail than most relationships I have struggled to keep alive. My refurbished ceiling makes me feel renewed, strengthened, and clean.

And with the urging of my son Weldon, I did get a new refrigerator—an "open box" stainless steel option at the Best Buy Outlet a few miles away. It was a little over $300 and it does work way better than the twenty-year-old white one it replaced. The only problem is the refrigerator moans and whistles. I am not kidding.

But my dreams are bigger for myself. I eschew time and effort spent on the next best dishwasher to work on my next book or essay, meet daily deadlines, mentor clients, connect with my grown sons, go to an art gallery or museum, and share pinot grigio on ice with friends—all while hoping to glimpse a sense of purpose and joy. I want my life to matter to someone other than me. I dream of being part of the shift to a world where hopelessness and fear are not routine.

I do not think my kitchen is part of any larger plan or life mission. COVID has not altered this position, other than making it more urgent for people other than me.

"Do you want to go on the Garden Walk this Sunday?"

I understand it was an innocent question, but I said no to the friend who shall remain nameless, nor was it a slight to my very kind neighbor whose garden was a stop on the walk and whose backyard was visited by 622 (yes, 622!) paying garden lovers. I have many planted flowers—perennial, annuals, and the kind that die just because they can—yet I do not dream of my garden, though I love it. Just as I do not dream of my kitchen, even though I do not love it. It is fine, it is in working order, and I reserve most of my love for people, perhaps places, but not all things.

I've read that the path to a Dream Kitchen is paved with an average cost of $23,400 and as much as $68,000. Now I know another reason I never got one; that is close to the cost range for yearly tuition at the three state schools that my sons attended for a total of twelve years—some years of double tuitions. For me, it was Dream Kitchen or Paid Tuition, couldn't be both. Tuition bills for three sons are behind me, yet I still don't yearn for a steep kitchen upgrade; I believe it is wiser to save for emergencies. I also didn't make $68,000 per year until I was in my late thirties. And yes, that was a long time ago, but that is a lot of money for a kitchen. Still.

* * *

OUR KITCHEN IN THE HOUSE ON JACKSON AVENUE WHERE the eight of us lived from 1964 to 1979 had multicolored carpeting at one point—thankfully not shag. If we had spilled cereal or potato chips, my mother would vacuum it with the electric broom that buzzed. More often she would require us to vacuum up the mess we'd made, because isn't that the proper way to raise children? Clean up your mess. It's literal and a metaphor.

The microwave in our kitchen was the showstopper—we were early adopters. My friend Julie came over after school when we were freshmen at Oak Park–River Forest High School in 1971, asking if she could watch a hot dog cook. I obliged. It didn't explode, but then we deposited a Milky Way inside and slammed the door to see it melt and later a cup of hot water to see it bubble and boil. This was before my mother told us to get out of the kitchen and go do something outside.

"Can't you find something better to do?" she asked, as if we were to answer.

This was one of hundreds of rhetorical questions my mother would ask each week. That and the classic, "Does that seem like a good idea to you?" I believe that would make a good T-shirt slogan; I also inherited the gene for asking that question of your children. I'm a firm believer in rhetorical questions posed to children as young as three. Just ask my sons.

"Is that true or not true? Do you really want to say it if it isn't?"

The center island was where we picked up the dinner plates upon which my mother had portioned out heaps from pots on the stove—mashed potatoes made from a box of potato buds scooped from the yellow Le Creuset iron pan (that I have now). A few steps away was the roasting pan with two or three pork tenderloins on tinfoil, smothered in caramelized onions— sitting atop the dormant burners.

The refrigerator was avocado green, as was the dishwasher. It was someone's job every day to empty the dishwasher, and those chores were rotated.

I cannot recall once my mother commenting on needing to improve on the stove, refrigerator, cabinets, or look of the kitchen. At one point the kitchen had wallpaper, but it was not as exquisite as the silver-flecked wallpaper with the exotic birds in the dining room.

Mom had other priorities beyond cooking for us and was more excited about a book assigned in her book club or a new painting she bought at an art fair—like the one I have in my hallway; four feet by three feet of a huge vase of flowers with a yellow background. It reminds me of her.

My mother would take me or another sibling to the Lyric Opera or the Chicago Symphony Orchestra along with my dad—and I often fell asleep an hour or so in. She and my father had four season tickets to both, usually taking another couple as guests, but occasionally if I begged, she would take me and another brother or sister. Often it was Madeleine or Paul. We also went to matinees at the Goodman Theatre and the Art Institute for a Saturday indulgence for a visiting exhibit, always ending the trip in the gift shop to browse, where I loved to look at the copies of Tiffany paperweights; we never bought one.

As a girl in the '60s, I saw the kitchen as a place women were trying to escape—like the models smoking in the Virginia Slims commercials—and though I did like to cook, I assessed that the ingredients and the chef made the difference, not the appliances. I watched Julia Child on public television and loved her peculiar laugh and the way she joked when Jacques Pépin came on as a guest. They seemed like real friends.

The kitchens of apartments I lived in during college in the '70s were not the focus; the dishwasher in the third-floor apartment on Clark Street leaked suds out the side—more geyser than trickle—and we took it as the time we would mop the kitchen floor. The house on Sherman Avenue had a decent kitchen but mostly we drank wine in it and ate pizza slices from boxes. The washing machine on the second floor sometimes leaked through the kitchen ceiling. I know.

After college, my apartments in the early '80s on Fullerton Avenue, Wrightwood Avenue, and then Cedar Street had nice enough kitchens, clean and all, but most of my single friends stored things in their apartment oven that were not pots and pans—files, vodka, cigarettes, maybe books and shoes.

I was an anomaly in my group of single women friends, as I made batches of apple butter for holiday gifts in my small Wrightwood studio apartment, where I could not fit a table or chair in the kitchen. Dozens of jars of apple butter tied with tartan ribbon that I gave to family and friends made the entire apartment smell of butter and cinnamon for days.

After I was married in 1986, we moved back from Dallas (the house on Oram Street had a very small kitchen and a predilection for rats) to the house on White Oak Drive in South Bend, Indiana, with kitchen cabinets that had no doors. We added cabinet doors and got our rent reduced. In Chicago, the house on Linden Avenue built in 1928—our first house—did not have a garbage disposal or dishwasher. My friends declared this was an abomination, as if it had no indoor plumbing.

"How can you live like this?"

The kitchen had a pale-yellow ceramic tile countertop with dark brown grout original to the house. I imagine it was not originally dark brown grout when the builder of the Tudor house with the small backyard installed it. I painted castles and knights on the walls of the older two boys' bedroom and made pillows for nearly every seating arrangement. I was trying to make the home we lived in be a buffer for my pain.

I spent considerable time in that kitchen making meals for my three small children and for a husband rarely home for dinner, always working late. I felt insulated with the reassurance that decades of meals had been prepared there in this space before me; I sometimes wondered about the lives of the people who lived there before us. Were they happy? Could I keep pretending to be?

The couple who sold us the house had lived in it for thirty years; she had dyed dark-black hair piled hive high in hairsprayed curls. She would stop to ask me how I was in the post office if I ran into her, always holding hands with her husband, whose name I forgot. The rumor on the block was their son had died in the house. I never asked.

I decided to paint the yellow countertop white because the clerk at Ace Hardware on Chicago Avenue told me that it would look nice if I did when I asked for help in cleaning the tile, you know, sprucing it up. Yes, it did look fresh and clean for a few weeks, and then it began peeling.

My life was peeling, too. It had actually been shredding for years, even before we landed on Linden Avenue after White Oak Drive in South Bend and Oram Street in Dallas. But now the swaths of heart wounds were showing, and it was far too hard to avoid the unveiling that getting myself unmarried was the only thing to do to save myself. And my family.

When I sold the house four years later as a newly divorced single mother to three boys ages six, four, and one, the couple who bought it had no children. They were nice enough—she was exuberant and a little overbubbly: they paid below the asking price and they commented in a condescending tone that the kitchen was original, but they bought the house anyway. There were white wooden flower boxes on the upstairs windows; I had filled them with geraniums, thinking if I tried harder, my life would be as it seemed. It was not.

For a while, I kept up to date on the changing hands of my house, though it was no longer my house. The couple who bought it divorced in a year—I was still close with my former neighbors, so they told me—and I wondered if it was the house that was cursed. I had walked through it burning sage—or was it thyme?—at the insistence of a friend after my divorce. She said it would help with the sale. Apparently it did not help with the new owners' marriage.

The next owner was a single woman, a chef who owned popular restaurants in the area. She gutted the kitchen, I heard, combining it with the little breakfast room by knocking down the wall where I had hung framed photos of the boys.

I was invited to a party there as a plus-one of a friend and didn't go: I thought seeing a sparkling modern kitchen in the place where my peeling white-painted tile was would make me sad. Not just for how much I imagined it cost—and how many trips to Europe or Asia or New Zealand you could take for that amount—but that it was a top priority. Yes, she was a restaurateur, fine, so perhaps she needed the latest kitchen to try out recipes, host fancy food parties, all of that.

I heard she also installed central air. As if the one in-window air conditioner in the hall at the top of the stairs and all the fans in each room would not suffice on a hundred-degree day. Splash cold water on your forehead, neck, and wrists, I would tell my sons.

The Kitchen Walk every fall in Oak Park, Illinois, a suburb near the one where I live, is a fundraiser for a children's charity, and it involves traipsing through kitchens of about a half dozen houses—gloriously modern and new and offering the latest everything! Similar to the Garden Walk, you must have a ticket in advance. You place blue paper booties over your shoes before going inside.

I went to one about twenty-five years ago when I was new to the neighborhood. My friends from the block said it was a good time, you know, looking at different kitchens and getting ideas for your own. As if those were ideas that I entertained.

I was so uncomfortable there because it made me feel like an outsider, wondering how I was disconnected from the rapture, the way everyone was oohing and aahing about the fixtures and the counters and the cabinets, taking notes and photos. I save my oohing and aahing for art museums and national parks.

There was also so much more in my life that needed fixing. A kitchen was not my priority.

To me the kitchens looked placid and dormant, not like anyone really ate there, let alone cooked there; the bottle of olive oil looked like a prop, and there were not enough good wooden spoons near the stove. I felt they tried to trick you into thinking it was a working kitchen with a bowl of fruit. There weren't even ripe bananas in the bowl, and that's what you need for banana bread, not the firm, bright-yellow ones. I wondered if anyone actually used the kitchen.

Maybe I was jealous—maybe it's downright lucid green envy that drives my disdain—but I felt like I could never have that kind of kitchen. I simply could not afford it. It was not that I felt I didn't deserve one; I felt I deserved more than a concentration on one room of the house. But I also wondered why I was the only one in proximity who thought an extravagantly and frequently updated kitchen was nice but unnecessary, sort of like when you go out for cocktails and someone asks for top shelf when a shot of the generic whiskey will do.

My friends and I went out for drinks after the house walk—we were, of course, alone and without children so why the hell not—and everyone but me planned how to buy a pizza oven. I thought it would be a fire hazard, and isn't the best part of pizza that you don't have to make it and it arrives at your door fully cooked?

Reserving adulation for an oven, sink, faucet, or center island with a grill seemed ridiculous to me then and now—so Donna

Reed, so Carol Brady, such antiquated antifeminist entrapment, so disconnected from what is important. I love to cook, I love to learn how to cook new delicacies from my favorite PBS shows, and I am in awe of Padma Lakshmi and all, but that is because I love to learn about, prepare, and eat different foods with their own glorious smells and histories, not because of the appliances. I don't feel that a Dream Kitchen is the secret ingredient to a life well lived. Maybe it improves the meal prep or the consumption but not your entire life.

I am decidedly not an ascetic or virtuous hair-shirt type, denying myself life's appliance pleasures: I do have a jones for shoes and I do like pretty things. I was in a Neiman Marcus—the original Neiman Marcus in Dallas—recently, and I floated through the designer department ogling the fabrics. The saleswoman followed me, insisting I try something on. No, I said, looking is enough. The top I was admiring cost $1,200. Yet still way cheaper than a Dream Kitchen.

This year, this month, this week, I think about a Dream Kitchen, and I think about my tombstone. It definitely will not say, "She had a Dream Kitchen" because that would be a lie, but I wager that not many people have "Achieved Dream Kitchen" on their tombstones either.

I think a lot about tombstones lately because who in the pandemic isn't thinking about death every day. We wear masks not just so we don't get sick, but so we don't die and so our family and friends and strangers on the bus don't die either. After millions were successfully vaccinated, along came the delta variant and then omicron and then the subvariant and now small children die from RSV and COVID and the flu, a triple pandemic. People we love die for many different reasons.

How can I not think of tombstones when protesters across the world have been shouting and sharing the names of the Black, brown, Muslim, Asian and Indigenous men and women killed yesterday, today, last year, last decade, last century? Ceremonies have been delayed for the families of loved ones dying in prison or in custody at the border. I am alerted to the murders of strangers buying groceries, waiting for their workplaces to open early in the morning, walking home from the store. I watch the news of the shootings of children playing outside or sleeping inside their homes or riding in the back seats of their parents' cars. The children in their classrooms in Uvalde, Texas, or Nashville, Tennessee, and hundreds of towns across the nation, the death tolls rising like tides—unavoidable and ubiquitous. I cannot reconcile the way the mothers are contorted in the stranglehold of grief on the 10:00 P.M. news, the way they file along slowly next to the small coffins, draped in carnations and roses. How do you survive the ones who don't?

* * *

THE PINK CERAMIC FLOOR TILES IN MY KITCHEN AND BREAKfast room are not original to the house, which was built in 1932. My sister-in-law Bernadette, Paul's wife, installed them—she loved pink. My late brother Paul and his family owned this house before us; I bought it from them when they moved to a bigger place and I was desperate to leave the house on Linden where my life broke open. I did not move to get a better kitchen, though it was a better kitchen. Now that both of them—Paul and his late wife Bernie—are gone, I feel it is an insult to their legacies to change the flooring they loved.

No, I was not crazy about the pink tiles at first, but I have since grown to love the floor. It is so hard and relentless that you can throw a twenty-pound bag of ice filled with melded cubes and the cubes will break instantly into their individual squares. You just can't drop anything fragile on it, because that, too, will break into many small pieces.

The cabinets are cream colored; I have repainted them a few times over the years and replaced the knobs with handles that are knives and forks—so clever, I know. I did take off the floral wallpaper, but I have the stove from the aughts, thank you.

I have a much smaller new microwave and a new refrigerator that moans and occasionally makes gasping and knocking noises.

My kitchen is clean and every night is engorged with smells of the dinner I prepare—roasted chicken with artichokes, broiled salmon with capers in a teriyaki ginger sauce, olive turkey burgers, spinach and kale sprinkled with garlic, olive oil, and parmesan. I have my framed paintings on two of the walls. I did get a granite countertop installed ten years ago because the Formica had bubbled and burned in one large spot when I was in a hurry and didn't use a trivet and my brother Paul got a deal. It's not a color I would have picked, but it's easy to clean.

I imagine whoever lives in this house after me will gut it all, and that makes me think and feel a few things. One is good for them; they can afford to have the best. The other is that I was always dreaming of bigger things than kitchens. Not that I would know anything about their dreams, but if their brain and heart space is occupied by Dream Kitchen dreams, then what else can they possibly have room to dream about? How many dreams can one heart accommodate?

I dream about inspiring someone other than myself, not the strangers who would traipse through my kitchen on a charity walk in blue paper booties dreaming of a second freezer. I dream that the work I do and have done has made a difference to anyone, anywhere, anytime. I dream I did an adequate job as a parent and that my three sons each have lives that are filled with purpose and love, that I did OK, that when I failed it was not too severely, and that they are grafted with a vision of something much bigger than themselves. That they learned how to love and that they use that lesson often with people who deserve them and for people who love them properly, generously, and deliciously.

I dream I am a good friend and that when someone texts me upset, they know I will text them right back or ask if they need a ride home. I dream of loving someone who loves me the way he says he will and the way I need. I dream of my sons having full, calm, and fulfilling lives in which they feel loved and seen. I dream of closing my eyes at night with a tired smile and waking up on the other side of a dream full of colors and soft music and clouds that paint a panorama of—if not bliss—then satisfaction.

January 2023

12

PHYSICAL THERAPY

HER GUM IS GREEN. HARD TO MISS, SPEARMINT, I IMAGINE, not that I was looking real closely or could smell the flavor, but it slid out of the side of her mouth like a mini salamander, a gecko maybe, yes, a kelly-green gecko, the kind of cute creature animated in the insurance commercials.

She seems not to notice and keeps talking through and around the gum—here in her workplace!—where I am her client and she's getting paid, I hope well because they charged my insurance a lot.

"So how do you feel?" she asks as I glide into the open-air space of my second physical therapy appointment, this for doctor-mandated treatment of bursitis, which I swear I am too young to get.

"It's sore," I tell her.

"So no pain, good." She smiles as if she has just delivered me an ice cream soda, the kind with fake whipped cream and the bright-red inorganic cherries.

"It's sore, so it hurts, so that is pain," I tell her, as I ponder pulling up the Wikipedia page for "pain" on my phone to define the term. I am definitely irritated, and it's showing.

"Sore is not pain," she says defensively, and this is when the gum begins protruding more aggressively.

Now I imagine that she will pull up mimeographed sheets of the round cartoon faces moving from smiley face at zero to full-on closed-eyes grimace at ten—the pain scale. She doesn't.

She goes into a three-minute explanation of how soreness is expected and goes away after one to two days and pain is stabbing and harsh and does not subside.

"It's both, then," I tell her. I try to breathe so someone in the open room doesn't record my reactions and I end up a video on someone's phone to be shared on social media.

It is 7:30 A.M., and I'm annoyed not because I am not a morning person—I am. I have been up almost two hours already, had coffee, even worried about my future and my next essay and my next book, made my bed, emptied the dishwasher, and decided to unfriend a work colleague on Facebook. I will consider whether blocking her on all social media apps is too aggressive.

But I am here, after suffering through six months of left-hip pain so sharp and bone on bone grinding that I cannot roller-skate any more or even entertain the thought of sleeping on my left side. At the last pre-COVID wedding I attended, I even exited the dance floor before the band played the last song, something I have not done in forty-five years. I am always the last one on the dance floor until they make you go home by turning the lights off and handing you your purse. My youngest son, Colin, once told me I "overdance." As if.

This is serious. I guess this is what it means to get old, older, oldish. I should have known?

All of a sudden I slipped into old. No warning! Yes, of course I know it happens, but it was sudden like a door slamming—no gradual hinting, no inch-by-inch increments of a little here, a little there, sliding down the hill to ancient history and obsolescence. I know, I know, it's inevitable. But until now, it was what happens to other people. I got thrown off the cliff of middle age into old age. Not that this was totally unexpected: I had made no deals with the devil, no *Picture of Dorian Gray* agreements here. But so soon? I am not ready to be old. Because being an old woman in this culture means you are invisible and mute. Unless you are Helen Mirren or Angela Bassett (who is my age) or a handful of other senior rock stars, it is likely no one sees you, listens to you, or thinks you matter. This is not OK with me. I am not ready to be sidelined and lumped into every crabby old lady trope imaginable. Even though the encounter this morning makes me a crabby old lady.

The physical therapy place looks like a scene from *One Flew over the Cuckoo's Nest.* The scene where everyone is bending and exercising in the recreation room and they look like puppets. And Jack Nicholson is not happy. Come to think of it, I have not seen a hint of Jack Nicholson in years. I wonder what he looks like.

Her name is Sara, she tells me. They all tell me their names: the guy at the front desk, the guy who hands out the towels. Sara's name is clearly on her nametag. She reminds me she does not have an *h* in Sara, and I find this unnecessary because I can see that from her nametag and I am not the kind of person who adds syllables or vowels unless otherwise directed. A few people have added an *h* to Weldon, as if Wheldon makes sense, and seven out of ten people will misspell my first name, adding two *l*'s. People who have known me for twenty, thirty, forty years spell my name with two *l*'s. It is a litmus test for me on how much people pay attention.

I know I sound ungrateful for the professional help. It's because I cannot reconcile my demise; the notion of decline and mortality shrouds a more reasonable, respectful attitude. I am not rational in my approach; I scorn the inevitable. I apologize.

Mine is not an athletic injury. It is an age consequence, an outcome of living this long. I am happy to have lived this long, yes, but I am not happy I'm in pain.

I am not averse to athleticism. I roller-skated in an amateur roller derby league for six years most every Tuesday night, two hours of skating in sequined hot pants with my derby girls, most a good ten to twenty-plus years younger. I haven't skated in a while. I swim in the summers.

When I was skating I felt like I was flying, literally flying, weightless, unencumbered. Free. I am not flying now. I'm at the mercy of a physical therapist who singsongs every phrase and chomps green gum and looks at me like I am a sad old lady with no life and nowhere to go in the day except for physical therapy.

Sara clearly does not know this about me—I am not old like everyone else here, retired and without anything on the daily agenda but a stroll through Whole Foods. She talks in slow motion and in that lyrical uptick that people her age generally do, ending every sentence with a question? Even when it's not a question?

"Come over he-ee-re?"

"Lie on your stomach?"

The gum is showing as Sara offers additional statement questions. "Three sets of ten?"

I am not and have never been a gum chewer. This is because my mother declared it "déclassé," which I thought was spelled "Day Class A" the way she pronounced it. I thought at the time that gum chewing was something that happened on the first day of school somewhere. I was always waiting for it. Where is Class A?

My mom said chewing gum makes you look foolish, as if you need to have something in your mouth at all times, slurping and chomping. It's disrespectful to those around you, she said, that they had to look at you gnawing on a piece of gum; for heaven's sake, it's like talking with your mouth full of food.

Chew gum in private, if you must.

I passed on the antigum rules to my three sons, and it backfired on me in their childhoods. They craved the chance to chew gum so much they would pick discarded, chewed bits of bubble gum off the street or from under restaurant tables and stick it in their mouths. So not so much a good lesson for them.

Physical therapy is crowded like a prepandemic Starbucks on a Sunday.

"It's all-female day!" Sara declares between orders to do twenty on this side and twenty on that side, asking me as I wince and gasp why I'm making that face.

I don't mean to be this irascible to Sara. Sara doesn't deserve this. I am not an unpleasant person—or at least not always. I don't want to be here. I started this process voluntarily when I agreed to go to the orthopedic surgeon for a consultation because friends told me she would give me a cortisone shot in my hip that would last a year. I'm up for anything that lasts a year—a new job, a man with all his own teeth and independence, or a pair of jeans that fit just right.

It was the orthopedic surgeon who said after X-rays that I needed to complete four to six weeks of physical therapy before she would consider giving me a shot. So here I am with Sara and her gum. And no, I am not being gracious. I'm the angry old lady everyone hates.

I believe I'm aging without the proper gradual buildup, the seamless transition. Just last winter I was youngish. You can see as much in pictures. Now it's summer, and I am oldish. I feel like one of those time-lapse videos of photographs that speed up the passage of time so you can see the clouds moving in and the storm raging. Like characters in every other episode of *This Is Us*.

It's not Sara's fault, but I don't believe it's my fault. I haven't been exercising every day like I said I would—and have the outfits for—and all of a sudden my joints and bones are rebelling, and I am ticked.

It's not like I've been idle all this time—waiting around, passively aging, holding on for retirement. I've been holding up my family and my home and my career. I work about fifty hours a week, traveled for work one to four times a month pre-COVID, and have learned not to fly Spirit or JetBlue and not to order the potato salad at diners in small towns.

I know that I should blow off these minor inconveniences and say I have a good life: I'm privileged and have good eyesight and all my limbs and teeth. I'm employed. My children are all healthy and working. My friends mostly like the movies I suggest. At all times, I have a stash of bubbly water in flavors from black cherry to peach and pineapple in the fridge. I'm a cancer survivor, for goodness' sake.

But the older I get the longer it takes me to recover, and not just from physical ailments. It takes me longer to recover from someone shouting at me in a conference call, sending a cruel email, or accusing me of something I didn't do in a meeting. I look tough, yes, real tough, but on the inside I'm a fourteen-year-old who is cursing herself under her breath, heart pounding, legs shaking, waiting for just the right moment to go in the bathroom and cry. Yes, I do go in the bathroom and cry, even when I'm working remotely and alone.

I am being unkind to Sara, and it's wrong.

The older I get, the more I feel I will never get to be who I dreamed I would be. The more time passes, the more it hurts when someone hurts me. COVID only made it worse: every moment feels finite; every day feels like another square x-ed off on a calendar, and the calendar's pages are numbered.

When I was younger I didn't let other people bother me so much. I would have laughed about Sara and her questions and then told the story at cocktail parties before going to the kitchen for another empanada. I thought when you got older you didn't give a damn about what people said or did. That's what the movies professed, anyway—at least a lot of the really old ones with Joan Crawford, Bette Davis, Sally Field, and Cher.

It's not true for me. I often have nightmares that I am kidnapped and have no voice. In the dreams that happen at least once a week, I don't know how to get out of the locked room I'm in—that sometimes is a locked house. You don't need to go to a dream-discussion group or google "dream meanings" to decipher the meaning of that one.

Getting old in the time of COVID especially makes me feel as if my youth and all possibility have been kidnapped: Not as if by an intruder, but by someone I knew all along was coming over to visit and to stay. Still, their presence is forced on me. And they will never leave.

August 2020

13

ICU

INTENSIVE CARE UNIT ROOM 3. THE EAGLES' "HOTEL California" is playing in my head, the part about how you can check out anytime you like, but you can never leave.

Apparently my subconscious has a sense of humor.

I'm lying in my narrow bed with the plastic guardrail barriers locked in place, an IV drip of heparin stemming from my left hand ("You're a hard stick," the first of a dozen nurses tells me). Heart monitors are connected by color-coded wires to a dozen adhesive circles across my chest and stomach; a blood pressure cuff encircles my right upper arm. I am still in crisis, but I'm slowly lifting out of it.

An invested entourage of doctors, nurses, hospitalists, radiologists, technicians, allergists, cardiologists, pulmonologists, and a primary care ICU specialist who is all business are making sure of that. I am white, and I am insured. I am in the ICU, but I do not have COVID.

My body has three blood clots—one the size of a child's fist in my left lung pressing against my left ventricle and the other two in my left leg. They all reportedly stem from repercussions of a minor ankle fracture that I unwisely kept immobile in a walking boot for up to sixteen hours a day for several weeks—oblivious to warning signs. No one told me keeping my foot immobile in a walking boot for sixteen hours at a time was a bad idea—for circulation's sake.

I break my ankle—a very minor fracture—three weeks earlier as I step off the front step of my house for my daily after-work walk. I'm on the phone, not paying attention. I hear it crack like a dry tree branch. I pull myself up and knock on our front door for my oldest son to let me back in. He drives me to the emergency room of a hospital close by—he drops me off because no one is allowed in the waiting room per COVID precautions—and the X-ray reveals a break.

It isn't really all that painful, and I make a few friends in the ER while I'm waiting for X-ray results: a young woman and her husband. She has a cough and is eight months pregnant; she's worried it's pneumonia. I'm worried I won't get out of there at a decent hour because I am coleading a Zoom training the next day, starting at 9:30 A.M. Sitting in the emergency room still waiting for the orthopedic specialist to declare whether I need surgery, I text the head of programming and tell her my predicament. I assure her I will let her know.

By 10 P.M., I'm released with follow-up instructions after they wrap my foot up to my knee in Ace bandages and give me crutches. Yes, I paid for the crutches; they were not a gift. I text back the program director and say yes, I will be able to be on Zoom all day. No surgery.

At first my ankle doesn't hurt so badly; it's just inconvenient. I crawl up the stairs in the evening and down the stairs in the morning to sit at my desk, foot propped, and work all day. I hobble around the house. I don't drive.

As prescribed, the next week I go to the orthopedic surgeon, who looks it over, assesses the minor fracture, leaves the room, and has a nurse hand me a walking boot that is extremely expensive.

His instructions are, "This is how you put it on. Do not sleep in it."

I do what he says. But I get no more information than that: no handouts, no warnings, no websites to check.

That is the problem. I keep my foot in the plastic boot for about sixteen hours a day for three weeks. No one tells me not to. I keep working, and with the immobility, the clots keep forming: first one, then two, then three. Of course, I don't know this.

I can map how I got here to the ICU. Try to make sense of my actions. Try to rationalize my choices and also hold myself accountable.

Yes, my leg has pain. Yes, I try to rub the pain away. I do not know about blood clots. Did I mention no one mentioned blood clots were a possibility? I am busy working. I hop around the house; I can walk with the boot on. I take the boot off to sleep. I figure out how to wash my hair in the bathtub with my left leg propped up and protruding over the side.

Three weeks after the fall that caused my minor ankle fracture, the cough that I attribute to allergies or a reaction to my second COVID shot has mushroomed into the nuclear cloud of a near-fatal event.

The downward dive in my health is fast; it's just a few days from a pain in my back that the immediate care doctor dismisses as a muscular problem and prescribes muscle relaxants for, to desperate breathlessness.

I visit my brother Paul that Saturday, bring him his weekly batch of my homemade soup, and am irritated by the pain in my back.

"Get that checked out," he says.

On my way home that afternoon, I go to the immediate care site in the strip mall that also has a Starbucks, a DSW, a Chico's, and an Ann Taylor Loft. The physician examines me and does not give me an X-ray. Instead she tells me after five minutes of questions that my pain is from my leg in a boot causing my gait to be off; I am straining different muscles. She prescribes muscle relaxants. I fill the prescription at Walgreens. I take the pills. They do not change the pain.

What I do not realize is this is part of what many call "medical gaslighting," which happens mostly to women and people of color. Their symptoms are dismissed.

But I think the doctor, who is likely twenty years younger than me and seems smart, knows better than I do. So I go home and work for the next five days, trying to rub the pain out of my leg and taking NyQuil for my cough at night and DayQuil in the day. With each day it gets worse and worse and worse.

Did I mention no one has brought up blood clots as a possibility?

Three days later, the pain is so intense in my chest and back that I can't inhale. I have spent a week of nights coughing so uncontrollably that I can't sleep.

By Thursday evening, I can no longer take in enough breath to speak. I text my sister Madeleine that I can't talk, and her husband, Mike, a retired physician, tells me to get to the hospital right away. I text my son Colin, who is maybe fifty feet away in his room, to take me to the ER because I don't have the wind or breath to speak and ask him.

I do notice as I pass the mirror in the hallway downstairs, before I slowly climb into the passenger seat of the Nissan Rogue for Colin to drive me to the ER, that my skin looks gray, the color of a storm-threatened sky before dusk. Colin drops me off, and drives away—COVID rules are no one can wait with you in the emergency room. I arrive at the hospital Thursday night after seven. In the X-ray the ER technicians and doctor almost immediately find the large pulmonary embolism in my left lung and two more blood clots in my left leg, the leg I kept unwisely immobile for too long.

"You could have died tonight," the ER nurse says, as I wait for transport to the ICU. "You look really terrible."

I know I look terrible; I didn't know I could have died. They start blood thinners immediately in the ER and tell me to stay as still as possible. Then they wheel me up to the ICU. Everyone is masked, and everyone is very nice. I'm tired, and I'm grateful, even if going to the bathroom in a bedpan is freaking me out.

I have now been in this hospital ICU since 1:00 A.M. Friday morning. It is Saturday morning in mid-April, and I have not slept yet. Lights are unforgivingly and perpetually on in my room; the large picture windows with a broad view of the hallway do not have privacy shades or drapes. I am the octopus inside a reef exhibit at the Shedd Aquarium. It is not quiet ever because I can hear everything in the hall, and I am rarely alone. There is no night and day. In the ICU people have to watch you all the time. Because, well, because you could die.

I'm scared. People are dying in the ICU. I see it every night on the news. They're dying of COVID, and it's a regular occurrence. They are dying around me.

I feel as if my body hosts a Mars mission in the hands of a highly trained NASA team or a billionaire space entourage created by Jeff Bezos or Richard Branson—everyone has access.

I'm relieved to be in this position; saving my injured body is their collective goal. Skilled hands touching me with intention and deliberate purpose—checking, poking, probing. The ultrasound technician pulls down my hospital gown, leaving my left breast exposed, and then senses my discomfort and apologizes, placing a towel over my breast.

The reality that I nearly died startles me every hour or so.

What is running through my head are all the videos I have watched over the past year of people with COVID in ICUs around the world—the frenzy, the tension, the anxiety, the grief. It's hard to believe that I'm here and harder to believe that I could have died over my own failure to monitor my time spent in a walking boot; such a simple solution.

"Love you. Sorry for your pain," my brother Paul texts me. And that makes me cry because he is not getting better. Ever. I am.

Madeleine calls and puts Mike on the phone. He explains more thoroughly the medical terms that the doctor has told me. He talks to the doctor if the doctor is in the room checking up on me. I feel safe.

Still, between coughing bouts, I sob tears of gratitude and tears of anguish unprompted and sprouting from within without warning. I cry about the distinct possibility of dying, of leaving my three grown sons, the work I will never finish, and the places I love that I will never see again—my backyard with the hydrangea bushes is one. I yearn for the places I've never seen beyond a laptop screen or a PBS travel commercial. Hawaii is one. Greece one more. Thailand another. Australia. Egypt. I have been to Quebec. I love Quebec, and I want to go again. My friends say Cabo is beautiful.

When I close my eyes and pretend to rest, I see intricate patterns in reddish gold, like velvet flocked wallpaper, the kind from an old Western TV show like *Gunsmoke*. I squeeze my eyes shut tighter to try to make the image go black and smooth, but the pattern is stubborn; I wonder if I'm losing my mind, too.

Scans by bedside radiology, an EKG, blood draws every six hours, staff check-in every twenty minutes, automatic blood pressure tests every hour on the hour through the cuff on my right lower arm. It buzzes and pinches, then relaxes.

"How you feeling?" Each new doctor, nurse, or technician questions me calmly, sweetly, tenderly, cautiously, as if my well-being is the highest priority in the universe.

After the need for surgery to remove the lung clot is dismissed as unnecessary because the blood thinners are working, I can now eat food. The person answering the phone at the hospital cafeteria when I order meals between 6:30 A.M. and 6:30 P.M. calls me "sweetheart" or "love" and has the congenial bearing of an old friend. I love her back. I check the calorie counts on the menu and then decide that is foolish, so I order a turkey burger with fries. I have not eaten in days, and when I return home I have lost ten pounds.

Code blue in ICU 1. Two doors down. A swift stampede of pale-blue-uniformed nurses and doctors race past in the hallway, noise and confusion erupt, a hustling flurry, multi-directional chaos for many minutes. And then it stops. I wonder who died. I ask; the nurse won't tell me. She just shakes her head. I'm sure it's COVID related. But then I'm not sure: I'm not here for COVID. And that could have been me.

I wonder how many people have died this week on this floor in this hospital. And whether anyone has died in my room. And then I think that it's not my room; it's only the room I'm in for now. I will leave this room in a few days, not because I have died, but because I am recovered. Then someone else will stay here. I hope they don't die.

My friends who are MDs and nurses tell me stories about the ER and the ICU and about some of their patients dying. The helplessness they feel. The tearful meetings on FaceTime with the loved ones. How COVID changed the nature of ICUs, hospitals, and care.

Like, I imagine, everyone else in the country, I am keeping tabs on death tolls from COVID and imagining the patients in ICUs all over the world, if they are lucky enough to be in ICUs.

Now I am in an ICU.

It's mid-April, and I have been in the ICU, the recipient of competent and meticulous care for nearly thirty-six hours.

I'm told not to get out of bed, not to move too much. I turn on CNN because why not. I watch the funeral ceremony extravagance for Prince Philip, the duke of Edinburgh.

His nearly century-old, hidden, lifeless body inside the flower-draped casket is treated as a sacred vessel, talked about as if he is a deity. His body is considered so globally and irrefutably sacrosanct that a parade of scores of staff, family, and soldiers—red uniformed, black clad, and weighed down by golden medals—walk slowly to St. George's Chapel to worship him. It is a procession worthy of sainthood or a resurrection.

It's all moving very slowly. And I think that I could have died just as he did. But my body would not be as celebrated as his. Few are.

I'm partially expecting him to rise out of the coffin and fly into the heavens. I'm trying to remember who played him in *The Crown*, which I binged-watched on Netflix. Whatever, there's a new Prince Philip now, an older one.

Someone has the job of standing to read Prince Philip's titles—forty-two of them. Later the national anthem, "God Save the Queen," plays. From the bagpipe player and chorus members to the pallbearers and family, everyone walks slowly and stiffly, so robotically regal that it feels like a *Monty Python* imitation of the silly walk. Gun salutes. Somber, tearless faces. Everyone everywhere is white.

Across the bottom of the TV screen mounted on the wall, next to the whiteboard where they have the name of my doctor and the nurses on shift, a chyron moves across bearing the news of the killing of Adam Toledo, a Latino thirteen-year-old in Chicago, at the hands of the police. He was in seventh grade and was killed near a wooden fence in Little Village after a police chase, with his hands raised, two shots to his chest. He was not old enough to drive.

Seventh grade is when you learn integers and linear functions in math class. In language arts you develop supporting arguments, learn conjunctions and sentence fragments. In social studies, you learn about US citizenship, the US Constitution, and the Civil War. Dying is not part of the official curriculum. I wonder if Adam Toledo had any crushes at school. I wonder what he had for dinner that day. I wonder what is in his locker at school and if his mother will have to go through it and when. I know she will cry.

In seventh grade, I worried about being invited to slumber parties and making the honor roll; I thought about whether I really wanted to wear bangs or let my hair grow longer and whether or not my sister Madeleine would know I borrowed her favorite white shirt for dancing school. I had a crush on a boy named Bruce, and it never occurred to me I could die. Grandparents died. Old aunts and uncles. Neighbors. People on TV news and in movies.

It is days before the verdict in the murder of George Floyd by police officer Derek Chauvin is announced, and a split screen of protests in Minneapolis, Chicago, and Oakland plays opposite the royal funeral of a man deemed untouchable from birth, immune to ill consequences.

I am acutely aware of my own body in this moment. And the bodies—or news of the bodies—with me on my screen in this room. We are all in this moment, our bodies public property; everyone is dead but me. We are all treated so differently.

The simultaneous news alerts of the demonstrations and latest shootings echo the ruling that the bodies of the men, women, and children who are historically, chronically, and repeatedly not respected by the systems in place are seen as having a different value, if any value at all. They're afforded a different value from mine, and I feel embarrassed, grateful, and ashamed all at once.

They insist their lives matter because not everyone believes it; many need to be reminded. Some are shocked that equity is a possibility—the same ones who believe critical race theory is an anti-American lie. The ones who scream for book bans and decry that The 1619 Project creator and Pulitzer Prize–winning journalist, author and academic Nikole Hannah-Jones, created is a lie. These are often the same people who think saying gay is dangerous and that if you read a book about love or transgender characters, you are doomed, damned.

It is a confluence of universally twisted contradictions. The list of names of those killed recently because of racist violence and police murders in the United States is longer than Prince Philip's list of titles. Infinitely longer and growing.

Deborah Douglas—author, Northwestern University Medill School of Journalism faculty, director of Midwest Solutions

Journalism Hub, and my friend—created the term "depresencing" to explain the habit of looking past and through so many Black women with "a failure to acknowledge your presence." The damage, she says, is that this "annihilates the hope of you."

My own hope of myself is what is cascading me forward to recovery. A trust is embedded in that hope—that the well-being of the patient in ICU Room 3 is on the agenda for many devoted health-care workers. I am not a celebrity; they are devoted to everyone on this floor, even the person in ICU Room 1, who I presume has passed.

For me, this is an unquestioned hope and trust that I rely on, one not shared automatically, one I know is mine as an insured person of privilege in America. It is given to me, not earned. I know that I am lucky.

Weeks later the bill to the insurance company for my stay arrives, and it is $36,582.86, including $18,762 for the ICU. My portion of the bill after insurance is $5,162. I try to arrange to pay it over time, negotiate with the insurance company. But I can afford to pay it over time. The hospital says I don't qualify for a payment plan. I begin paying $200 payments one at a time, and they inform me by letter that I can't do that. They inform me that the total of nearly $5,000 is due now. They send a notice from a collection agency. The collection agency calls. I try to explain. They say it doesn't matter.

I charge the remainder of the bill to Visa. My credit score goes down a few points.

FAIR Health reports that in 2021 the average hospital costs for a COVID-19 patient were $24,012 for people in their fifties, which is comparable to what the Centers for Medicare and Medicaid Services found for the average COVID hospitalization. The Kaiser Family Foundation analysis estimated the average hospitalization at nearly $21,000.

This is less than mine and more than I earned annually on my first job out of college in 1979. It is also cheaper than many estimate; Ed Bastian, CEO of Delta Airlines, says the average cost of an employee hospitalized for COVID is close to $40,000, which is what I made on my fifth job out of college.

For someone uninsured, the hospitalization costs are closer to $70,000, FAIR Health reports. Nearly thirty million Americans who are working do not have health insurance, the US Census Bureau reports, with more than one million losing their health insurance due to COVID.

But I guess the numbers depend on the data and the source. The Economic Policy Institute estimates twelve million people lost workplace health insurance for themselves or a family member. The $1,300 a month I pay as an independent contractor to Blue Cross Blue Shield of Illinois is not only saving my life, it's saving my solvency.

Because I was cocooned within the health-care system that cares for all those who enter with morally bound dedication, I lived. I am here for today and also for tomorrow.

Of course the ICU team serves everyone regardless of identity, as I witness directly, but getting here? There are hurdles I did not face because I am working, insured. I was admitted through the ER because of my insurance card; my symptoms were taken seriously this time.

Access to such care in the United States is blocked for millions, whether they are undocumented, unemployed, or uninsured. They will go bankrupt from the debt. Or they will die from random internal medical events, just like the one I had. They might not have a physician brother-in-law who could read between the lines about their complaints. They might not have a son with a car who lives in the same house and could immediately drive them to the hospital a few miles away.

They will die perhaps because no one will take their symptoms seriously; they will be told by impatient doctors stymied by bias—unconscious, deliberate, or both—to go home and rest. Or they will never seek medical help because they are afraid of the consequences of discovery, shaming, or disbelief. Or they simply cannot get a ride to the hospital. Or they are in a care facility where they are routinely ignored. Or they will be in prison where the lead-laced water might kill them first. They will have a myriad of social determinants of health that ensure they will not have access to health treatment.

Deemed dangerous from birth with an identity as Black, brown, Asian, Indigenous, Native, or any combination not assigned "Anglo-Saxon" immunity, they are frequently seized upon, destroyed, caged, annihilated. Without protection or prediction of health events, their bodies are often branded for extinction. It is only the specifics of the incidents of erasure and harm that vary—and not by much.

My survival is a direct result of my identity triggering into action a system that pays keen medical attention to my body.

Prince Philip's body received a ceremony worthy of a heavenly savior, his glorification a result of centuries of randomly assigned, historic royal birthrights. The following year his wife, Queen Elizabeth, is celebrated in an elaborate funeral that gathers the world's attention and conveniently dismisses—or pauses—recognition of the legacy of colonization's cruelties.

But people like Adam Toledo, George Floyd, and many more—who inhabit bodies randomly and irrationally deemed dangerous—endured each day with a quaking fear of dying.

I am forever spared this fear.

Four days after I arrive, I am released. The nurses wave as I am wheeled past the center desk on the ICU floor. Colin is waiting outside to take me home after my discharge; a nurse with a kind demeanor wheels me to the curb.

As I settle into the front seat, all I can think to say is, "I didn't die." But I guess that's obvious.

April 2021

14

SHAME

"SHAME ON YOU."

Many of us may have heard that diminishing scolding from a parent or grandparent as a child, perhaps as an adult. It is a scorching insult with a mean-spirited, finger-wagging damnation.

Public shaming is having its cultural moment—again and still—while the gender divides appear distinct. More women are refusing to stay silently embalmed in shame for what has happened to them personally and professionally, while many men are declaring they are immune to feeling shame about their own acts.

At least seven women so far including Lindsey Boylan, Charlotte Bennett, Anna Ruch, and more recently Jessica Bakeman have transcended the intended shaming and told their stories of harassment and assault at the hands of New York governor Andrew Cuomo. Even as he faces calls for his resignation and a complaint filed to Albany police, Cuomo's statements demonstrate he is impervious to any shame—or accountability—for what he is accused of doing.

Boylan writes, "I spontaneously decided to share a small part of the truth I had hidden for so long in shame and never planned to disclose."

Cuomo has a notably shameless response: "I have never done anything like this."

In her book *Assume Nothing: A Story of Intimate Violence*, award-winning filmmaker Tanya Selvaratnam writes of the abuse she endured from her intimate partner, former New York State Attorney General Eric Schneiderman. In a *New Yorker* interview, Selvaratnam says, "And I hope that my book sparks more people to share their stories, so that we take the shame and the stigma out of it."

A global chorus of voices upholds such humiliation as normative, while a counteroffensive emboldened by the universal validation of global movements such as #MeToo, #BlackLivesMatter, and #Time'sUp stands for truth and eradicating shame.

In her book *Prey Tell: Why We Silence Women Who Tell the Truth and How Everyone Can Speak Up*, author Tiffany Bluhm writes: "If we are to care for women who've endured sexual misconduct, it will take a radical shift away from shameful theology that believes women are second, when in fact, they are created with equal dignity to share in authority over the earth (Genesis 1:26–28.)"

Yes, gender is fluid and nonbinary, but the brutal violence, shaming, and discrimination against transgender individuals also demonstrate that the hovering universal lesson is that shame is unequally distributed over a power hierarchy connected to gender identity. Anyone defined as "other" is more frequently the target of humiliation—including men who are marginalized.

From the Garden of Eden to body-shaming on Insta, shame has been used to humiliate, silence, punish, deter, and diminish anyone who strays outside the lines professionally or personally.

In her 2019 book, *Eve Was Shamed: How British Justice is Failing Women*, author Helena Kennedy writes, "The way women have to live their lives and the debasing wretchedness of continuing gender inequality" is a factor in the ubiquity of shaming.

Author Ute Frevert, managing director of the Max Planck Institute for Human Development in Berlin, recounts in her latest book, *The Politics of Humiliation: A Modern History*, the long tale of the shaming of women.

Frevert writes, "In England, women who mistreated their husbands were forced to go on so-called skimmington rides in which they sat backwards on a donkey and were paraded around while neighbors and other village people mocked them. Even in 1971, during the Northern Irish troubles, Catholic women who dated British soldiers ran the risk of being tied to streetlamps, having their hair cut off, and being tarred and feathered."

On college campuses, "the walk of shame" refers to any woman walking home Saturday or Sunday morning after staying over at a partner's place the night before—with the presumption of sex. Rarely is the label used when talking about men.

Twenty-first-century shaming features the dangerously dark side of social media with revenge porn, vicious verbal attacks, IRL death threats, and fearless trolls targeting women more frequently than men for personal, political, professional, and public acts—even if that targeting is based on false information.

Yet often men accused of outrageous acts seem immune to both shaming and accountability.

Piers Morgan is neither embarrassed nor ashamed of his racist comments about Meghan Markle; rather he is indignant, as confirmed by his power walk off the set of his British morning show.

Chris Harrison, once the king of *The Bachelor* and *Bachelorette* enterprise, has shown no remorse; his apology lite has been too thin for his repeated racist-leaning remarks and attitudes.

Woody Allen is forever shameless for his marriage to his stepdaughter: the HBO docuseries *Allen v. Farrow* is a testament to his righteous indignation about the allegations of assault on his daughter Dylan.

In the workplace, you can be shamed for a career lapse, a career jump, a demotion, even a comment in a meeting. You can be shamed for being tired—which in the COVID era of homeschooling, elder care, childcare, layoffs, economic uncertainty, remote work, health fears, injustice, and mental health stress seems unavoidable.

At work, women are blamed for errors more often than men are, even if they are working on the same projects, according to a 2020 Women in the Workplace report from McKinsey & Company. It is one reason why 54 percent of women in senior leadership positions say they are exhausted.

In a 2017 study, the Workplace Bullying Institute reported 60.4 million Americans are affected by workplace shaming. Even more worrisome, the survey found "dramatic gender and racial differences appeared in the key findings; as 70% of the perpetrators were men and 60% of the targets are women, while Hispanics were identified as the most frequently bullied race."

Shame can be rigorously and randomly distributed for failure and difference as well as excellence. Certainly, shaming is a key component of racial injustice, with deliberate, institutionalized frameworks that shame and punish entire populations, generations, and communities for just being who they are.

You can be shamed for sexuality, gender identity, race, skin tone, size, career paths, education, degrees, homes, cars, religion, zip codes, accents, families, friends, children, job titles, mental health status, disabilities, wardrobes, introversion, extroversion, even your backdrop on Zoom.

I understand the power of shame. I was married to a man who was physically violent, and though I am a journalist, for years I hid in plain sight. I dared not say the truth out loud because I had internalized the shame.

That's ironic, as my livelihood was based on reporting and telling the truth. If I wrote about my experience with domestic violence with a man who seemed perfect to everyone else, how would I ever be taken seriously in my career? How would I ever be trusted as a leader? Could I outrun the shame?

After years of silence, I wrote *I Closed My Eyes,* my memoir published in 1999. I braced myself for pity and judgments because the shame I assigned myself was leaking out of me. The opposite happened—telling the truth eradicated my shame.

After I appeared on *The Oprah Winfrey Show* for the book, one of my students at Northwestern University approached me in the hallway. "Professor Weldon, I had no idea you had a past."

"Everyone has a past," I told her.

But not everyone is shamed for their past, and no one needs to be. The antidote to shaming for anyone is owning the truth and being accountable. Yes, shame can be assigned to us, but only we can take it in.

March 2021

15

ZOOM

JANE JETSON DID LITTLE MORE IN HER ORBIT CITY DAYS THAN press buttons, shop at the local mall, dictate orders to her children, Judy and Elroy, inside their space home, and tolerate her inexplicably Brooklyn-accented husband, George.

Jane also Zoomed sixty years before it was a thing.

I loved *The Jetsons*, the cartoon show that debuted in 1962, and I would watch on the color console TV in the basement of our house—lying on the floor, head propped up by a large pillow—when I was just four years old. Jane was glamorous, with her upturned red-headed hairdo, bangle bracelets, and sharply angled purple dress and tights—that she never changed, ever. But she took an interactive Zoom exercise class before there was such a thing and spoke often to her mother on her TV screen. Jane was a pioneer in Zoom family meetings. I wanted to be her when I grew up, even though I did not imagine we would be doing exactly what she was doing six decades later.

Imaginary friends, robots, and aliens dotted the TV landscape of my childhood, from *My Favorite Martian* to *Lost in Space*, in which the red-flag warning, "Danger, Will Robinson, danger!" is what my brothers and sisters and I would shout to each other if we did something provocative to get a response, like steal the favorite spot in front of the TV in the basement, threaten to tell Mom about anything, or grab the last Oreo from the plastic and cardboard package in the pantry off the kitchen.

Like that of most everyone in my age-group, my childhood imagination was infiltrated by these unreal, robotic, alien, or otherworldly relationships from the portals of TV and movies like *2001: A Space Odyssey* and *Planet of the Apes* with Charlton Heston (a.k.a. Moses) bare chested with scraps of fabric draped on his lower torso. Both of those films, in theaters in 1968, instilled the notion that virtual and alien friendships could be deadly. But these fabricated small- and large-screen characters were also key in normalizing how connections could exist even if the person you were talking to wasn't standing right in front of you—in the flesh.

For many of those early years, I harbored Betty Sally, my own imaginary friend, whom my parents and siblings treated respectfully as if she were really there until I declared her suddenly departed when I was about six or seven. Add to this phantasmagoric existence the Easter Bunny, Santa Claus, the Tooth Fairy, and the ubiquitous Holy Spirit for all of us guilt-centered Catholics, and there was a culturally reinforced system of pretend protectors and benefactors you would never meet but trusted were always there.

You didn't need to be able to see, touch, or feel the presence of a person to believe they were real.

More than six decades later, in real life, the pandemic ushered in the necessity to exist virtually within the spaces of work, friends, family, and community with Zoom (or Microsoft Teams, FaceTime, or Google Meet) becoming the cursed platforms as well as the tangible lifelines that connected us to each other. The virtual nonlocation allowed everyone to stay in touch from anywhere. Like Jane Jetson and her mom.

By January 2022, three hundred million people were meeting on Zoom each day, an increase of nearly 3000 percent since the final day of 2019. There are 3.3 trillion Zoom meeting minutes every year.

For millions living a COVID-affected remote life, those meetings were elective and work related: you got paid to participate. For millions more, they were obligatory for education or health-care requirements. And they did not always go as planned or intended.

By spring 2020, Zoom was the mandate of schools and universities. Remote learning became a curse for working parents with small children who needed constant supervision. For university instructors who needed to redesign course work and develop systems that did not allow cheating and encouraged participation and learning, the situation was near impossible.

The students also didn't universally approve of remote learning, even though many whose race or gender identities marginalized them reported a relief from daily IRL bullying, bias, and cruelty. But the switch to Zoom learning made a classic and classist presumption that online access was available to all. It is not. Zooming is a privilege. Millions of households do not harbor an extra laptop for a child, teen, or college student to use all day for learning. Many areas—rural and urban—do not have reliable internet access, if any.

A pair of researchers at California State Fullerton conducted a study in the fall of 2020 and found that "60% of our students had not taken online coursework prior to the pandemic, with Hispanic students being the most unfamiliar with online courses. Some students did not have an appropriate home environment conducive to attending online lectures and taking exams. Media reports have focused on the challenges experienced by younger students, from kindergarten (ages 5–6) to grade 12 (ages 17–18), with crowded study and living spaces being a particular issue. But this was also a problem for our student body, a large proportion of whom are commuters and working students, living in an urban region of expensive housing. Many of our students live with several family members (the median household size is 4, with 63% of students living with 4 or more members). Some also had children to care for in the absence of daycare, all of which could create distractions leading to a lack of focus, attention and motivation during class."

The researchers concluded, "Only 4% of those surveyed said that their learning in the new situation was the same as in the face-to-face context; 36% responded that the change in learning was substantially different (worse); and 48% rated their overall learning in the virtual format as average or poor."

For so many millions of students across the country from kindergarten through twelfth grade and in higher education, in public and private schools, there was no tuition reimbursement, refund, or accommodation for the remote switch. Costs for education—completely disrupted—remained the same throughout the pandemic. By the declared end of COVID, nearly every student from kindergarten through high school had fallen behind in measurable expectations of learning.

Grateful my sons were adults and I did not have to supervise remote learning as well as complete my daily workload, I was way luckier than so many whose work lives suffered. Mostly the burden was on mothers; for single parents it was brutal. It was no longer a quaint interruption caught on video when a child ran in a room to interrupt a parent in a meeting. The interruptions were nonstop and tiresome.

I had already been Zooming weekly in meetings with colleagues in different cities for the past five years for two different organizations that employ me, but COVID guillotined the possibility of in-person anything. No water cooler talk, no happy hours, no trainings at hotels with breakfast meetings beforehand, no retreats, no conferences, no work events, no awards ceremonies, no board meetings, no chats by the elevator before you get to the meeting room. No spontaneous going out for lunch, no laughing by the coffee machine. No jokes in the elevator when you press the button. "Which floor?"

It was just me dressed appropriately from the waist up (jeans and yoga pants from the waist down), without shoes and in the warm days without socks, clicking on the Zoom-meeting address in the calendar invite from my home office next to the backyard (and the neighbors' backyard, where the parents shout often and loudly at their four small children). I dread the early meetings, when the mom next door is scream-corralling her sons into one of their three enormous SUVs for school. There is almost always a bloodcurdling shouting match getting them in or out of the car, resulting in threats to take away video games, bicycles, basketballs, or the bouncy house. They own a bouncy house.

When the neighbors are home and I am on Zoom, I get concerned queries: "Where are you? Who is screaming in the background?" "Are you OK?" As if I am in a fistfight in a casino.

Launch meeting. Turn on the ring light. Adjust the lighting and the camera position. Windows behind me in my office make me forever backlit, so the lighting is trickier. A skylight also turns high noon into high shadows. Make sure the audio is working. Test speakers.

Zoom fatigue is a phenomenon because it is tiring to stare at a screen for up to eight hours a day with different people jumping in and out, many not turning on their cameras, some forgetting to unmute, sharing screens awkwardly, and taking what feels like forever to scroll down when you need them to.

"You're muted."

"Can't hear you."

"Put your comments in the chat."

"Do you have to have that soup right now?"

And dear God, can people please respect that a 9:00 A.M. meeting means 9:00 A.M. and not 9:04 or 9:06, forcing you to answer all your other emails on your phone while cursing the key person who is leading the meeting and is running late. I developed a ten-minute rule; I will wait ten minutes for a no-show for an interview or an update meeting, and I will wait longer if there is pleading for forgiveness and a promise of being there soon by email or text. If not, then I'm gone.

Leave meeting.

The weariness I found—and millions of others did as well—was that Zooming for two, three, four, eight hours a day was about sitting in a chair at your desk, the same chair, the same desk, and looking at the screen, the same screen. Some had standing desks, but you stood at the same desk all day, so not really that much different. There was no new visual information coming at you—unless of course a child ran in or a dog started barking or a cat crawled across the keyboard. If the person you were Zooming with was in a public place, then it was invariably too loud, and you could barely make out what they were saying. But you could hear the orders being served up by number or customer name.

"Lost you for a moment."

Sometimes the timing is comical: The leader of the meeting would say, "The most important takeaway here is . . ." and then the connection would fail. And you'd wonder for a second if that was a joke or planned or if you just got fired.

I was coleading a seminar from my home office, and in the final hour of the eight-hour day, my internet went out, after messages had been warning me throughout the day that "your connection is unstable." I tried to get back in, hardwiring the cable to the laptop. I tried to call in, but I couldn't hear them, though they could hear me. My hot spot from my phone was oddly not working (it works in airports!). I drove to the local church a block away and figured they had Wi-Fi that I could connect to from the parking lot, but I didn't know the password. So I drove to the Starbucks six blocks away, but couldn't connect to the Wi-Fi without going in for the code. Then I drove to a small university about a mile away and tried to connect as a guest, but I didn't know the code. Finally, I drove a few miles to

Whole Foods and connected from the parking lot and was able to finish the last thirty minutes in the car. Church, café, university, grocery store. Connect.

Only one person in the virtual convening asked me directly in the chat, "Why are you driving?"

I wasn't. I was parked, but no one else noticed.

All that Zooming was apparently bad for all of our mental health. And opting out was not an option, that is if you wanted to keep your job.

Health magazine reported in May 2020 that video-conferencing or Zoom burnout was affecting men and women poorly—and women more than men.

Dr. Brian Wind, cochair of the American Psychological Association and adjunct professor in Vanderbilt University's psychology department, told *Health*, "When we're on Zoom . . . the brain has to work overtime to process information. It isn't picking up the social cues it's used to identifying [like hand movements, body movements and even a person's energy]. This places stress on the mind and uses up a lot of energy."

In an April 2021 study, Stanford University researchers found that women were more deeply affected—deleteriously—by zoom fatigue than men. Some of it had to do with performance anxiety. Much of that anxiety was because of looking at ourselves, that is until many got smart and clicked "Hide Self View."

I hear you there. I planned what shirt, blouse, jacket, earrings, and necklace I would wear for a virtual speech, podcast, book talk, or training. I worried about my hair, straightening or curling it depending on mood—not the usual practice of pulling my hair into an elastic rubber band because so what. I didn't care so much what I wore in the weekly forever meetings, though I did wear lipstick and comb my hair for those.

The Social Science Research Network published the results of their study on "Zoom Exhaustion & Fatigue" with 10,591 participants. The problem, the scientists allege, arrives from "associations between five theoretical nonverbal mechanisms and Zoom Fatigue—mirror anxiety, being physically trapped, hyper gaze from a grid of staring faces, and the cognitive load from producing and interpreting nonverbal cues."

Aah, the hyper gaze from a grid of staring faces. That deserves its own warning sign.

They also discovered that "exploratory research shows that race, age, and personality relate to fatigue."

As a woman I am at higher risk for Zoom fatigue. Being white and older helps on the anxiety range. Another thing that may save me is personality; I am not an introvert, not in the least. But alas, no celebrating yet, as the researchers conclude, "Finally, exploratory analyses showed less fatigue for extraverts than for introverts, for older people than for younger people, for social contexts than for work contexts, and for white people compared to other races. The greater fatigue for women compared to men, however, remained even when controlling for these additional variables."

Zoom doom.

Along with that there was also a reportedly correlated "Zoom boom," or the "unanticipated rise in cosmetic procedures propelled by the ubiquity of video conferencing. While the term quickly became a generic catchphrase for society's heightened interest in pandemic plastic surgery, video chats were hardly the only factor nudging patients into exam rooms," Refinery 29 reported.

Maybe you could hide your healing scars under a mask?

In her 2022 book, *Connected in Isolation: Digital Privilege in Unsettled Times*, Eszter Hargittai—former Northwestern colleague, social scientist, University of Zurich professor and chair of the Department of Internet Use and Society, and my friend—writes, "For large portions of the population, the Internet became an essential lifeline." In her study of participants in the United States, Italy, and Switzerland in 2020, Hargittai writes, "What made the pandemic events unprecedented in the realm of the digital is that it was the first time in the Internet's history that it became completely front and center for the digitally connected parts of the world that were suddenly relying on it for the most essential of daily needs."

The downside of the digital reliance was that 50 percent of those in the United States with children reported feeling trapped in lockdown, while just over 40 percent of the respondents without children reported the same, Hargittai writes.

Agreed. I do miss meeting in person for work. I had a few in-person work trainings in 2022 and 2023, but only a few. I loved the happy hours after work events and going out to dinner with colleagues I had never met in real life.

Give me a conference room with a pot of coffee, too many water bottles, a plate of bagels neatly halved, and a tub of cream cheese—always plain, never chives—please. I miss the old days, the chitter chatter, the part about having a backstory and a real life with a body that existed past your sternum. (Never mind that Jeffrey Toobin of CNN-contributor infamy did not heed that sternum rule or many other rules of privacy, decency, and common sense when he exposed himself to his coworkers in the middle of pleasuring himself.) Give me an in-person book signing with wine, cheese cubes, and celery sticks. Those little cocktail napkins spread out on the table; I love those.

But Zoom was not all exasperation and desperation because of the person going over the allotted time and the lack of a potty break.

Yes, Zoom was lifesaving and affirming at times and still can be. It was also inclusive and safe—for some. You could Zoom from anywhere on the planet—anywhere that had internet access. You did not have to be physically in an office or even your own home office. You could apply for a job out of state, out of the country, out of reach. And you could land it.

For the disability, Deaf, and neurodivergent communities, Zoom meetings at least approached the creation of a level playing field. Adding in transcription as a given was a boost. Except breakout rooms do not have transcription capability. Why?

Courtney Wade, founder of the Disability, Autistic, Mad, & Neuroqueer Solidarity Project, wrote on North Carolina State University's website, "Zoom's remote work functionality was the manifestation of what disabled communities fought for —and were denied—for decades. Remote access provides an opportunity for disabled and neurodivergent people to be employed without having to deal with access barriers often present in the physical workplace environment. But while the widespread availability of Zoom had a positive impact on many disabled and neurodivergent users, it was not a panacea."

Access is not the same as accessibility, Wade writes. And granting access should not be seen as an eye-rolling accommodation.

Telehealth also boomed because of the pandemic, supposedly giving everyone access to medical professionals when in-person care wasn't possible. This actually created a barrier for those in rural or internet-blighted communities, forcing many to connect in the parking lots of fast-food places, grocery stores, or libraries, if they were open, that is. And if they could leave their homes.

I had a few follow-up telehealth visits during the pandemic, as a cancer survivor with some other complications, oh yes, and the cardiology follow up after the ICU trip, and on one call I waited forty minutes past the appointment time for my doctor.

From what I understand, on the other side of the equation, scheduling telehealth visits was at times logistical chaos, and health-care providers were not often able to discern accurately the patient's status or needs. And again, as with blanket home-schooling demands, it was impossible for everyone to Zoom from home without a working laptop or internet access.

In February 2022, Senator Catherine Cortez Masto of Nevada, a Democrat, and Senator Todd Young of Indiana, a Republican, introduced the Telemedicine Extension and Evaluation Act "to ensure predictable patient access to telehealth following the end of the public health emergency, allow more time to gather data around virtual care utilization and efficacy, and avoid a sudden drop-off in access to care (known as the telehealth cliff)."

This was a request for more funding, a continuation of the Centers for Medicare and Medicaid Services' Hospitals Without Walls initiative launched in March 2020 to offer telehealth services during and after COVID, assuming there was going to be an after.

While telehealth services were part of the approved massive $1.5 trillion Consolidated Appropriations Act in 2022, the naming of COVID as a public health emergency needed to happen every ninety days to keep the funding in place.

American Medical Association president Gerald E. Harmon, MD, issued this statement: "The dramatic increase in adoption of telehealth that occurred in 2020 has allowed medical care that combines in-person and virtual services to become the new standard of care. This new legislation guarantees that patients with Medicare will continue to benefit from this important innovation in health care delivery."

Did COVID permanently shift doctor-patient rapport to mimic the calls Jane Jetson made to her mom or George Jetson made to his boss, Mr. Spacely? Perhaps.

Zoom also made nonwork gatherings possible.

Early in the pandemic in 2020, my friend Teresa invited me to a Zoom dance party with a DJ and scores of strangers saying hello and waving madly, even though we were spread out across the country from California to Illinois and New York. It was like a real party without the cover charge. I stood up and danced and then remembered to close the shades in my home office so my neighbors would not see me dancing with myself, so Billy Idol.

My family held a few multigenerational Zoom meetings on holidays, as we were scattered across the country and my brother Paul was in the final stages of multiple myeloma. Several months before he passed, he was able to Zoom with as many of us as could attend, joking and waving from his leather recliner in the den. That was before he fell into the cliff drop that was the last several weeks of his life.

I attended conferences on Zoom—organized portions of a few—and was able to meet up with good friends whom I would normally see in person. Maybe next year.

The pandemic forced my beloved writing group online instead of our weekly in-person gatherings; the core four of us have met now for more than twenty years. Mondays at 6:00 P.M. central standard time we logged in and shared our written work—upcoming books, plays in progress, essays, chapters, poetry, speeches, all of it—and we critiqued, honored, improved with laughter, and invested care. But now we got to add in new writers from around the country, something we never could have done in person. On our calls, as we did for the many years in person, we talked about our whole lives, not just our writing lives, sharing the ups and downs of the week, the wrecking ball tragedies with deaths of parents and siblings, the exclamation points of book deals and new agents, the shared hurrahs of freshly found love. Those Zoom meetings didn't make me feel fatigued.

My art classes on Saturdays via Zoom were often the best part of my week. I took classes in portrait drawing, landscapes, figure drawing using pastels, pen and ink, charcoal, pencils. The instructor was generous and affable, praising everyone for just the right touch. We shared our efforts on Cluster, and she commented on how we could improve and what was already perfect.

I have heard from friends and acquaintances that Zoom was the final meeting place for friends, parents, siblings, aunts, uncles, spouses strangled by COVID, who leaned in from hospital rooms, where visitors were not allowed. I heard that it was both glorious and damned; the block to access in person was heartbreaking, but the digital breakthrough was at least a small consolation.

Older parents and relatives could see their loved ones every day if they cared to, while they were blocked from traveling or were relegated to a group home or long-term care space. They could feel the love: even octogenarians who claimed to be less than tech savvy conquered the Zoom divide.

Along with my sons and many friends, I attended the Zoom memorial of close friends, a couple who were brutally murdered in their home—a case unsolved—and more than seven hundred people logged in for the choreographed tribute with live music, poetry readings, planned eulogies, and comments from their three sons. We could see them and demonstrate our concerned condolences bound in love for their parents, holding these young men in our hearts, even though we couldn't hold them in our arms.

Zoom was a place to grieve and come together.

One Sunday a month—or every six weeks—I Zoom with my friends from the *Daily Northwestern*, the campus newspaper where we worked together at Northwestern University, and I truly look forward to those one-hour chats we call "Daily Edit Board" meetings, even though we graduated in 1979. Zooming from sites across the country and Europe, we catch each other up on work and family and—in one fell swoop—an avalanche of retirements. We tell old jokes and some new ones, update the old jokes, and remind each other that who we were at our cores at nineteen, twenty, and twenty-one years old is really much the same as who we are now. Different hair—if we still have hair. At least we are all still those same souls to each other.

Zoom virtual backdrops became a contest—not for me, I just changed bouquets of fresh flowers behind me—and I spent more than a small amount of time obliging friends by casting votes on favorites. I was never a fan of the popular colorful-library backdrop, as some people color coordinated the book covers and some had libraries filled with books that had all been covered in pale gray paper. How would you ever pick out your favorite book?

My Zoom schedules each week are not letting up, but I have learned a few key survival tricks. Log on early with a colleague and share nonwork updates before the recording begins. For a minute or two you can compliment each other on hair, lipstick, top, or even a new pillow in the background. You can also text during meetings that are not going well, though I have found that in a meeting of ten people, if two burst into grins at the same time, it's a giveaway that there is probably some behind-the-scenes texting. I learned from a friend's mistake that you never DM in the chat because those transcripts are available to the hosts. So if you think you are private messaging about how the host of the meeting is driving you batty, then oops. Zoom texting on your phones can save the day.

As a colleague was recently going way, way over their allotted time to answer a question, another colleague texted me, "Twenty-five thousand years later . . ."

I almost spit out my coffee.

It's cliché to call something a blessing and a curse because you can say that about anything, from denim jackets to boxed mac 'n' cheese. But Zoom is both of those; it's also a million other things, and it's a connection to people—sometimes the only one we have. And it's free. There's no high gas price to pay to commute, no parking fees, no price of admission. No need to find your vaccination card in your purse or on your phone.

The pandemic did not usher in virtual relationships or create them; it at once damaged and enhanced them, elevating some virtual conversations to the necessary level of universal crisis management. Ukrainian president Volodymyr Zelenskyy addressed the US Congress on Zoom nearly a month into the Russian invasion of his country in 2022. "There has never been a speech quite like it," Dan Balz wrote in the *Washington Post*.

Zoom enabled outreach to global leaders on a platform that is dismissed for trivializing human connections. Zoom also brought the war crimes and horrifying destruction and images of death and tragedy onto our laptops, livestreaming a new twenty-first-century mass murder, reconnecting us all to the capacity of inhumanity.

You can be with anyone anywhere in the world anytime.

A decade ago, I watched the Spike Jonze 2013 movie *Her*, with Joaquin Phoenix and the voice of Scarlett Johansson as his love interest. I was a bit confused as to how and why Joaquin's character Theodore, an intelligent and attractive—though emotionally stunted—person fell in love with the ethereal voice of Scarlett playing Samantha, rejecting at first the real-life encounters with partners. The movie was a critical success, earning five Academy Award nominations and the statue for Best Original Screenplay. A BBC poll in 2016 listed *Her* as the eighty-fourth greatest film made since 2000. So maybe Spike Jonze was prescient about the possibilities for virtual relationships replacing real ones, or at least simulating their depth and intricacies. It was years before ChatGPT.

Virtual is better than nothing. Or is it?

Many assumed that because of the pandemic everyone would fall on the side of declaring a video substitute for face-to-face interaction the next best thing, or perhaps even the best thing, or the worst thing. It's an ongoing conversation. But we have all been changed irreversibly.

Six decades ago, before there was *Star Trek* and *Star Wars*, Jane Jetson spoke to George on a TV screen to see when he was coming home for dinner. George talked to Mr. Spacely on a screen to get his next assignment or learn that he's in trouble and must explain himself.

I silence my Google calendar alert and head into the third Zoom meeting of the day, turn on my ring light, and pull up the documents I need on my second screen. Start video.

May 2022

16

WITHIN

"CONSTITUTIONAL: SHE'S ORIENTED TO PERSON, PLACE AND time. Well-developed and well-groomed female in no acute psychiatric distress. She has a normal mood and affect. Her behavior is normal. Judgment and thought content normal."

Well, at least I come off as normal when I'm in a hospital gown that ties in the front while my bare legs and sweat-socked feet are primed for stirrups.

I was switching doctors (this particular gynecologist in this practice I had been visiting for decades was now oddly declared out of network and no longer covered by my very expensive insurance) and so I requested my medical records. Upon downloading the scores of pages covering thirty years of my surgery-pocked medical history in very small type, I discovered this was my doctor's description of me on my recent annual visit.

Normal?

Yes, I am contemplating having "well-developed and well-groomed female in no acute psychiatric distress" printed on a

T-shirt, or maybe a pillow. Perhaps on a future dating profile, that is if I ever create a dating profile again.

What I appreciate in this very brief summary of my existence on the planet is that in the space of a few minutes, a medical professional declared me normal—during a pandemic, no less. Yet normal is not always what I feel, and at any moment, I feel an untenable tug-of-war between my exterior and interior lives. What I project defiantly to the outside world feels at times grossly dissimilar from what is within—sort of like I'm a tearful toddler afraid to walk out the door while pretending to be Nancy Pelosi.

The pandemic has changed my inner and outer selves, and at the same time my small world collides with the larger world in ways that are not always uplifting or, more honestly, in ways that can inspire despair. It is akin to the feeling you get when you open the neat kitchen cabinet door to reveal a gross disarray of erratically placed spices, cans of soup from the aughts, and stale granola from who knows when.

In response to an innocent inquiry, "How are you?" I can choose to answer at once that I am fine and that I am not fine, depending on the time and the place and how well I know the person asking the question.

"Who needs to know?" "Why you asking?"

Regardless of what I say out loud, it is the conflict of colliding realities within me that is always present; I know I'm not alone. This feeling of not normal may indeed be a new normal. But then that is a presumption of normalcy.

For many the pandemic rearranged our self-views, our worldviews, our exterior lives, and our interior selves, but not in a way that makes feng shui sense, with rearranged items of furniture having designated purposes. There are no neat philosophically inspired assignments for the end table now placed under the window or the standing desk away from the door. These nonelective recasts of how I spend the hours and days of my life have not yet received starred reviews. The outer world is populated with complications and difficulties, inconveniences and demands about how we can and cannot touch each other and where we can and cannot go.

COVID and the too many years following its bombastic arrival into all our lives gave me more time to reflect on what I do day-to-day and the stinging slap in the face that these days for all of us are numbered. Yes, the realities of an end-time were always there, but I didn't measure my mortality every day until now. I didn't think about holidays as the last act of a play or a job opportunity as my swan song. I didn't see the possibility of the tidy last chapter in every encounter—and for sure not every day of the week.

But the stunning realization inspired by COVID that all this is leading up to the last curtain call is a lot to take in. You simply cannot squander or savor as much time alone, with so many hours spent going to wakes, funerals, memorial services, and celebrations of life in person and online without feeling that the ill-mannered grim reaper is lurking just around the corner calling your name. You cannot bury loved ones at this frequency and endure the news of so many more forever lost and ever feel the same again.

The pandemic shoved me out of alignment with who I was before.

Some mornings I look in the bathroom mirror and feel I am not connected to my physical self. I am standing above me, watching, observing, a third party to the lady in yoga pants and her late mother's soft camisole. I call these my out-of-register times, when I mentally and intellectually don't line up with the person brushing her teeth madly from a tube that promises teeth-whitening brilliance and who then is rhythmically swishing the gum-protection rinse aggressively in her mouth. All to the tune of Kelly Clarkson's "Since U Been Gone" or the Bee Gees' "Stayin' Alive." I know.

This separation of consciousness feels imposed—definitely not elective—and feels assigned to me as a defense mechanism. Time to step away, we've got this.

These are times of stress brought on by work, deadlines, sometimes demanding and disrespectful clients, conflict, or intense and at times irrational arguments with my sons in the form of unkindness shouted or texted with axe-throwing deliberateness.

I was just trying to finish this on deadline, I wasn't expecting this conflagration at 3:30 in the afternoon on a Tuesday. I didn't wake up this morning and expect to have the equivalent of a dead fish dropped through the mail slot by a stranger.

Sometimes I'm tired and just want to rest: lie down in the quiet of my four fluffy pillows in soft cotton with crisp sheets around me, the ones I wash every Sunday with a scoop of scent beads. And then I wonder how I lived before there was such a thing as scent beads. How could anyone?

Sometimes I want to scream (and I understand that is not peaceful) that someone else's elective conflict, whether at work or home, inserts itself in my day like a sharp sword—uninvited and unprovoked. Why does anyone waste a moment of this life and this day butting heads like goats on a hilltop? It unnerves me because if I have learned nothing else from the pandemic and from the illogical randomness of illness, death, economic landslides, and eggs that cost more than roast beef, it is that we are in control of only a spoonful of outcomes in an ocean of possibilities. So why would you fill that spoon with poison?

What I would tell my sons when they were younger and then when they were older and even this past week is that it is best not to do or say something you will eventually need to apologize for saying or doing. That is not the smarmy, "Love means never having to say you're sorry" blithering from the 1970 blockbuster movie *Love Story* with Ali MacGraw and Ryan O'Neal. I saw that one in the theater in eighth grade and cried, even though way back then I thought some of the dialogue was not even worthy of saying to my eighth-grade crush. Spoiler alert, in the movie, she dies. And my eighth-grade crush gave me a ring with his initials on it. We kissed behind the gym at school.

What not needing to apologize for your actions is really about, I concede, is stopping yourself from spewing something or doing something that will cause pain—in any form, to anyone. You don't get a hall pass to run through the halls shouting your viciousness.

My friend Ann Marie takes this notion another cha-cha-cha by asking herself before she makes a comment whether it's about something the person she is telling can change in the moment or not change right then. Like a bad haircut. If not, she keeps mum. And yes, that's why she chose not to tell me how completely terrible I looked one Sunday when we were painting floral arrangements in oil on canvas in my kitchen and my hair looked like I had just emerged from a three-year nap. I caught a glimpse of myself in the bathroom mirror and gasped.

"Why would I hurt your feelings?" she asked.

Life is too brief to create problems of your own volition—the world offers enough of them randomly and without warning. Have we learned nothing the past few years?

Easier said than done. And yes, this is coming from a woman whose hands shake involuntarily under stress and whose heart pounds when someone is verbally cruel. I cry in the car on the way home from parties or events if someone was harsh. I still regularly have the dream of running through the hallways of my high school looking for the classroom where the final exam is happening right now, and this test is what I need to graduate. It has been almost fifty years since I graduated from Oak Park–River Forest High School, so I did find the classroom in real life. But then, I know this particular brand of recurring nightmare is about imposter syndrome, self-doubt, fear about performance, and fear of everything you need to accomplish to prove yourself in the time allowed. It is about the forever theme of not being enough. Oh, yes, sometimes I dream I'm running naked northbound in the southbound lanes of Lake Shore Drive, and it's winter. So not only am I exposed, I'm freezing and barefoot and likely going to be hit by a car, bus, or FedEx truck. I wake up before that happens.

The never saying you're sorry part of my preachiness to myself and occasionally to others is that I try to live in a way that I don't need to apologize to others but also don't need to apologize to myself. Of course this is the lifestyle of the flawless and saintly, but I can try. Ideally, I attempt to move from sunup to sundown without acting in ways that require recovery—physical, emotional, or economic. No, this doesn't apply to exercising a little harder with extra planks or another mile added to the brisk walk so that my muscles twinge and ache. That's a good brand of hurt, like the roller derby hurt I had every Tuesday night skating with my amateur roller derby friends for six years. We called bruises "rink rash" and bragged about them.

Recovering from your own behavior choices feels like a huge waste of time, and many of these are lessons I learned in college and don't need to keep relearning. It's like listening to the same Rosetta Stone app of introductory Spanish over and over for years and never advancing to intermediate and advanced versions of the lessons. You never get past asking, "How much does that cost?"

What it means is knowing that too many alcoholic drinks—more than two glasses of wine for me in an evening—lead to a hangover and a rotten night's sleep. Never mind you may commit a regrettable text. Or worse.

Too much food—mostly too much fresh, warm bread brought to the table and dipped in olive oil and freshly grated parmesan cheese—leads to a stomachache for me, and that is another reason why I dare not go to all-you-can-eat buffets (the pandemic wiped those off the face of the earth for a time).

Too much verbal conflict leads to a schism in a relationship. There are words you can't take back or unhear, so best never to say them. I write them down on a Post-it and throw away the evidence. Sometimes I hang up the phone and scream swear words to no one in particular. I make sure the windows are closed. You can't behave like the family members in *Succession*.

Having no regrets can also mean not pressing "add to cart" for those bright-pink pants I can't afford right now. I learned a long time ago that no matter how much I want those bright-pink pants, blue satin wrap dress, or platform pumps, I don't need them. I try to ignore the ads on Facebook that I know are targeting me and say, is this really worth the money? What I learned in my twenties, when I would buy more clothes than food, is that by the end of the month I would be hunting for happy hours after work where they served free appetizers in order to eat that day, even if the appetizers were the little wieners wrapped in crescent rolls that I abhor. I don't know who invented them and why after so many years they are still a thing. Goodness, some people dip them in bright-yellow mustard.

All of these regrettable missteps in judgment and action may seem minor, but they need holistic mending and time to heal: time that is better spent doing something that adds value to my life or that of others or benefits the planet or the universe. Or maybe just smells good. I have more time for the boards I volunteer on. I can take a walk in the late afternoon. I can go on more plein air painting excursions with fellow painters who are ten thousand times better at it than I am. But we can chat about brushstrokes and how they so exquisitely captured the tone of the faded wood on that bench, right there, yes, right there.

A professor in a fellowship I co-led recently told me about a concept I had never heard of before and have been advised is part of Al-Anon: QTIP. It stands for quit taking it personally. Amen, but easier said than done.

The pandemic gave me time to think and to look inward, even if I feel separate and disconnected to the me that is within. So I want the look inward not to be filled with grime and regret, like the basement after a rain of several inches in an hour where it seeps through the cracks and I place bath towels on the floor just in case. I want the inward look to be redemptive and clean, thinking of new ways to have a life that feels full and whole.

A friend recently introduced me to the work of poet, instructor, and author Jeff Foster, who wrote *You Were Never Broken* and other books. He writes: "Everything that seems permanent is impermanent and will be smashed. Experience will gradually, or not so gradually, strip away everything that it can strip away. Waking up means facing this reality with open eyes and no longer turning away."

Foster continues, "But right now, we stand on sacred and holy ground, for that which will be lost has not yet been lost, and realizing this is the key to unspeakable joy. Impermanence has already rendered everything and everyone around you so deeply holy and significant and worthy of your heartbreaking gratitude."

Maybe I can be realistic about the life I have and the time I have and maybe, just maybe, I can venture to use that time well. Perhaps bingeing on seven episodes of *Yellowstone* or *Succession* in one night into the early morning is not the best use of the time I have, even though I totally want to be Beth Dutton or Siobhan Roy for at least five minutes—without the swearing, yelling, infidelity, and constant drinking—when someone says something rude and I come back with a one-liner that makes everyone gasp. Beth's strawberry-blond hair that is never neat and her swagger across a room or a field in a floral, flowy dress or worn jeans and cowboy boots reflect a person who owns her demons and defends her right to be who she is in every moment. Siobhan—Shiv—has the best pantsuits, and she lights up every meeting and party with her wit; her red hair is always perfectly coiffed, even after an all-night flight. Both of them say whatever the heck they please to anyone, and their words land like a lightning strike. I admire both, even though I know acting like either one of them is something I would regret.

My health concerns are manageable, and I have good insurance. If I eat right and walk every day, I feel OK. My son Colin signed me up for long-term home health-care insurance a few years ago, and I'm guaranteed that toward the end—and may it please be a little bit off in the future—there will be funds for someone to care for me.

Yet I do feel full and hungry at the same time. And when I'm deeply hurt, suffering from a relationship bruising or a conflict with one of my sons or a mistake I made, my throat closes in tension, and I can't eat or breathe deeply.

As it did to most everyone on the globe, COVID shuffled the expectations and outcomes of my life in very tangible ways. It canceled the work-travel schedule that I relied on for personal connection with colleagues and friends as well as experiences in new cities—beloved familiar stops and excitingly unfamiliar places like museums in Toronto, art galleries in Savannah, Georgia, and a small bistro in Providence, Rhode Island, that smells like butter, garlic, slow-roasted vegetables, and history. I miss the newness of exploration, the art of awe and discovery, the indoor pool on the third floor of the hotel that is empty at six in the morning so I can float on my back and sigh.

The pandemic also canceled my nonwork expeditions, however infrequent. I did attend my nephew's wedding in 2022 in Miami and danced like it was 1975. I took off my shoes.

I miss the privately haughty practice in airports in which I would silently unwrap my carefully packed breakfast or lunch that I made in my own kitchen—cold chicken breast on a pretzel roll—so proud of myself for planning ahead and not having to spend twenty-five dollars on breakfast pizza. For that moment, holding the food I made, I felt in control: of what I spent, of what I ate, and of what filled my body. There were no surprises. I didn't even have to worry that I would spill on my shirt because I never added sauce.

Looking at my fellow passengers, I wouldn't exactly tsk-tsk at other people, but I would smile as I glanced at the patrons around me noshing on their egg sandwiches or toasted submarines, calculating them to be worth about a thousand calories, six days' worth of sodium, and a twenty-dollar bill, that is without coffee or a soda, and feel proud of myself for not spending the money on the nutrition-negative indulgence. Really, how petty in the scheme of things, but I felt power over one meal.

Of course that feeling of personal triumph was only on the departure side of a trip, as most of the time, coming home from a business trip involved me racing to the airport after a conference or training ended, and I had no access to make a meal. So yes, on the return I was one of those people with a twenty-dollar bowl of soup, trying to decide if I could wait three hours until I got home to eat something else.

So who am I if I never leave the house?

When I don't have to regularly walk through a world of other people, engage in gentle, polite conversation, or even offer kind pleasantries about whether or not the sun is shining and it sure is cold today, eh, then what in the solitude of my life can fill in those gaps?

I have found that saluting the stalemate of stillness within when I feel so separate from my own self requires me to perform wellness. The disconnectedness I have—the looking in the mirror and not knowing who she is—may be sharp and fleeting or dull and clinging like a dry cough; it can last for hours, days, or weeks. I am objectifying myself, unzipped from my own humanity. And then after time, rest, and some resolutions, I can reinsert myself, and the slide back into my skin feels comfortable. That feeling of disconnection is temporary, and what brings me back, guides my return to hand-holding with the real world, is intention. When I have ridden out the long train ride of stress, I can lay my head on the pillow—my head, this pillow, my hair, my neck, my smile.

I am trying to be the normal that the doctor decided that I am.

So many of us, apparently, are trying to do the same. Yes, I fully appreciate the global movement of self-care as helpful for the physical and mental wellness of everyone on the planet, yet sometimes I see the Gwyneth Paltrow goopiness branding of wellness as an act of insincerity. She did herself no favors with that ski-slope accident legal mess and her haughty eyebrow-raised looks of mockery, oh my. And then her confession of what she eats—mostly doesn't eat—in one day was alarming.

I want my wellness to be free of charge and something I can be in charge of, that I can set into motion by deliberate and intentional action. I do not have to fly somewhere, pay for a spa treatment, or order an unbearably expensive meal. I can breathe myself into bliss.

I can do that. I can go for a walk. I can read, sketch, paint, draw, call a close friend, write a story, binge watch *Schitt's Creek*, and laugh like I'm at a party filled with people I like and who like me back. I just can't pretend that I feel good all the time, even if my lucky circumstances demand that I should.

Just being conscious of my internal dialogue is an important step, even if the dialogue at times feels like a screaming match with myself.

* * *

"DON'T BE SO SELF-CENTERED," MY MOTHER WOULD SAY. Though she has been gone since 2002, I can hear her voice in my head still, reminding me not to be a selfish toad.

That phrase is somewhat amusing now because it was a damning accusation back then, but centering on yourself today does not mean you are a selfish, myopic brute but that you are paying attention to yourself and that you deserve it. Being centered is a good thing. Being self-centered means you are at peace.

How my mother and her generation viewed the world and lived in the world was so different. Sometimes it feels like very little of how that generation survived applies to today. They didn't speak of things that traumatized them. They let it go. They hid. They denied. They tried to create a finite world that was manageable and filled with persons, places, and things they loved.

Among the many things in my house that I have from my mother are the Battenberg lace tablecloths—one is enormous, at one hundred inches by sixty-two inches—plus the ten matching napkins and the literally dozens upon dozens of other linen napkins, embroidered and lace-edged. One set of ten cocktail napkins has a tiny yellow daisy in one corner. Everything needs to be ironed.

There are pale-blue linen napkins and placemats with shiny striped edges and blue floral dinner napkins, colorfully embroidered breadbasket liners in the shape of a X. White lace, beige lace, ivory lace, some are French, some Irish, all seem fragile, yet I know some of them are from my grandmother (my mother's mother), so they must be nearly a hundred years old. They are still beautiful, and I want to use them when I have a family party. But I don't want to iron them.

The reality of all those lace inheritances is that they endured; they are not fragile. The lace was created by women alone or a team of women in a factory or women sitting on dining room chairs together smiling, talking, and concentrating on what was in front of them. I wonder if they imagined who would use their work and when. I wonder if they pictured people laughing as they settled in, crowding at the tables, elbow to elbow, mothers and fathers and cousins holding the exquisitely artful napkins bordered in lace to their lips wet with gravy and butter and crumbs from biscuits. Such beauty used to wipe our mouths and hands. For a century. Did they know their work would last?

My life is different from my mother's; I doubt my mother ever felt out of register with her body when she looked in the mirror and brushed her teeth. She probably didn't want to seem self-centered; she didn't have time.

My mother also frequently offered the caveat "Don't be such a worrywart."

I brought that notion forward to my own children.

"It doesn't help to preworry," I would tell my sons, whether they were nervous over a wrestling match or, later, job interviews or relationships.

I realize that is hypocritical coming from someone who catastrophizes at regular intervals. Every time I would click into a Zoom meeting or step on a stage I would worry it was going to end badly if I hadn't prepared deeply and fully. I worry that the person I trust with my heart will trample it. I worry that this book means nothing. I worry that my sons will not always love me back.

But then COVID and the years following in its deadly wake show me you can never be fully prepared for everything anyway. It does not help to preworry.

What I know is I want to keep my life clean—literally and figuratively. I'm enamored with the smell of Fabuloso in the morning in my home and lemon Pledge on weekends, with some scented candles filling the air at all times. And I aim to have clean, clear boundaries and intentions in my encounters with the people in this world and with myself. No hangovers. No leftover regrets. No grief and despair I cause. I want to be that person people walk away from with a smile, or at least not with a frown. I try.

That's not always possible, says the woman who eats more dark-chocolate-covered dried cherries in one sitting than is advisable and occasionally blurts out what she really thinks, and some of it is not so nice or polite.

"Our one task is to make friends with reality," writes Pico Iyer in his book *The Half Known Life: In Search of Paradise.* "With impermanence and suffering and death; the unrest you feel will always have more to do with you than with what's around you."

I am trying to make friends with reality. To do that, I make it my mission to behave in a way that is clean—clean margins in the life I lead and the relationships I sustain, an interior life that is calm and smooth like the gray plush blanket on the edge of my bed, clean as the lovely inherited delicate lace napkins in the living room hutch from my mother and my grandmother. Clean as I can promise to be to the world and to myself so I can look in the mirror and brush my teeth and know who the hell I am. At least some days.

Judgment and thought content normal. It's a goal.

February 2023

PART THREE

THINGS

.

17

PINK COUCHES

I COULD SEE HER SEATED SILHOUETTE FROM THE LIVING room through the sheer curtains over the large bay window as I pulled into the driveway, the headlights illuminating her in a halo of my intrusion. She was sitting on the left pink silk settee, one in the pair of fuchsia love seats facing each other in the brick ranch house on Ashland Avenue, the one where I did not grow up, the one where my parents were growing older.

Damn. Mom was waiting up for me.

Twenty-one years old and fresh out of graduate school with the last quarter spent in Washington, DC, doing whatever I damn well pleased in my free time, I was now living at my parents' home temporarily for a few months, working and getting together the two months' rent needed to put down an apartment security deposit and move out. Yes, this was my parents' car, and yes, this was my parents' house. But it was 1979, and I was an adult, and if I wanted to come home at three in the morning, then I could come home at three in the morning on a Sunday.

This was not going to go well.

My mother sat rigid and alert in her white nightgown and butterfly bathrobe, her short black-and-silver hair held in tight concentric circles around her head, a constellation of carefully placed bobby pins under her hairnet, her hands in her lap, softened by years of grooming with a jar of Ponds on her nightstand. By my calculations, she had probably been sitting on the pink couch for three hours at least, after checking the time and imagining that I had been kidnapped, killed on the expressway in a 152-car pileup, or, worse, been drinking too much, lying unconscious in an alley, or, God forbid, being with a boy (she never called them men), though S-E-X was never spoken of directly, or even indirectly. Ever.

"Nothing good ever happens after midnight." This was a mother mantra she repeated often. Little did she know.

My father slept through all her calamitous end-of-the-world foreshadowing, as he had for all of our curfew-busting adolescences and now early adulthoods. All five of my brothers and sisters were out of the house, and with just me on the daily in-her-face worry list, my mother moved slowly and independently through the stages of maternal worry, prompted by the time on the kitchen clock above the steel double sink and the white wooden grandfather clock in the front hallway that chimed every fifteen minutes. Confusion, annoyance, indignation, anguish, grief, and the final stage of relief that turns to rage when she finally sees her youngest daughter is OK. In one piece. Unharmed.

Cell phones did not exist, but as I learned later, they did little to influence the stages of her worry, only perhaps accelerating the transmutations from confusion to rage.

"I lost track of time, Mom."

"I was worried sick."

"I'm OK, sorry, Mom."

"You should have called."

"I couldn't find a pay phone."

"You could have tried."

"I didn't want to wake you."

"I was awake."

With ivory-painted wooden armrests and carved curvy legs, the pink settees were the center of the worry nucleus in the living room and the perfect embodiment of my mother's style: assertive, boldly feminine, confident, unapologetic, and certainly out of the ordinary.

There is a photograph of me on my wedding day in 1986 seated on the left pink couch, wearing the wedding dress all my sisters wore before me, the alençon lace veil draped over my shoulder as I stared wistfully at the bouquet of calla lilies in my hands. I was clueless as to what was ahead.

In a Christmas card from 1987, my mother and father are sitting on one pink couch, each with a squirming grandchild in their lap, the first eight of the eventual twenty-one grandchildren draped across the back or leaning on the sides. One of my nieces is younger than a year old and is screeching in my father's lap, clearly opposed to the pose, and my father is squinting with laughter. None of my three sons were born yet, and it was the last Christmas card my parents sent before my father died a month later.

Those two pink couches are in my living room now and have been since my mother passed in 2002. My brothers and sisters and I divided up her very heavily furnished home, dispersing over the years the couches and desks and tables and mirrors to our own homes and those of our children.

Like my mother, I am a maximalist.

Her mother was not one: she was more practical, less ostentatious, and the living room couch in their apartment on Wisconsin Avenue in Oak Park had thick plastic covers our thighs stuck to in the summers on the days we visited—which were frequent. The wooden floors creaked when my grandfather walked in to sit in his armchair by the window in their third-floor east-facing apartment in the six-flat they owned, staring out and occasionally joining the conversation with a terse comment or a joke, most often at someone else's expense.

Their couch was a dark-green brocade, thick and imposing, stifled by the squeaking, reflective plastic covers that zipped out the dirt and the germs. Germs were everywhere, I was always told, and my mother, the oldest of eight in her family, was always washing our hands—not gently.

"Wash your hands. Here, I'll wash them for you."

It was as if such a ritual would keep us safe from everything. I can't imagine how much handwashing she would have done during COVID.

The pink couches have been in my living room in this house for more than twenty years, surviving my three sons' childhoods and now their early adulthoods. At six feet tall, when they sit on them, each of them is too big for the tufted back cushion. Their arms are too long for the armrests. If they lie down, their legs hang off the sides from the knees, sideways, and it looks like a scene from the 1988 Tom Hanks movie *Big*.

All the couches in my house—and there are six more than these two settees—I have inherited from my mother and brother Paul except one, and that one is in the basement. I bought it for my first solo apartment on Wrightwood Avenue, a studio, and the couch was $150, a huge expense at the time. I love it still, though it has been recovered twice, now with one of those pale beige removable sofa covers you get at Target for maybe $50 if they are on sale. The good news is you can wash them. My sons do not want any of my couches, even though I insist that the ones they have recently bought from IKEA for their own apartments may not last out the year.

The eight-foot—yes, I said eight-foot—couch in the center of the living room (the pink couches are by the front windows) is also from my mother. It is white wool with three down-filled back cushions and needs to be cleaned frequently. I do that, or rather I call the Stanley Steemer people to do that. I find them to be very nice and polite (they arrive on time and wear plastic shoe covers), and they never say mean things or pass judgment. I gather they have seen a lot of interiors that would send chills up the spines of infectious disease specialists or psychologists. They give me coupons, and in return I gush about them by name on the feedback forms. They wear masks when they come in during COVID.

My middle son, Brendan, worked for Best Buy for a bit as a member of Geek Squad and installed appliances like dishwashers, washing machines, and dryers. He said the insides of some homes and apartments are terrifying, like episodes of *Hoarders*, or show sad vistas of dirt and disarray, making him wonder, "Why did you buy this huge, expensive TV?"

Americans buy a lot of TVs and couches and mattresses and end tables, $114.5 billion worth in 2019, to be exact; you can tell that every President's Day and Memorial Day when the TV and radio airwaves are full of ads for discounts for one day only. How Abraham Lincoln and his successors became associated with furniture sales, I do not know. Or why so many people need a new mattress frequently stumps me; I think the one I sleep on now is almost ten years old. I recently bought a poufy mattress pad from Target, and it is magnificent.

In 2020, the average furniture expenditure per household was $534 a year, with some higher income households shelling out up to $1,092. That is maybe one cheap couch or a really cheap dining room set, or one very nice couch, perhaps used.

The pandemic shifted millions to call home the new workplace, and that likely meant new desks and comfortable chairs—Weldon gave me a comfy fake-leather desk chair on wheels with a seat that adjusts.

Global Workplace Analytics reported that one in four Americans, or more than thirty-six million, were working remotely in the second year of the pandemic. The initial quarantining, remote work, and homeschooling mandated more staying at home for all generations: the living room became a literal hot spot and the communal areas got more attention and use. Beanbag chairs wouldn't cut it. Couches were crucial in the mix. I understand that from the local Walter E. Smithe furniture commercials.

If they are lucky and privileged enough to have a place to call home and to furnish, it is likely that a person's furniture acquisition stage lasts from young adulthood to old age. For those of us who were able to inherit furniture—and wanted to keep it all—the creation of a home was more about accessories and incidentals than big-ticket items. I am lucky to be house-full, and I am beyond lucky to have my house full of items I love— furniture, my paintings, lamps. Nothing in my house is brand spanking new—well, except for food and toilet paper, toothpaste, those kinds of things.

The things in my home have a history.

I am in the phase when many of my friends—and siblings— are tossing and storing the contents of their lives to downsize. While I do try to get broken and useless items into the trash weekly, I am not there yet, and I admit that the life-clearance phase scares me. Because what it really is about is the end. My end.

For four days recently, an estate sale was in progress in the home across the street that belonged to my friend's parents; both of them have passed. Cars were parked on both sides of the street, north and south, filling up the block and stretching around the corner. I peered out the window to see a younger woman trying to get a four-foot red-and-white plastic Santa lawn decoration, likely from the '60s, into the trunk of her blue Hyundai. She gave up and threw it sideways into the back seat, with his head sticking out the window. A couple hoisted together a set of two wooden and leather storage chests—they looked like pirates' chests—to a waiting van. I wondered if there was gold inside or old clothes. Days later the rest of what was in the house filled an enormous dumpster in the driveway. I couldn't watch.

Not an estate sale lover—though I do occasionally go to flea markets—I find the posthumous display of abandoned belongings very saddening. I want to demonstrate reverence for every side chair in flame stitch or red plaid because it meant something, maybe a lot of somethings, to the late owner, but now they are gone and what remains has no meaning for strangers. Estate sales are sometimes like the scene in Charles Dickens's *A Christmas Carol*, with the servants ransacking Ebeneezer Scrooge's bedroom while the Ghost of Christmas Yet to Come is morosely ominous and silently foreboding.

"Is there anyone who feels emotion at this man's death?" Scrooge cries.

I know how he feels.

On Harlem Avenue near the Riverside Mall a few miles from my house is a secondhand furniture store I stroll through occasionally to pick up something I need like a bookcase, or just to admire the inventory of other people's choices. The store is bright and freshly painted in the space of a former sports equipment store that went bankrupt. A honey-colored dresser with a price tag of $747.50 is staged near a side chair with a peacock on the back and another on the seat, priced at $49.50. A peacock! How many people can say they have a chair with a peacock? I eye a fuchsia glass bowl with wavy sides and decide it's for me at $14.

A couple moves through the store with a little girl who looks to be about six and is skipping in snow boots and a pale blue chenille jacket. They pass by the chair and linger at the driftwood table lamps on dressers near the rows of bar stools, a swath of six in bright orange plastic—or are they red?

Toward the back, near the rugs—ninety-six by forty-eight—hanging on the wall, is a vintage bright purple leather, down-filled sofa from the Kreiss Collection, the price tag announces, at $1,599.65. A custom ottoman with a center black pole looks as if it was lifted from a midcentury hotel in north Florida; it's priced at $1,265. A red leather sofa by Bernhardt has a $1,381 price tag swinging from its arm, and nearby is a white suede sofa—surprisingly clean—boasting a pre-owned deal at $1,380. The Chinese screens leaning against the wall that look similar to the ones I have in my house from my mother are priced at $149.

Every piece of furniture in my house looks as if it belongs here; I assume the values have been researched by someone. I hope so.

Many, many of my friends in my age bracket of late fifties, early sixties, have already completed the excruciating process of narrowing, throwing out, selling on eBay, or donating to Goodwill everything that will not fit in the neat new condo in Arizona, the farmhouse in Michigan, or the tidy place downtown that requires more modern furnishings. Most all of my friends have lost their parents; some of us have compounded that grief with lost siblings, spouses, partners, best friends, or children; COVID claimed some but not all. Many of us have sorted through their things swallowing tears.

We are familiar as a generation with the shedding of all that you can't take with you, cursing those whose legacies we inherited who perhaps did not see fit to throw out restaurant receipts or printed bank statements since the '70s. Or plastic Santa Claus figures from fifty years ago.

I think this concept is harder for me now, particularly since my brother Paul's death, because the final dispersal of my parents' possessions was twenty years ago. My sister Madeleine was in charge of that; she was excessively efficient, and every item was marked with preferences and found a home with one of us.

I have a fresh grief about things beloved by someone who has passed. Perhaps irrationally, I feel as if the things they owned harbor tiny pieces of their identity.

So many memories and emotions inhabit the items in my home, the gifts I was given, the people whom I love. Is it irrational? If I keep this couch, if I hold on to this table, they are not fully gone. It is not that their ghosts haunt me, it is that their memories fill me.

Inside the drawers of two desks in bedrooms upstairs are sacred relics of my past. Notes and cards from each son. Report cards. Photos of them smiling by the garage, posing on the beach. Brendan in his T-ball uniform, smiling. Colin barefoot and laughing in the backyard. Weldon's Mother's Day card from 1993. So many school photos; I remember the mandatory ordering each year of eight-by-ten or five-by-seven shots and scores of wallet-sized photos. The packages were always priced too high, and you would never need all those photos; it didn't matter, I bought packages every year for each son.

It feels as if every inch of my home holds family history.

Maybe this is the reason I'm fascinated by the intricacies of the sets on episodes of *The Gilded Age*, *Bridgerton*, *Victoria*, or even *Mary Berry's Country House Secrets*; none of these interiors are remotely attainable, but the opulence of colors and textures, the bold pairings of patterns, even the wallpapers and frames on the enormous oil paintings along the staircases make me sigh.

I could watch these shows with the sound off, oozing with joy at every new room. Not that I want to duplicate this extravagance, or even want something like it. I just want to witness it and for a moment imagine what it would be like to be the person living within those cobalt blue walls. Did they love that turquoise vase over on the bookcase? I want the story behind the lamp. I have a parrot lamp from my mother in my dining room; most people think it's strange.

In the PBS series *Legacy List with Matt Paxton*, each episode features a home whose owners are looking to "keep the memories, lose the stuff." It's a fascinating adventure through time and stories, a narrative encompassing acquisition and gifting that is not about compulsive accumulation for the sake of accumulation.

Unlike the reality-show glimpses into the lives of billionaires that applaud accruing things for the sake of things, these episodes reach back through decades and sometimes centuries to the stories of people whose life moments are contained in concrete objects. These sacred talismans are about survival or devastation, loss and gain, curated in boxes in a basement or storage bins in an attic. The stories are of families dragged through slavery, trauma, escape, and reclamation. These are the memory-embossed treasures mothers and fathers carried with them across borders, holy trinkets from their homelands, reminders of who they are and where they have been. The refugees escaping crisis only to find new hate inside US borders, clutching the belongings that contain their pasts. So many tales are tinged with sorrow but also the celebration of strength.

I want people who come into my home to feel the love of the people before me whom I love. I want them to feel the love I have for these people, even in their absence, perhaps especially in their absence.

It was important to me to stay in this house where Paul lived before me and where I raised my sons because I wanted my sons to have a solid, if infrequently updated, base. They could rely on me, a permanent address that would always be safe and known. They could store their memories here. No one would abandon or erase their pasts; they and their things have value.

Chloé Zhao's 2020 film *Nomadland*, based on Jessica Bruder's 2017 book *Nomadland: Surviving America in the Twenty-First Century*, filled me with voyeuristic amazement. I could never be the person whose entire life was contained in a van. Many were forced there out of need; for others it was their choice. But in those community members I could also see the sanctity assigned to what they owned, the love they had for the few things they held on to, and the meaning they found in each other. Each dish was a record of a life. The contents of their lives were few, but they seemed limitless.

I have friends who talk about their bucket lists filled with places to go, people to meet, things to do and accumulate before, you know, the end. It is probably appropriate and certainly the topic of many podcasts that I do not subscribe to. I have an unofficial list, written down nowhere, that includes Croatia and Thailand and every museum in every city in the universe. I am resistant to the notion of bucket lists because I feel somewhat squeamish about making even more finite and limited what is already finite and limited. This is the time we have. We have to make the best of our lives in the time allowed.

People you love die; people you love leave—each one and all of them for a billion different complicated reasons or irrational quirks, many specifics we will never know because no one will tell us.

Their things stay, whether gifted or left behind.

* * *

I WROTE "I LOVE YOU, DAD" IN THE LEAVES, IN MINUSCULE, careful capital letters in black acrylic paint, completely indiscernible unless you knew it was there. The leaves boast black, gold, yellow, white, and multiple shades of green swaths. It is a small acrylic painting, on an eleven-by-fourteen canvas board. The vase is squat and colorful, red with yellow and blue flowers, and it holds a fern with a dozen or so curvaceous leaves that seem to sway. I signed and dated the painting on the lower left side: "Michele '84." I painted it for my father for his office before I left Chicago to work in Dallas in 1984; I wanted him to look at it every day and know I loved him.

I believe he did.

My father kept this painting—and others by my sister Madeleine and me—framed in his office at the manufacturing company founded in 1919 that he inherited from his father. The company made starter drives and other automobile parts, and he ran it until he died in 1988. My mother started working there with my father in the '70s, when I went to college and she earned her masters in business administration; she was chief financial officer. My brother Paul went to work there in the early '80s and ran the company until he died in 2021. His daughter Marirose carried on his business after his passing. The painting is now in my office at home.

My house has scores of my paintings from the time I was in high school to the present. One of the sun breaking through clouds over an ocean—I think it was an ocean, it was from a photograph—makes me smile. I painted it in acrylic on stretched canvas in art class at Oak Park–River Forest High School in 1971, my freshman year. It has a silver-tone metal frame (that was the style back then), and it has hung on the walls in all the apartments and houses in cities where I have lived. It's now in my dining room.

These framed expressions are pieces of me—of my heart, mind, and creative soul—and when I look at them I can recall the mood I was in and the setting of when and where I was as I worked on them. Sometimes I painted, sketched, or drew to mask what I was feeling. Sometimes I painted to escape. I frame them all to remember that what I do matters.

"That's worth framing" is a throwaway phrase that for amateur artists is either a compliment or a mockery. Framing is what you do for a work of significance, whether it's a charcoal sketch, a pastel, an oil, or an acrylic work with a secret in the leaves. Framing is what you do with the experiences of your life.

You also keep within the framework of your life things that have helped establish who you are and where you have been. And you honor the things your parents, grandparents, and loved ones have left in your custodial care.

If we are lucky and do not need to cash in on their pasts to pay their medical bills, they leave us their untouched things. Willingly or not, we are left to assume, tidy up, and proceed. This is just as the people we leave behind will have to cope and tidy up after us. Hopefully they remember us and these objects as evidence that we were here and that we mattered. I want to matter.

My mother's pink couches are so like her: flamboyant, bold, filled with a zest for proclaiming a point of view. They were one way she expressed herself, but not the only way. I hope I am like her.

My three sons have indeed expressed unequivocally that they do not want these pink couches I adore. I hold out hope that perhaps their partners will, or someone strolling through the pre-owned furniture store on a weekend afternoon will alight on them and sigh, "Yes. These are perfect."

January 2024

18

WATCHES

I AM ALWAYS ON TIME. ACKNOWLEDGING THAT USING ABSO-lutes like forever, never, and always is a dangerously boastful and inauthentic thing to do, I revise that to say I am mostly on time—or try really hard to be on time save an unplanned delay from a major accident, train crossing, or weather hazard. That is because I am the daughter of a man who loved watches and clocks—having them, giving them as gifts, admiring them in public. For his own timepieces, he diligently made sure they were in working order and kept perfect time.

Over the years I have known many friends who were often hours late for a party—even the big occasions like surprise parties and reunions, not just your run-of-the-mill come over when you feel like it impromptu gatherings.

Some friends' tardy practices were predictably recurrent and always forgiven, so I gather they were supposed to be fine, you know, like expecting the toast will burn if you put the setting too high. But it made me upset on principle, especially when it was me hosting the event when my three boys were small.

Preparing and planning was not at all seamless, particularly if naptime was abbreviated or abandoned.

"No, they're not here yet."

"No, I don't know when they're coming."

"No, you can't take off your good pants."

"Please stop eating the chips."

"Stop hitting your brother."

I timed every menu offering for when it was going to be piping hot (lasagna, pork tenderloin, quiches) plus what needed to be cold (salads, cheeses, dips) and how I could keep the boys from doing something that needed to be undone, like shoving one another against a table or jumping from the top of the dryer to the concrete basement floor. Yes, it was a game, with points.

The way I looked at this tardiness was that it was an inconsiderate habit, like putting your feet on the table or chewing food with your mouth open. Did no one tell them not to? It was, of course, a tax on the time of the person hosting or expecting promptness, but being so late was disrespectful to everyone in a larger circle, a way of saying, "I'm OK even if you're not." It discounts the fact that other people have other things to do. There's a reason the invite was 4:00 P.M. and not 8:00 P.M. It's not just impolite, it's the middle finger thrust in the air to your requests.

"I will do as I please."

This is an issue on *Bling Empire*. So I'm not alone.

My own father would never intentionally be late, at least that's how I saw it.

"Gentlemen are on time," he told me once as I waited in the front hall on Jackson Avenue for a high school sophomore date to pick me up, It was required that my father meet him before I was allowed to leave the house. And I could go only if my father approved. My date was fifteen minutes late.

No matter what, if my dad said he would be there, he would be there—and at the time requested or preferred. He timed the drive, left allowances for traffic—this is before our phones could tell us in the accent we choose if the traffic is heavy or light and why and offer alternative routes. "Recalculating route."

Dad left for work at 7:15 every morning and returned home at 4:30 every late afternoon.

So I wanted to be like him, in anything I could emulate. I never wanted to be late for other people, and I wanted to raise my children to be on time, like I was raised: not exactly drill sergeant strict, but observant of the niceties of polite society. Being on time was one of those niceties, up there with never saying the f-word out loud. Well. All I can say about that is my son Brendan recently gifted me a refrigerator magnet that says, "Good moms say bad words."

When my sons were all under ten, I set the clocks in the house ahead forty-five minutes—you realize, of course, that this is way before everyone had cell phones and when people had wall clocks and wristwatches, before the current watch revival that followed the previous watch abandonment. We looked at the wall to see what time it was. Or called time and weather on the house phone that was heavy and clunky and had a cord that stretched maybe five feet. The kind with a rotary dial. Or later the push buttons in a square grid that made a loud noise when you pressed each one.

I am on time.

Pre–digital age, in the '90s, my sons dawdled as children do, so I built in dawdle time and they were never late for school or practice or church—yes, church—or parties (family and other-wise). They were always (alright, alright, frequently) surprised that we left the house at 6:45 P.M., drove the three or four miles to the theater, and still made it to the movie theater for the 6:30 show, and that included time to park. I told them there many minutes of movie trailers: yes, I lied. Mothers get to do these things, but only on things like movie times.

They figured out I lied about the clocks in the house when they got cell phones, which was in eighth grade for Weldon, sixth grade for Brendan, and third grade for Colin. But they

were used to being on time, so they liked it. You get a bad repu-
tation even as a preteen or teenager if you are not time-reliable.

"Why does it say 9:00 on the kitchen clock when it's
only 8:15?"

I believe part of my impatience about tardiness and my love
for timeliness comes from my dad.

Perhaps it was his service in the US Army in the '40s, maybe
before then, but my late father (I mean my father who passed,
not my tardy father, because he was never late) loved any and
all timekeeping devices—ones he would wear on his wrist,
clocks on the wall, freestanding grandfather clocks, large public clocks in the center of public spaces and squares, church bells
ringing on the hour, clocks in the car. I am sure at one point in
his life, Dad must have also had a pocket watch; I can picture
him pulling it from a vest pocket, opening it with a snap, and
peering at its face for the reassurance it offered.

He gave me a portable alarm clock after I graduated college
for when I traveled for work and walked me through how to set
the alarm.

"I always ask the front desk for a wake-up call," I told him.

You would think I'd told him that I didn't believe in God or
that it was OK to eat meat on Fridays during Lent.

"You can't rely on that! What if you miss your meeting?
What if they forget? No, be in charge of your own alarm."

I could see the disappointment in his face.

You can't lie about time. It's the ultimate truth, even if you
alter it twice a year—spring forward, fall back—except for the
states that don't, and people who live there always need clari-
fication. I guess eventually the country will all be in one time
zone? Imagine.

Time is the great equalizer. Or is it?

I'm not sure where Dad got his timekeeping fascination from,
but it was embodied in the large white grandfather clock in the
front hallway on Clinton Place and later on Jackson Avenue,
then on Ashland Avenue. It chimed an ethereal, regal ring—a

reliable and soothing song every fifteen minutes, around the clock. I remember my father winding the chains with their brass-colored weights once a week, shutting the glass door with a smile and a sense of accomplishment. His first task when we came home from a family trip was to wind the clock, set it to its proper time. It was important to respect time—yours and everyone else's.

After my father passed, my brothers, Bill and Paul, would wind the clock in the hall when visiting Mom.

Each one of my brothers and sisters has a gift from our Dad in our homes, a forever clock. The size of a small toaster, it says LeCoultre on its face, and its gold trim sparkles. The hours on its round face are marked in Roman numerals, and it has a moon dial beneath it that spins constantly. You have to stop the dial to move it, or the time will be off. My sister Maureen says her clock chimes. Mine doesn't, or maybe I have forgotten how to make it chime.

My father gave me my forever clock when I moved with my then-husband and our first two children into our first house on Linden Avenue in Oak Park. Like my dad, the clock was steady, reliable, forever. I learned that these traits are not universal.

Wristwatches were also a love of my dad's, and he collected them—from Timex to Rolex. I have a few of his silver stainless steel large wristwatches—not Rolex—and they don't work, but they remind me of him, so I keep them. I can't bear to throw them away.

My dad would have scoffed at people who looked at their phones to see what time it is; I think he would have thought it absurd. It's something about the intimacy of a watch attached to your body—your wrist—so it's a part of you. It helps you to be precise and respectful of other people's time but also your own. Your watch is your own personal compact with the universe that you will heed and abide by its ticking decrees. I'm not sure what he would think about Apple wristwatches that can do everything from take your pulse to deliver emails. He might love them, or he might despise the complications. Or maybe he would have rolled his eyes at something that did not respect the royalty of sparce elegance.

I begged for a watch and got one for my eighth-grade graduation from the Convent of the Sacred Heart on Sheridan Road in 1971; it was bold and bright with a huge round face that had only four numbers on it—twelve, three, six, and nine. It had a thick, bright-green fake-leather wristband. Having a watch was very adult, an indication you had somewhere to go, someplace to be, like the Mad Hatter in *Alice's Adventures in Wonderland* chattering, "I'm late, I'm late, for a very important date."

In college, I bought myself watches at Walgreens or whatever drugstore was nearby: always under ten dollars, changing the wristbands to different colors as was the style back then in the '70s and '80s. I didn't have enough money for the really expensive watches, but I knew people who did and worried about them getting mugged for their watches on public transportation. I was grateful my watches were cheap and efficient. You had to wind them often when they stopped moving forward, and I learned much later that sometimes you just had to get a new battery. The watch wasn't broken.

Watches seemed to disappear from most everyone's wrists in the early aughts, when cell phones told the time more accurately and your phone was out anyway: why not just glance at it? In 2016, news stories declared that smart phones had killed the watch industry, but maybe not the luxury-watch industry.

The pandemic temporarily gouged the retail watch industry, as retail stores closed down during the initial COVID wave, dropping US sales to less than $10 million in 2020, from $12.3 million in 2019. Swiss exports of watches to China fell more than 51 percent in 2020, as exports of Swiss watches to Hong Kong plummeted 42 percent. Who needs a fancy watch if you never leave your home?

The average person in 2022 spent $35.60 on a watch, though the new Gem Dior sells for $77,000, which in salary terms is the same as earning $40 an hour for almost forty hours of work every week for a year. Minimum wage in 2022 is $9.30 in Ohio and $13.20 in New York.

But then in 2020, reports were that people went crazy for secondhand high-end watches during the pandemic. I'm not sure why, but I read that a McKinsey report estimated pre owned luxury-watch sales were $18 billion in 2018 and will hit $30 billion in 2025 for the fancy-pants brands of Rolex, Patek Philippe, and the like.

Even Benedict Cumberbatch is in a Jaeger-LeCoultre watch commercial (the company that makes the forever clock my father gave each one of us). He's alternately meditating and diving deep into the ocean; I guess his gorgeous watch helps him do all that, or is it just his arm that's gorgeous? Uma Thurman, Maria Sharapova, Charlize Theron, Serena Williams, Daniel Craig, and Kate Winslet all sing the praises of expensive timepieces, even though they likely have assistants to keep them on time.

My father would love the fact that these incredibly expensive and exquisite salutes to the past of watchmaking are having a recurrence of popularity. Because it is a trend that directly opposes the Apple Watch craze that marries innovation with obsolescence. I read that the Apple WatchOS 7 (I had to read about it because I will never own one) could endeavor to complete sixty-five tasks you may or may not need ever, including track your sleep, monitor your heart rate, open and start your car, check your email, translate phrases, be a compass, open your garage door, check your blood oxygen level, or pay a bill. I can open my email on my phone and also check my Facebook messages there, so can my watch just leave my social media alone?

Then, in a blink of an eye, there was a WatchOS 8. Then in December 2023 Apple Watch Series 9 and Apple Watch Ultra were banned from being sold in the U.S. By the time you read this, there may be a WatchOS 22.

Time doesn't change. Timekeeping does.

At the Beijing Olympics in the winter of 2022, the reality that lives and medals were on the line over a few milliseconds in the timing of a finish in each competition gave me anxiety as I sat on my bed watching NBC's trumpet-blaring about the most popular sports. For an hour or so before I tried to drift off to sleep, I cheered for US team superstars Nathan Chen, Chloe Kim, and Erin Jackson, the first Black woman in history to win gold in speedskating. Watching the competitors fly, defy the laws of the universe, and contort in the air in freestyle skiing, snowboard slopestyle, and giant slalom, I watched the tears and the grins in sports in which time is almost everything. That and doping, or not.

The official Olympics website explained the burden of time-keeping assigned to OMEGA, the official Olympic timekeeper: "60 tons of equipment were placed on the competition sites with the presence of 150 people managing the entire timing system, which was developed entirely in Switzerland. Technological developments have made it possible to computerize a process that for a long time was manual. And to avoid any problems in the event of a technical glitch, the main system naturally has several back-up sources." There are two people standing at the finish line, and, of course, cameras, just in case the tech goes poof.

The pandemic threw time into the food processor, and we're all still adjusting. Remote working, remote learning, quarantining, and isolation eliminate the time it takes to commute, get dressed, and get prepared. COVID elongated and transformed time for everyone except essential workers in hospitals, grocery stores, nursing homes, or wherever else they had no respite. For those whose time was still required on-site, those hours were compounded with danger, as real face time became possibly infection time, maybe even leading to death.

Many of us changed our relationship with time during the pandemic. Every fleeting morsel of seconds, minutes and hours bore impact not just for ourselves, but for our families, communities, strangers on the train.

How long have you had these symptoms?

When was your last COVID test?

When will you get the results?

How long were you exposed to the person with COVID?

When does the booster become effective?

Does long COVID last forever?

All of these forced changes related to how we spend time, save time, use up our time, reclaim our time, invest in time, and disregard time, have altered not just individual time spending, but how culture values and accounts for time spent. Who is ultimately in charge of the time we have to spend? Or even the time we have left?

The technological innovations have complicated and improved how we keep time, but they have so many add-ons and extra amenities that perhaps the original intent is lost.

We are measuring time. We are keeping time. We are telling time. Time use is not the same for everyone; it is a privilege to have "downtime," to even consider that you can have "me time." We each create a story, a narrative about time and how we use it.

For work-from-home single parents strangled by the around-the-clock, minute-by-minute demands of homeschooling, childcare, elder care, and a management structure that does not imagine or even respect that you are never "off the clock," time is hijacked by everyone and everything else.

Time is of the essence. That belongs on a T-shirt. Wait, I'm sure it already is.

What we can do with time is light-years away from what it was. In 1873, Jules Verne published the novel *Around the World in 80 Days,* and the journey of Phileas Fogg in those eleven-and-a-half weeks became a recent PBS Masterpiece remake. Eighty days to get around the world was worth the bet because it was unfathomably fast, improbable, even a ludicrous consideration.

In theory, *Flying* magazine reports, a Cessna Citation X+ can make it around the world in thirty-five hours, give or take a few minutes, flying at 717 miles per hour. But it's a grand hypothetical because that calculates flying time, not stopping and refueling time. Imagine how many trips to the teeny tiny bathroom that would be, let alone how many of those inedible little biscuits you would ingest.

In the hundred years since my father was born in 1922, the way the world and everyone in it tells time and measures time has changed.

Yes, times have changed, too, and that is a cliché that is at once dismissive and consoling. But time itself has not. Forever is an impossibility, though so much of what we do feels as if it lasts forever. Even if we declare we will keep things in our minds and hearts forever, we forget.

My father's forever clock tells time in my dining room—still—but it doesn't chime.

December 2023

19

NICKNAMES

DAD CALLED ME MICH AND WAS THE FIRST PERSON EVER TO do so; he said it with a tenderness, a kind of reverence. It was reserved for when he would compliment me, congratulate me, or urge me on.

He also called my mother Patsy instead of Patricia; all six of his children got their own nicknames. He passed away before any of my children were born—but not before his other eight grandchildren, courtesy of my five older brothers and sisters, created his own nickname: Papa Bill.

When I first began the relationship with the man who would become my husband (and later my ex-husband), he called me Lovey. The only other time I'd heard that nickname was when the Professor on *Gilligan's Island* called his wife that. I tolerated it for a few years from him because he was kind when he said it.

But at one point, when describing an argument he'd had with an ex-girlfriend, he mentioned her nickname: Lovey. I don't know why I was so shocked that he'd called someone else by the nickname he'd insisted on using with me. Even then, it felt like only a small brick in a cathedral of betrayals from him. I asked him not to call me that again; he did anyway. It no longer felt like a kindness.

Still, it didn't turn me away from nicknames. When I had children, I had nicknames for all my boys—who are men now at thirty-two, thirty, and twenty-seven. Brendan was Sugar Dumpling Pie, B-Man, and Boo Boo Bear. Weldon was Kissy Button Bear Pie, Dub, and Dubaroonio.

And Colin, well, he was Coleyville, Coley Bear, and one slightly more embarrassing name his friends all discovered when he was seven and playing youth baseball.

At the time, I was a single parent and eager to cheer Colin on but also watching the time, as I had to get to two other games on two other local baseball fields for my other two sons. After passing on a series of balls at his first at-bat of the game, Colin slammed one pitched down the middle of the plate, and it flew right past the outfielders.

I screamed his nickname in sheer elated youth-baseball-mother ecstasy: "Go, Sugar Buns!"

There was an instant hush in the stands. "Sugar Buns?" asked the mother sitting next to me. "That one will never die."

All the boys on his team turned to stare at me, and then guffawed, screeching in high-pitched voices: "Ahhhh, Sugar Buns!"

I had ruined his life.

Rounding the bases, Colin glared at me in disbelief. But approaching home plate, Colin acted impervious to their disdain. "That's me, Sugar Buns!" he smiled, high-fiving his teammates.

In recent years, he has repeatedly reminded me not to call him any nickname in public, particularly at work events, even though these days for my sons I use the banal, affectionate nicknames of Dub, B, and C-Ster.

Still, my oldest son, Weldon, was recently recovering from surgery at my home and, when I went to check on him and feel his head for a fever, I smoothed his hair and sighed, "My little Baby Snookie Boy." Without opening his eyes, he smiled.

The cherished nicknames for my sons cannot erase the torrential conflicts we've had over the years—every parent and child has those—but they smooth the edges of our disagreements and serve as quick reminders of what is truly at stake. Love, after all, is not one straight line from birth to death, filled solely with kind expressions and Instagram shots of birthday cakes, anniversaries, weddings, and Halloweens.

But intermittently—along the more complicated timelines of our lives as families—are the reasons we come up with the special names that both parties hold in our hearts, the ones we assign to each other and only each other that signify more than what's on our birth certificates. They can overshadow some of the hurt we can't help but inflict. There's an embroidered connection contained in the sounds of the words.

Whispered at bedside or shouted from bleachers, a nickname is an assignment of love so heartily ostentatious it is meant to be consumed; it's a literal translation of the sweetness it manifests.

One day, after my parents were gone, when my siblings were far away, Mich became the core of my amateur roller derby name—when I skated every week for six glorious years until 2018. They called me Mich the Masher, and the derby girls call me Mich to this day.

"Mich." It calms me still.

March 2021

20

SHOES

I HOPE TO WEAR THE BUTTERFLY SLIDES WITH THE WOODEN wedge and the emerald-green accents again.

I have treasured them since I purchased those pointed-toe miracles at a small boutique in Cambridge, Massachusetts, where I was in town to speak on a panel at a narrative journalism conference held at Massachusetts Institute of Technology. It was 2006, and they have aged well, if at all.

The shoes are still perfect. The times for them are not.

Since the onslaught of the global pandemic, the economic failure that ensued, and the days of upheaval in response to the cumulative racist murders, mass shootings and worldwide violence I have not worn them or any other pair of shoes besides my running shoes. Or winter boots. Slip-on sandals or flip-flops if it's warm. I am not a slippers person. Worrying about shoes seems absurd.

Each prolonged COVID day I am working long hours from home, mostly barefoot or in socks. I put on shoes maybe for an hour or two each day—or every other. I leave the house wary and masked to go for a walk or to the small grocery store for cauliflower pretzels, CVS for gum care mouthwash, or Walgreens to pick up my prescriptions. Zoom shots on conference calls are from the chest up; no one sees my feet.

As a sixty-something cancer survivor with asthma, high blood pressure, fear of COVID, and a dislike of huge crowds, I have not protested outside in this pandemic, though I believe in many of the causes. But I would need to wear shoes.

I understand fully my privilege of working healthy from home with checks still coming in, as millions face furloughs, unemployment, personal, professional, and economic disaster, health catastrophes, and unspeakable loss.

And I also understand my privilege as a white person not inhabiting the paralysis from the weight of grief and trauma caused by the murder of George Floyd added to the roster and the widespread injustices exposed again following his killing.

Yes, my footwear focus is vain, shallow, meaningless, and absurd. They don't matter.

As shallow as it sounds, I miss the shoes.

So many have spoken eloquently about the liberation the shelter at home mandate has hatched for those of us who WFH, and how freeing it is to wear pajamas all day, and (for those who did wear them) to boycott bras and makeup.

Certainly in the face of the collapse of democracy and the upending of the systems of injustice condoning violence against more than half of Americans and the silent complicity of many others, worrying about shoes is ridiculous. Appearance is immaterial, a disconnect from what is important.

But I miss them. I miss who I was in them. I miss what I wore when I went outside—not for necessity, but for fun and for work. Having dinner or drinks in a bustling café, attending a conference, giving a training, going to work, traveling for work. I regularly wore fishnets with cowboy boots. Yes I did.

It was a different world. No one really cares what they look like during the apocalypse.

Each day that I am not Zooming I fumble to pull on leggings, a tunic, and a coated rubber band to convince my hair into a ponytail and head to my laptop in my home office. Yes, I could elect to wear shoes in isolation. But I don't.

I read recently in an excerpt from Donald A. Norman, a cognitive scientist and author of the book *Emotional Design: Why We Love (or Hate) Everyday Things*, that there are three levels of brain processing. He writes, "Love for Shoes would be at the visceral level, which is responsible for quick judgments, attraction and where the physical characteristics prevail."

This scientific theory of shoes is further explained in a 2012 research paper "Protection or Pleasure: Female Footwear." The Brazilian researchers also ascribe to Norman that "Love for the Shoe is in the reflexive level, which is contemplative, sophisticated, comes to the perceived rarity, experience, exclusivity, self-image and about the messages that a product sends to people."

In plain language, when you love shoes, research shows you also love what your choice of footwear tells the world about you. Yes, for me, I want to project confidence by wearing red plaid pumps with thick heels while giving a speech. So it is true, Donald Norman, I have experienced love of shoes at both visceral and reflexive levels. I appreciate the craftsmanship and creativity of an exquisite shoe but also the identity I adopt when I am in them: Cinderella without the bothersome prince.

* * *

AS A YOUNG GIRL I WORE PATENT LEATHER MARY JANES: white and black, the only colors available. It was Keds in the summers, ordered from the Sears Roebuck catalog. Platforms defined high school for me—cork or suede, some as high as six inches. College in the '70s was tight pants tucked into high boots—I loved my tan suede pair with heels that did not fare well in the snow. I dated a man sophomore year who wore earth shoes. We broke up. Yes, there were other issues as well.

Later, like most every other woman my age, I was awed by celebrities parading about in Manolo Blahnik pumps, though I would never be able to afford them. While Beyoncé ventured into athletic shoes with Ivy Park, I directly related to her other impressive shoe game—the spiked heels with the dangling beads. She could dance in them.

I have orange, fuchsia, and cobalt-blue suede sandals in my closet. I have multiple pairs of leopard print shoes—flats, heels, and a pair of French suede ankle boots my friend Katherine made me buy. All of them, for the COVID time being, go unworn. I refuse to throw them away.

The protests continue with curfews attached, another surge of COVID is expected as a result. The phases of quarantine may take months or longer to move from lockdown toward re-entry. Yes, the shoes seem a narcissistic demonstration of complete and utter oblivion.

The world must change.

I loved the shoes before. I wonder if I will love them as much after.

June 2020

21

SOUNDS

THE THUD AGAINST THE FRONT DOOR WAKES ME ABOUT 4:15 or 4:30 A.M. It is followed by the dozen or so rubber-soled rushed footsteps of the person who has been delivering the Sunday printed newspaper to my house for more than twenty years, the slam of his car door, and the loud growling of his car as he pulls out of the driveway and vanishes down the street, headed south.

I lie there in my mismatched percale sheets, determined not to check email on my phone. Soon enough the birds start to chirp in the lilac trees flanking the front of the house; their call and response is soothing and bright. It is the first summer of the pandemic.

Since the near end of the world began in March 2020, the street sounds of cars passing in the suburb of Chicago where I live have nearly evaporated. The deep drumming of lawn mowers and hedge trimmers fills the afternoons and weekends. Occasional barks from dogs punctuate the hours that slide past. I understand these are the sounds of insulated privilege.

No one in my neighborhood applauds the health-care workers from apartment balconies; we tie white ribbons around the trees. There are few ambulance sirens pronouncing catastrophes; two people have died in this small suburb since March. The sounds went missing from the outside in.

It's odd when the expected sounds of daily life disappear; it's as if you're seeing what is in the back of the cupboard for the first time, reminding yourself of how you placed it there long ago, wondering if it has gone stale, past its usefulness.

I live in this 1932 house in a compliant, quarantining neighborhood where people shelter at home, indoors mostly, except when they garden or play in their yards. I am indoors working, as I imagine my neighbors are as well. I go for a walk alone in the evening—four miles round trip—after I stop working about six or so. I often wave to the sometimes-masked walkers, bikers, skaters, and joggers. They sometimes wave back.

Save for the Saturday backyard-pool-splashing children, the crying toddlers, the parents reprimanding, the neighbor with his rare and random illegally begotten fireworks aglare every few weeks from the yard facing one door to the south, and the daily shouting from the parents next door, the block is mostly quiet. Good.

I have grown to be noise intolerant.

Sudden loud noises startle me—in a cartoonish way, like Elmer Fudd jumping back at the burst of his shotgun. Unpredictable sounds that erupt without warning scare me. I am not crazy about dogs who bark ferociously. Aside from the allergy issue, if I had a dog the barking in my house would unravel me to the point of sobbing in a locked closet whispering, "Please stop." I don't like amusement parks; they do not amuse me. It's the screaming I despise.

My workday is quiet and long—save the Zoom meetings where I put myself on mute most of the time unless I am speaking, answering questions, or delivering the instruction module. I write, edit, and type for maybe eight hours a day or more, sometimes nine or ten. The only sounds are my fingers tapping on the keyboard and the whirr of the portable fan nearby. I am not one of those who works while listening to music in the background, never have been. If I loved the music, I would get up and dance. I would never get any work done in a coffee shop.

In the evenings, most of the things on network, cable, and subscription TV are loud—the cop shows, the SWAT shows, the fire department and hospital shows, even the music shows, the competition for the next champion whatever shows, finding the next best Taylor Swift, all that. There was one network show earlier in the spring with a lot of crying and snuggling about couples finding their perfect singing partner and also the love of their lives. Talk about high standards. Even the documentaries and the historic remakes are too loud: so much war, so many bombs, so much gunfire. And crying. I opt out.

Oh, yes, I love *The Great British Baking Show*. It's like life in slow motion, with cubes of butter. And they are ruthlessly polite.

Not so many friends of mine like to go to the movies with me anymore because of my low decibel criterion. If I won't go to a war movie or one with car chases and screaming and shooting—that leaves the sappy romance movies, the costume dramas, and the foreign films where all that happens is people change clothes, partners, and restaurants. If you can't remember *My Dinner with Andre*, look it up—that's the ideal. People just talk over dinner.

But no one is going to the movies anymore. At least until Disney says we can.

I do love music, though, and dancing. If the music is loud and thumping through my body, that is different than the sudden, unpredictable outbursts from an angry person or a car crash or gunfire. I hate fireworks.

With music, it's my choice, and I can control the volume.

* * *

GROWING UP, OUR HOUSE ON CLINTON PLACE AND THEN THE one on Jackson Avenue was what some may say was loud—the natural noise from six of us children born in fewer than eight years. There was a white baby grand piano in the living room, and all I could play was "Chopsticks," though I played the viola in middle school, rushing down to serenade my mother by scratching my bow across the strings as she placed damp clothes in the dryer. We played records on the console. We each had a transistor radio.

My two brothers would be in the backyard or the driveway playing basketball as they oomphed and grunted and dribbled a ball they would never throw to me. My sisters Mary and Maureen would be in their third-floor bedroom we called Blue Heaven, setting their hair at night in pink plastic rollers, the blue princess phone on the nightstand between their twin beds with the shiny blue bedspreads. My sister Madeleine would be cajoling me into doing her chores—saying she would time me.

We played pool and Ping-Pong and danced in the basement, had friends over. It was crowded at our house and loud, but it was a good loud. There was mandated quiet when we were doing our homework in our bedrooms or in the library with the marble table off the living room. No TV or music playing during the week at night. I had a record player in my room for the forty-fives I bought with allowance money, saving up for the albums, switching the toggle to thirty-three. It was always homework quiet time from after dinner until bedtime.

The library on the first floor of the house with the leather club chairs had shelves filled with two different kinds of encyclopedias that my father bought from a door-to-door ency-clopedia salesman. My father said yes because we asked, and the six of us thought we would never have to go to the library to do our homework after that because we would always have the answers at home.

My parents expected us to be quiet and told us to be quiet; they never shouted for us to shut up like I heard some other fathers do to their daughters or mothers do to their sons.

The sounds in the house on Jackson were predictable—even the weekend sounds of *American Bandstand* or *Soul Train* and *The Ed Sullivan Show* on Sunday night. I remember watching the Beatles and being astounded by how loud the girls in the audience were screaming. Were those happy screams? Is there such a thing?

My mother sang to herself when she did the laundry—she was always doing the laundry. My father whistled when he came home; I heard the electric garage door going up, the car pulling in, the engine stopping, him opening the door and walking briskly to the back door. Whistling.

"Hi, Mich. Where's your mother?"

With him it was always your mother, not Mom, I guess so we would not forget who she belonged to. Mrs. B, he called my grandmother, short for Mrs. Butler, who ate dinner with us most every night after my grandfather died. JJ was his name; "John," my grandmother called him, so that it was soft and marshmallow sweet, so unlike him. I never knew his middle name was Joseph until I read his obituary.

JJ was thin and hunched over like an apostrophe, lifting himself up off his armchair by the picture window, covered in plastic like all the other crinkly, sweat-sticking furniture in the six-flat on Wisconsin Avenue. He smelled spicy and sharp and would throw word darts at people he disliked; I remember thinking my father sounded nothing like him, and I was grateful.

* * *

I FIRST NOTICED THAT THE SOUNDS OF A BUSY FAMILY WENT missing eight years ago when I was alone in this house for the first time. The sounds disappeared, not gradually like the fade of sunlight at the end of the day from a sweet pink to blue to a black denouement. My oldest son was studying abroad, earning his masters. My middle son was away in his final year of college. My youngest son was away in his first year of college. The sounds disappeared, not gently like a rowboat gliding to shore, oars lifted into the boat, waiting for the time it's prudent to jump out and wade ankle deep when the bottom scrapes the sand. But suddenly, like the flick of a light switch or the slamming of a door, punctuating the before and the after, separating them mercilessly so there is no confusion.

It was foreign—the silence, the un-noise—so much so that I couldn't identify why I felt upended, disoriented, and fluish, like the time an inner-ear infection made me unable to stand without falling.

But that silence lasted just nine months, until two sons moved back home again. I have not been alone for more than a few months since.

Because of COVID, my house is only quiet again when Weldon and Colin are out, most every weekend. Then I can hear the sounds I couldn't hear before—the undertones, the backdrop of the air conditioner humming, cars pulling into other driveways. There is very little honking outside.

The years of my sons growing up were the loudest yet: the *thudthud thudthud* of an impromptu wrestling match upstairs in Colin's room—Colin against one of his brothers or Sammy or Joey or Ellis or any of the muscled athletes who ate, showered, and slept at our house every week, sometimes every day.

The heavy gait on the basement stairs *plodplodplodplod* and the accompanying yank of the railing, rattling its screws and bolts from the wall. The clanging of pots and pans—pizza or grilled cheese sandwiches made at one, two, three, or four in the morning. The shower water running long, long, long, so long I knew there would be no hot water left to wash my hair. The shouting on the phone, music from laptops, and video game din with machine guns and bells and clinking and shouts. The swearing, no matter how many times I said, "Stop, please."

I no longer have one ear perked for the White Nissan Altima (the White Knight, they called it) in the driveway, Colin or Brendan coming home late, the relief of the back door opening, the alarm buzzing once as the door opened. Then the clanking of the keys on the butcher block, the shoes thrown one at a time on the floor, the refrigerator opening, the cupboards, the clanking of plates and glasses. The water in the sink running, the teeth brushing, the toilet flushing.

I do not miss the sharp things they shouted to me and to each other. I yelled at them, too; I don't miss my own angry voice.

Shouting reminded me of him and the lifetime ago when I couldn't predict the volume or the moods of the man I was married to. As foolish as it seems, I was mostly caught off guard. Even the tornadoes warn you with the yellow sky and the eerie stillness. The early-warning sirens go off because our suburb has that system, and that's why the property taxes are high—or one of the reasons.

I need the yellow sky.

It's not too quiet now. I don't miss the sounds; I'm relieved. But it is just strange, unnatural, as if I've been treading water neck-deep in an ocean for so many years and suddenly I'm on dry land, standing. Where did the water go? It was just here.

August 2020

11

SOUP

THE TRICK IS TO WHIP THE EGGS FULLY AND MIGHTILY WITH
the juice squeezed from the fresh lemons—carefully so as not
to drop in any seeds—and add them to the chicken broth steam-
ing and promising, slowly, like someone afraid to fall off the
edge of a tightrope, stretched across the canyon.

Careful: otherwise the eggs start to cook and they leave
behind streams of egg as happens in egg drop soup, and this
is not that. I add three times as much lemon juice as the recipe demands because I know feeling the tart smack in your
mouth full of creamy, sunny yellow richness will be a surprise
reminder that someone did not follow the rules.

There are only three ingredients in egg lemon soup: chicken
broth, eggs, and lemon juice. I need to make things simple, even
though they are not. I am making this for my brother Paul, one
year older than me, fifth sibling in a tribe of six fewer than eight
years apart, who is dying of multiple myeloma. He is sixty-four.

I pour the daffodil-colored hot soup into the blue ceramic
pot, tape down the lid with black electrician's tape, and head

to his house in a nearby Chicago suburb—a twenty-minute drive from mine—for Saturday soup delivery. This has been my routine every weekend for the past year, five years after his diagnosis. In the past six months, his symptoms and pain have crescendoed.

"You know this is not about the soup," my older sister Madeleine says to me after I call her panicked that I don't have ham for the split pea soup I was making for Paul one Saturday, months earlier. "It's that you *make* him the soup."

Five years ago, Paul switched insurance companies and had the required physical, which uncovered multiple myeloma through a blood test. No symptoms. Projected survival is five years for 53 percent of patients; 35 percent survive ten years. Some lucky patients last longer.

Paul won't be one of them, though he doggedly pursued chemotherapies and early on had a stem cell transplant. He is weak and has lost close to a hundred pounds; now six foot three and about 130 pounds, he has arms thin as broomsticks, his cheekbones steel-angled, pronounced.

During his last visit to the hospital following a seizure—his fifth visit in as many months—the doctor called a family end-of-life meeting. We cried, asked questions, listened, held hands, planned for what we couldn't imagine.

In my earlier batches of egg lemon soup this winter, I would make the rice separately in the rice steamer, with brown rice, not white, and spoon the clumps of downy warmth into the soup, stirring wishfully, tenderly. It is late spring, and in the past week, Paul can no longer swallow food; it's liquids only, and I add extra broth to this batch to make it leaner, easier for him to sip when I hold the spoon to his lips.

I am not his caretaker; I am the sister Saturday soup maker offering a different soup each week, from tomato to mushroom, French onion, chicken vegetable, and white bean. I am one of the four sisters plus one brother who visit him and offer him what we can as often as we can.

His second wife, whom he married six years earlier, organizes some details. He had only been married to her for one year when he was diagnosed, their wedding coming after eleven years of Paul raising his three children alone as a widower; his late wife, Bernadette, died from an undiagnosed brain tumor in 2004.

His two daughters and a health-care worker who stays overnight have been doing the bulk of his daily care, including the buffet of medications delivered and logged onto a whiteboard with a blue marker.

He's in the first-floor den full time now, off the family room, the hospital bed facing the huge picture window onto his tree-draped yard, luscious and hopeful as far as you can see. There are family photo albums piled onto the side tables, framed photos of him from childhood and pictures of recent family weddings offer a parade of grins on the windowsill.

Too quickly following his last hospital stay, within weeks, the tempo switches to hospice care. Paul remains in the den, but it's different; *he* is different. The future has a different shape.

His youngest daughter, Marirose, is most always by his side; she moved from Los Angeles the year before to be with him and help with his business. His oldest daughter, Treacy, arrives with her husband, Dan, from their house a few miles away each day to help. She is in the kitchen. His son, Matt, is upstairs, in from Florida.

Everyone is waiting, and everyone is wounded; it feels inappropriate to laugh but also urgent. So I try to sprinkle in a joke just to feel something other than desperation.

"Remember when Dad used to go upstairs before the parties at our house ended and just lie on the guests' coats to go to sleep?" I ask.

Paul smiles. I am positioned near him on his left side so I can stroke his face; his four-day beard is reddish-blond stubble, but soft.

I don't heat up the soup anymore after I arrive, as I have for most of the past year. He loved it piping hot, an extra minute in the microwave. It's OK at room temperature now. I tell him I have egg lemon soup, and he mouths the words, "Oh, good."

Four spoonfuls is all I can manage for him, urging him to swallow each time, reminding him to close his lips. Marirose can usually get ten to fifteen spoonfuls accomplished; that's what we hope for.

"Our Father who art in heaven, hallowed be thy name." I start a decade of the rosary, holding the rosary draped over the guardrail. Paul is more fully devotional than I am, more authentic in his faith, though we share the same beginnings. We said the rosary every night as a family in the house on Clinton Place, then the house on Jackson Avenue.

Paul was my middle-school protector from bullies, my companion on double dates for his high school's prom, when he set me up with his friends, or my high school homecoming, when I set him up with mine. Later, he was my business adviser, my life and parenting coach, my friend. He kept secrets. He did imitations. He loved to dance.

Paul says he promised my mother before she died that he would watch out for me as a single mother raising three sons; that promise to her was nearly twenty years ago. Every time Paul helped me or my sons—hiring a clean-up crew after a basement flood, helping find a roof contractor, referring clients to me, advising Brendan on school, Colin on work, Weldon on life—he would say, "I promised Mom I would."

Paul is breathing through his mouth; I worry that his lips are chapped and his mouth is dry, but he doesn't seem to notice. I make a note to ask Treacy to swab his mouth and put Vaseline on his lips because that's my way of trying to help. She knows and doesn't need my reminders. I'm trying to help, but it's like trying to stop a speeding train with rose petals.

I finish the ten Hail Marys and say, "Glory be to the Father, to the Son, and to the Holy Spirit, as it was, is now, and ever shall be, world without end. Amen."

"Hi, Daddy."

Marirose comes in from the side door off the kitchen, picks up the bowl of soup, and tells Paul she needs him to swallow after she gently places the spoon to his lips and pours a spoonful of soup into his mouth. She gets him to swallow thirty-eight spoonfuls. Thirty-eight. We count them one by one softly. It is the most he has eaten in several days.

*　*　*

IT'S 2005, AND WE DRIVE A SHORT DISTANCE TO TARPON Springs, Florida, from his house in Palm Harbor to enjoy a Greek dinner at Mykonos, one of the many restaurants in what is called an "authentic Greek fishing village."

It was one of several times my three sons and I visited him and his three children in Florida for spring break—both of us single and combining our families after the death of his wife and my divorce. Motherless, fatherless children together for a week when all six of them could enjoy two parents.

"U. P.," my sons called him, for Uncle Paul. I was just Aunt Michele.

We order the egg lemon soup and mounds of other dishes—some flaming—and devour them all with such craving it was as if we knew this moment would soon be just a memory and that it would make us laugh every time for many years.

I was hoping this batch of soup would remind him of our jaunts to Tarpon Springs, when we walked by the piers, my sons begging for new T-shirts, sandals, or whatever was fluttering on ropes in small kiosks feet from the water, handprinted signs declaring they were on sale for $5.99.

I ask Paul if he remembers the rap song my sons made for him—and performed—for his surprise fiftieth birthday party. Their chorus was, "Where the palm trees sway and the girls say, 'Hey.'" I sing the chorus for him, and Paul smiles broadly, his eyes still closed.

It is my last batch of soup for Paul, our last Saturday. He dies early the next Monday morning.

Months later, I can't bring myself to make another batch of egg lemon soup for my family or his children just yet; it's too soon. But when I am ready, I will buy extra lemons and stir in the eggs slowly, carefully, and imagine his smile.

October 2021

23

BLUE

IT IS THE COLOR BLUE THAT MY FATHER ONCE CALLED "DEEP, dark, rich, pale blue" to describe a favorite rug. It is the color of the lane stripes at the bottom of the park district pool, the color of a late August sky against full tree branches, the color of his eyes.

The hospice nurse has silent-sealed him breathless inside the cobalt-blue plastic bag that fits his six-foot-three body, reduced to less than a hundred pounds, half of his weight nine months ago. The zippered bag is unreasonably thin, static, narrow, and compressed, as if it holds only neatly folded, ironed twin sheets.

Two kind-faced funeral home attendants wheel my brother Paul on a silver steel gurney out the wide white wooden front door inside a flattened bag the color of electrician's tape.

"I can't watch this," says his youngest daughter, Marirose, who retreats to the family room with my sisters Mary and Maureen. His oldest daughter, Treacy, moves to the kitchen with her husband.

Several of us stand in the hall in tearful vigilance; Paul's son, Matt, my brother Bill, my sister Madeleine, my brother-in-law Mike, two of my sons.

I can't not watch this.

Paul has been fast-forward dying for a year from multiple myeloma, randomly diagnosed five years earlier—symptomless—because of a full physical required to change insurance companies. This is our last glimpse of him in this house, his home for more than twenty years.

Blue is the background color in the family photo of him Treacy chose for the obituary. It matches the highlight color in his glen plaid suit jacket.

Over the decades, I mourned family members, close friends, and in-laws claimed by disease, accidents, violence. Both my parents have died; my father from a stroke in 1988, my mom from heart disease in 2002. I never knew my father's parents: his mother died before I was born, his father when I was a toddler. My mother's father died when I was a teen, her mother when I was in my twenties.

The man who was my senior year of high school boyfriend dies of AIDS after college in the '80s. His mother tells me the news of his death as we both stand in the checkout line at the local Dominick's grocery store. I am engaged to the man I would later marry and in town for the ten-year reunion of Oak Park–River Forest High School. I ask her coyly if he will be there, hoping.

"Oh, dear, he died," she says, with weary grief so palpable it seems like a forever necklace she wears around her neck. I didn't know.

Blue is the color of Paul's favorite shirt: soft, cotton, short-sleeved, collared. He's wearing it in photos of family parties for graduations, birthdays, celebrations, holidays.

The funerals of sons and daughters of friends lost to suicide are excruciating, and the lunches afterward are apocalyptic, infected with unfathomable disbelief that life can go on for anyone else.

An unsolved double murder carves head-shaking grief into our family. Parents to my sons' friends are killed in their red brick home on a late summer night after a bike ride through the neighborhood.

I am lucky so far not to lose family members or loved ones among the millions who have died globally from COVID-19. Pandemic deaths for me are cautionary tales, updates on Instagram or Facebook; I witness the grief from a polite but solemn distance.

I know it is impossible to assert equivalence on any death, and I dare not.

Blue is the color of most morning skies when he calls me from the car on his way to work at the manufacturing company that was my father's, where he is owner and CEO. He asks first how I am, then recounts a long-ago memory to make us both laugh. If I had a disagreement with one of my sons that week, I seek his advice. He later calls that son to say, "Calm always wins."

Many of the deaths that have intersected my life are older relatives in their seventies, eighties, nineties, a few one hundreds, with predictable expirations like timed train departures. Some friends and acquaintances pass who were long-suffering, beleaguered by disease. We waited, knowing.

Perhaps it is because of the relative rarity of death for me that Paul's death is changing me. Perhaps I haven't lost enough in my lifetime to have full perspective. I haven't lost enough to understand better how to accommodate, how to stand upright in this new life minus one more.

Of course, there is the murmured, brittle critique: "About time; you've had it so good."

Blue is the color of the Blessed Virgin Mary. His children, my sons, our siblings, we repeat Hail Marys together in the months before his death, holding his thin hand, the rosary draped around the guardrail of the temporary hospital bed in the den.

In the months since my brother's death, I am missing my patience and my filter. I can't abide friends with petty complaints.

I dismiss conflicts with coworkers or clients as time-wasting. I do not return angry texts or voicemails. I screen old friends and new acquaintances for illogical high drama and press Delete, editing my inner circle. I seethe silently at betrayal.

I am hollowed, subdued; my former fierce ambition feels as if it is packed away in a forgotten suitcase, unmarked, unnoticed. I work but feel tepidly uninspired. His death ushers in a prickly cascade of new ways to witness, feel, respond, live. Die.

Mine is not the loss of a father or son or husband. Mine is the loss of a brother who breaks his hand defending me against a bully in fifth grade. He puts cash in the kitchen cookie jar in my house on Linden Avenue when I'm a newly single mother with three sons all under five years old. He cheers at my sons' wrestling meets. He opens savings accounts in their names for their college expenses. He sells me his second car for a dollar so my three sons can share a car as teens to get to their practices, workouts, and wrestling camps when I can't accommodate driving them to all of it while working an hour away.

Losing a sibling is unlike other losses I have known. The intimacy is emotional and intellectual, historically cumulative, bound in a lifetime of shared experiences, similarities, knowns, crisscrossing over each other as if we are running bases in a game of softball in the backyard on Clinton Place.

Blue is the color Treacy chooses for her wedding colors in 2019, the year before Paul is avalanching downward, before the frequent collapses and stays in the hospital every few weeks. His toast to the bride and groom is so soul-felt it makes me sigh.

A brother's love is unlike the bond of a lover, partner, or spouse; there are no romantic secrets, only DNA shared responses and embedded memories. There is more pragmatism and practicality, less illusion. Paul's death is the first, and it's out of order; he is the fifth of six, one year older than I am. I am the sixth. As a cancer survivor, I wonder if Paul's death is a dress rehearsal for my own.

It is the early morning of May 24; Marirose calls before seven to say that her father has died and to come to the house. For several days prior she and her siblings have slept on couches in the next room, knowing it is soon.

In the last two months, his decline hosts a daily rapid deep dive erasure of abilities and functions. Every day is remarkably worse than the day before; there is no direction change.

Tuesday he is sipping water from a straw; Thursday he can't swallow.

The day before he dies, he can't speak or keep his eyes open for more than a few minutes from his hospice bed in the den, the one with the oil portrait of our father on one wall, a framed Michael Jordan jersey signed to his son, Matt, on another. Bookshelves of favorite books by Winston Churchill, Franklin D. Roosevelt, and Mother Teresa, flank the central picture window looking to the backyard.

Blue is the periwinkle that his late first wife, Bernadette, chooses for the family room in the house they own that I later buy from him, that I live in now. When she dies in her sleep in 2004 from an undiagnosed brain tumor, he can only say that she passed; he can't say the word die.

Until the last few weeks his memory and his words are clear. I dread the time when cognitive reduction may rob us of our conversations. I fearfully look for signs.

A month before the end I tell him about a difficult work exchange on the phone.

"What time was this?"

I bristle, frightened that his thinking is irreversibly fogged.

"About two, I think."

"Makes sense. Most people can't handle difficult conversations in the afternoon. Try to have those tough calls and meetings in the morning," Paul says. "I call the ones who want to argue 'afternoon people.' So I deal with them first thing."

Blue is the color of his aging Chevy van that we pile all six of the children into—his three, my three—on adventures in Florida on spring breaks after he is widowed. We are parents alone together, filling in for the children's other absent parent;

Paul shouting hello to strangers on the sidewalk, waving out the window, all of us crowded and laughing.

Grief is a stranger who lets himself in a back door with the easily hijacked keycode password that is your name and birthdate. He sneaks behind you as you type on deadline, words on a screen that feel vaporous, empty. Grief spoons you in your bed as you try to sleep and will not release you until you cry, letting out a tiny wail, inaudible over the ceiling fan.

Grief sits beside you in your Nissan Rogue in the parking lot of the grocery store where you think you see him pushing a cart to a car. Grief is standing near you when you have to tell him about your oldest son's new job, knowing he will smile. When you pick up the phone, you remember he is gone.

Blue is the color of Lake Michigan waves from the deck at his home in New Buffalo, Michigan, where he grills pork chops and burgers, chicken and corn, a bounty of smiles, providing for us all.

Grief is next to you in the kitchen when you halve brussels sprouts to bake in the way that he loved at Thanksgiving—balsamic vinegar, olive oil, walnuts, sun-dried tomatoes, panko breadcrumbs, shredded parmesan, 425 degrees for twenty minutes. You dread the first cluster of holiday absences.

Death is expected for each of us; we are born with a deadline, ignorant of precisely when that will be. It is an uneven distribution of longevity. Of course it is haughty to expect preferential treatment on the mortality guarantee. We all die; it is at times the when and how that are surprising, quirkily haphazard, and yes, unjust.

Blue is the color of the winning ribbons at the Michigan State Fair, where he and Bernadette, their three children, plus me and my three sons go for a jaunt one summer afternoon when they are all small and demand hot dogs, popcorn, ice cream, and pie.

I am incredulous that four years following his diagnosis his fast-forwarding into death is so physically gruesome and boldly immune to all his lifesaving efforts: years of treatment and chemotherapy, procedures, medications, radiation, experiments.

Brainwashed by the warrior narrative embalmed in every cancer diagnosis I anticipate a positive cause and effect for treatments that allows you to will the outcome. This is also a selfish delusion; my first bout with breast cancer fifteen years ago was treated successfully. Paul embraces all procedures, recommendations, and options with bottomless hope. The last doctor who treats him says he is still alive out of sheer willfulness. Marirose says a few weeks before he dies that when she comes downstairs in the morning she finds him walking a few agonized steps in the kitchen, wincing in pain. It is the first time in several days he has been out of bed.

"I have to show the doctor I can walk."

I do not believe Paul thought he was going to die until only days before his death; always envisioning recovery, he had faith that tricked him into an ambitious belief in miracles and grace.

Some days I feel energized and I want to act more like my brother: be purposeful, empathic, generous, kind, devout, making time for people who need help, ambitiously solving problems, offering tangible next steps.

"I'll get someone to give you an estimate. Let me take care of it. I'll make some calls."

His children, his nephews and nieces, his siblings, me, his friends, his neighbors, his employees, his second wife have all been on the receiving end of his graciousness. Some reciprocate, and some deserve his generosity less than others; some take ruthless advantage of him, but he is relentless in his kindness.

"Keep the peace," Paul says, more often in the months, weeks, and days before his death—reminding me, his children, and his siblings, that his legacy is to always aim to do just that. He routinely pauses before responding to a conflict or provocation and rarely reacts in anger to his family, friends, employees, customers, suppliers, or strangers.

"Wait before you answer," he says.

I am trying. Grateful for a lifetime of his examples, I shrink with defeat because I am not as fine a person; I am a fallow imitation of his goodness.

Blue is the color of the Chicago Bears jersey he wears when my father takes him, my brother Bill, and occasionally me to the snowy football games at Soldier Field.

"Everything happens for a reason" is not a mantra I can tolerate when someone offers rushed, clichéd condolences.

Everything happens. But you must find the reason to keep going; it is not assigned or delivered neatly.

Blue is the color of his sweater. The six of us are seated on a boat's bench, a trip by ferry crossing Lake Michigan from Chicago to Michigan for a vacation week, our mother posing us and our father taking our grainy picture.

I do not believe there is one grand scheme of things. I do not believe horrors—or glorious rewards—are predetermined, laid out, some glorified God-wisdom to teach you lessons and inspire your faith. It is abominably cruel to decree rigidly that every malady, crime, trauma, pandemic, or egregious act is an intentional lesson that should strengthen your character.

Sometimes there is no reason.

Yes, you can create reason after the fact by controlling what you do, how you behave and react. But a life is decided by so many external circumstances that are minor and major, catastrophic and glorious, historic and systemic, uncontrollable, unreasonable.

The silhouette of my life is changed; I no longer feel there is time to waste on people, places, things, or habits that have no future—dead ends. Time is rubber-slick, elastic, and swiftly evaporates. I must respect that it cannot be regained or negotiated. I must spend it frugally before it is gone forever.

What is irrevocably reinforced with Paul's death is that each of my siblings are angel guardians: that our love for each other is unconditional, that we are reliable and trustworthy, present. Together we comprise a seawall of boulders supporting any request, every need spoken or imagined, holding despair at bay. Unyielding and assuring, we have each other, just as our parents would have wanted.

Losing Paul decrees as my testament to him that I reassess, realign, and make over who and how I am in the world and why. It shapes the choices I make.

Sometimes the choice is as simple as a favorite color. Paul's was blue.

August 2021

24

BREATH

IT REMINDS ME OF THE FRESHEST AIR—SOFT OCEAN WIND— that waltzes smoothly across your skin as you pace a quiet beach: embedded with a muted saltiness but also a steadfast stillness. Not a blatant flowery scent like magnolias, roses, or lilacs, nor as distinguishable as fresh spring grass resurrected from winter or newly turned dirt, though it is assuredly all-natural, untouched.

Perhaps the smell is like trees, not regimentedly planted trees on a street busy with traffic, but trees in a forest, miles from interruptions and discord. This only-one-of-its-kind scent holds a determined earthiness, a saline tint that is clean, pure, and unlike any other smell I have experienced outside of a moment like this. Untouched, uncontaminated, and unimaginably intoxicating. Hopeful.

John Paul, the day-old newborn of my niece Treacy and her husband, Dan, radiates this magnificent scent like an invisible aura. I greedily hold his small, blanket-swaddled body in Treacy's fourth floor hospital room, her husband beaming nearby, the late afternoon sun shining after the long pale winter. He is my brother Paul's first grandchild, born almost a year after his death. John Paul is perfect, like a fifteenth-century cherub painting—round, symmetrical, and cheerful.

I am not here to do anything more than drink in the relief, gratitude, and wonder of the occasion, the triumph of his health. I am here to hold a one-day-old baby boy and marvel at how perfect he smells. How miraculously perfect he is.

Even the gravitas of the pandemic and every worldly concern has stepped aside temporarily to allow the happiness its own separate space in this one small hospital room. It is one room on one maternity floor in one hospital in one COVID-weary world where exhaustion dances into ecstasy with the welcomed birth of each new miracle. You can smell the relief. As if each exhalation explodes into beaming gratitude.

I think of the bravery of shepherding in a new baby during a pandemic, how inescapably frightening it was for so many who were literally hosting double vulnerability within their bodies: conflicting information on vaccines bombarding them during pregnancy and a weighty worry over random infection from a stranger's breath when their baby was born. How brave.

But here, now, everyone is safe in this one room at this one moment. Hold the baby gently. Breathe in his scent; remember this exact feeling. Honor the preciousness.

The first time I was able to notice this smell was in 1988 when my oldest son, Weldon, was born. His birth was complicated, but I took note as soon as he was born that he smelled like nothing I had ever smelled before—salty, clean, protected, new.

When Brendan was born two years later, I eagerly took in a deep breath of his pale-pink, soft skin and felt filled with dueling emotions of power in what my body was capable of doing and overwhelming joy at what was possible for him, for his future now that he had arrived.

Three years to the day later, Colin arrived with a deliberate confidence and self-assuredness he still owns. Smelling the same as his brothers did—fresh—as if nothing ever could pollute his purity. I remember he smiled almost immediately, and I couldn't stop smiling when I held his face up to mine and took him in. Breathing in my newest son.

Each son was born in a different hospital in a different city—Dallas, South Bend, Chicago. The births were all different experiences emotionally, physically, and mentally: nothing like the five-minute scripted labors on *Call the Midwife*, in which the process of labor and delivery often moves from water breaking to baby in arms in less time than you can say, "May I have a cup of tea?"

But my own babies, my three sons, all smelled the same when they were brand new, the same way that John Paul smells today. No one told me about this wildly fresh new baby smell—not my mother or my sisters—and I wonder why. Perhaps the secret is so dear every mother wants to keep it as a surprise.

The images of the pandemic and the challenges of the past few years have made me temporarily forget that people every second of every day are born in hospitals, they get better in hospitals—and they recover, their lives are saved, transformed, renewed. The baby is healthy. The transplant went well. The chemotherapy worked. Grateful, happy people are wheeled out of the hospital with balloons in their hands, hospital staff clapping and cheering. In cancer centers, patients ring a bell for the last treatment. The families go home with tiny infants carried in car seats, bristling with anticipation.

Dedicated, brilliantly selfless people work in hospitals and health-care facilities. Physicians, nurses, volunteers, administrators, technicians, scientists, researchers, faculty, residents, and students all choose to be in a profession that they believe will save lives, improve lives, and change health outcomes—not just of single individual patients who come under their care, but for any and all patients. Gifting them a future. Like I was given.

Because of COVID they were called heroes and celebrated in parades with gifts of doughnuts and food donated by grateful neighbors and nearby restaurants, all caught on the local news. Still they struggled and worked through their own fears and sorrows, logging on for shifts that exposed their own lives to tragedy. Some sacrificed their lives for the sake of others. So many reported they felt burned out from the pandemic and the stress of managing critically ill patients who would die at a rate they had not seen or experienced. Many left their professions; they had always been heroes.

From what I saw, the guardians of every person's health are almost always cheerful, even in the ICU, even in the middle of the night—perhaps more so, because they are in the ICU in the middle of the night and they want to be good to you. They want to save you. They want to honor your existence.

This is a different hospital from the one where I was admitted to the ICU—and recovered—from that pulmonary embolism and the two other blood clots that happened after my broken ankle. That was the same hospital where my oldest son recovered from surgeries, two in the space of a few months.

John Paul was born in a different hospital from the one where the grandfather he will never know recovered from seizure episodes, a handful in as many months. This is a different hospital from the one where Paul—who never saw the moment when he would be called GrandPaul—had a stem-cell transplant earlier in his diagnosis of multiple myeloma, a different hospital from the one where we had the end-of-life meeting with his doctor, twenty-one days before he passed and where my sisters, older brother, and I tearfully hugged in the parking lot.

We wore masks that day, and everyone in the hospital wore masks that day. The family meeting area was not private; it was punctuated with the comings and goings of people in other families wearing masks—the blue paper disposable kind, the white pointed versions, the colorful homemade ones—that didn't cover their tear-soaked eyes when they trudged to the vending machines and pressed the button for potato chips. Or coffee. Or Mountain Dew.

I suspect many people on that floor in the hospital were dying of COVID; Paul was not dying of COVID, but the specifics didn't matter. Everyone, it seems, was dying that day in that hospital on that floor. Everyone who was visiting knew that was the case. Many cried at the elevator, waiting for the doors to open. There was a resignation, a sorrow permeating each breath.

The smell was an antiseptic-laden sorrow. It felt heavy and thick, the air almost stifling. Today is different.

* * *

SCENT IS A WAY OF FRAMING OUR LIVES AND OUR memories—it punctuates the years or phases we strain to remember or dare never forget. It was particularly puzzling and worrisome in the dawn of COVID's entrenchment in the world that some of the most stark symptoms were of a loss of smell because it is so deeply intertwined with how we experience the world.

Researchers from New York University's Langone Health in the departments of medicine and microbiology published in the journal *Cell* a discovery that the COVID loss of smell and taste is temporary for many, just a few weeks. But for more than 12 percent of those who had COVID-19, the loss of small persists. How long that will be the case is unclear.

At Virginia Commonwealth University, *USA Today* reported that Dr. Daniel Coelho, professor of otolaryngology, researched the loss of taste and smell during the pandemic and found up to 80 percent had these senses return a month or so after COVID subsided. For those who did not have their sense of smell revived, depression was often a result.

"Smell is a very primitive and very powerful sense," Coelho reported.

COVID stole our senses and also marks the origin of so many smells that are wrapped in collaborative and collective memory. This may be how we immortalize the pandemic for ourselves.

For me and perhaps many others, COVID memory is embedded in the smell of antibacterial wipes, hand sanitizer, your own breath inside a well-worn mask, tears in a kerchief. It is also there in the sounds of sirens and ambulances, the hymns sung at funerals, the laughter during virtual family reunions that were forbidden in person.

At a conference for Women in Medicine in April 2022 at Northwestern University's Feinberg School of Medicine, where I was invited by my friend Dr. Angira Patel to speak, a cardiologist I met confided over the lunch break that she believed COVID would last forever. It will mimic the flu, she surmised, mutating each year to a new variant, but it won't be deadly for those vaccinated. Its recurrence would require seasonal vaccines each year like the flu.

Forever is a very long time.

In the first years of the pandemic, living our lives invaded by a contagion we didn't fully understand shaped each facet of our present and future. Agencies and institutions were still arguing over the cause more than three years after the outbreak—a lab leak or human contamination from an animal source.

When we look back, what we take away will be wholly unique, informed by the moments of loss and gain, hurt and laughter. It carves its own history. The impact on each of us is unique, yet oddly similar. It is how we recover—and with whom—that will engrave its meaning and interpretations on our hearts. Few of us will be untouched; most all of us will be different.

* * *

IT IS ONE OF MY MANY VISITS TO PAUL IN THE HOSPITAL IN the months before he died. I see his smile is the same. His laugh, too. But his body is drastically reduced; he stretches his chiseled-thin frame across the hospital bed, the one on the fourteenth floor in the tower of the cancer center at the hospital that you instantly discern from the mood, tone, and disposition of nurses, doctors, and visitors is often each patient's last residence.

Paul winces when he moves a leg or tries to slide his body up higher on the bed; he moves too much—red lights and alarms ring. Nurses buzz in to check if he's OK.

"They're afraid I'm going to escape," he says dryly. We both laugh in small, contained bursts.

A nurse arrives in moments and asks if he was trying to get up. Paul asks whether the alarm can be turned off while I'm in the room with him. The nurse says no. Later we go for a walk with a nurse, who puts a pastel-striped belt around his narrow waist and holds onto him, grabbing the belt with a fist and steadying his back with her other arm. I hold his hand.

I bring him chicken vegetable soup I made the night before; I heated it to boiling before taking the twenty-five-minute drive to the hospital, and it's still warm. When I take off the plastic cover of the bowl, the coiling smell of roasted chicken broth and vegetables swirls around the plastic tray attached to his bed. Paul readies his spoon to take a sip.

He is in room 1472. The same room he was in a few weeks ago, a different room from the one he was in last July. Same floor.

There's a gorgeous grand piano at the end of the hallway, placed by the floor-to-ceiling windows outside the empty family visitor center. The slick mahogany sides of the piano look as if they are glistening with olive oil. There is a bench with books of sheet music on it; I can't see what music.

"Does anyone play?" I ask the nurse as we round the floor again on our evening walk.

"Sometimes," she says.

I think this is a nice touch and probably a gift from a foundation that secures pianos for people in cancer centers on the top floor at the end of their lives so they can enjoy some moments of beauty, calm, escape. I am thinking they should also provide funding for someone to play. It's very quiet here. The air needs melody.

When we walk past it, Paul says he remembers Mom made us all take piano lessons in the house on Jackson Avenue, on the white baby grand in the living room. We obliged, but no one was any good. The piano teacher came on Saturdays, and the lessons were back-to-back for the six of us. As the youngest, I was last. Right before lunch.

"Heart and Soul," I say to Paul.

"That's right," he says softly.

The view from his hospital room is of downtown Chicago from the south; you see the skyline and you also see the United Center to the west and the new building going up just across the street. It's pretty out tonight. He won't see the outside for a few more days. He's not well enough for a vaccine. He will never get a vaccine. He will never be well. We all know it. I don't think he believes it.

* * *

HOSPITALS, IT SEEMS TO ME, HAVE THE SAME GENERAL PHYS-ical feel about them, the same simple unpretentious angles, the same pale-tiled floors, mostly neutral-tinted or tiled walls, similar uncomfortable chairs in the rooms, stiff benches underneath windows, if you're lucky enough to have a window, that mostly peer onto parking lots or the sides of other buildings. The colors are nondescript, the wall art has a mimeographed blandness, as if the choice of art centers on trying too hard not to offend or distract. It is as if designers determined that the room itself must be so simple because what is inside is often too complicated, and it must not compete with the priorities of caring for the person within its walls. You have to leave room for all the machines and equipment employed to keep life going, to guarantee, to maintain, to document the surrender. Or to usher in the brilliance of the unwritten unknowns of the world's newest residents.

The pediatric hospitals are a bit different; the walls are deliberately cheery, painted yellow or blue or green. I have been in a few of them for my sons, who always got better and went home.

Spiked with the experiences of the last few years, hospitals have not felt solely like places that can be sources of joy. Despite the frequently sugarcoated happy endings on *Chicago Med*, *Grey's Anatomy*, *The Good Doctor*, or any of the other one-hour dips into fabricated medical realities, real-life hospitals often breed for me a restless worry.

I am going to visit someone who is injured or ill or dying. Perhaps I am headed to a hospital myself for a procedure or treatment that is terrifying no matter whether it is unexpected or expected. As a cancer survivor, I always fear cancer is coming back or already here and I just don't know it. My chest can start to pound pulling into the parking space. My father died in a hospital; my mother died in a pseudo-hospital, long-term care facility. Paul died not in a hospital but in a hospital bed in his den. Millions died in hospitals due to COVID. Many never made it to the hospital.

But today is different.

This is the first time I have been in a hospital room in more than two years and not felt anxious, fearful, grieving, or angry—not pushing down my sadness to smile and project strength or wiping tears to make room for resolve. I am not here to fight or surrender. I am not here to gather information, settle conflict, or worry about my recovery, my son's surgery, or my brother's rapid decline. I am here to meet a new baby. To marvel at his perfect face.

I read recently that smell is the only fully developed sense that a baby has in the womb; it is the most developed of all the senses until the age of ten, when vision—for those who have vision—becomes more acutely refined. I read in a Harvard University article that Dawn Goldworm, cofounder and director of 12.29, an olfactory branding company, professes that "smell and emotion are stored as one memory."

For me, memories are time-capsuled within each distinct smell—the scent becomes the vehicle to cross time and space, arriving at the flashing moments of personal history. My mother's Chanel No. 5 as she dressed for an evening out with my father. Her perfume bottles lined up on a mirrored tray with ornate gold trim and handles on her dresser—blue with silver drawer pulls. I would sneak into her room and spray a brave touch of perfume on my wrist and dream of being grown-up and loved.

My father smelled like shaving cream mixed with Aramis aftershave, and I associated that with being a respected gentleman; if I was next up after him to brush my teeth in the upstairs bathroom, the scent he left behind was clear and defined, as he was.

Downstairs the smell of bacon sizzling each morning in the electric frying pan in the kitchen; each of us headed to school feeling prepared and loved.

"You have to get your brain working with a good breakfast," my mother would pronounce, turning the slices of Oscar Mayer bacon with tongs, another copper pan on the stove filled with eggs frying, circles of orderly sustenance.

In classrooms from first grade through high school, the omnipresent smell of chalk dust—years before the smell of dry-erase marker on whiteboard was even a thought—mingles with dusty wood floors warm and worn, except for the days when the floors were freshly mopped. Then it smelled like strong detergent and bleach.

After a trip to the beach, the sand in our sandals and between our toes smelled faintly like fish, reminders of the alewives that had been dutifully raked aside to make way for the family Sundays, when a pile of beach towels held the memories until the next load of laundry was complete.

The smell of chlorine in my hair, on our sweatshirts, bathing caps in the back seat of the burgundy Lincoln convertible after a summer day spent at the pool. My older sister Mary Pat driving us back home after an afternoon, now dreaming of dinner; maybe tonight we would eat outside on the patio where rose bushes bobbing in the wind lined the wooden fence to the north.

I learned from watching my three older sisters where to spray Love's Baby Soft—behind your ears, in your hair, and on your neck—so that I smelled fresh and maybe lovable, because I wanted to be lovable. I wanted to be loved. I ranked that high on the hierarchy of life goals, below being a world-famous writer or prima ballerina, whichever came first, and above cleaning my room. Then I saw a commercial on Yves Saint Laurent's Rive Gauche, and without knowing at all how it smelled, I decided it was for me. I saved my money for months to buy myself a spray bottle at Marshall Field's. I wore it every day for years.

It's odd how the mingling of scent memories for me are both manufactured and natural, contrived as well as spontaneous. I remember the spray of Lysol and Vicks VapoRub in our bedrooms if one of us was sick; the scent of pot roast with onions in late afternoons, reminding us that dinner was soon and that our family was reliable and together, solid, each seat at the table filled each night. We were loved.

In my own house when my sons were small, I cooked and baked often on the weekends especially, hoping to fill the house with good memories of what our lives were and could be, trying to crowd out and erase what was painful. I baked apple pies, lemon bars, and triple chocolate lemon brownies, the house filled with surges of butter, vanilla, and chocolate.

I loved the smell of my young sons fresh out of their baths with gentle soap and baby shampoo, wrapping them in fluffed towels smelling like Dreft detergent, the American scent of early childhood.

Lilac trees caress both sides of my front stoop, like fragrant parentheses. For a few weeks in May, you can't enter or exit without feeling the whole embrace of their scent.

More recently, the smell of turpentine punctuates the surroundings in the yard or on the back porch from a small plastic container where I dip my brushes to thin the paint or to erase the color before moving on to paint the next swath in a scene. The sharp pungency of a freshly opened tube of oil paint or the faint residue of charcoal dust, swelling to fill the canvas with my oil painting or sketchbooks on art Saturdays, the rescues of my week.

Yellow onions burnishing to dark brown in pools of butter, before I join them in the large pot with the copper-tinted broth of beef and vegetables. The smell fills my house until I load it in the car to bring to my brother.

So many years or days ago, or so recent, near and far, yet these scent memories are still within reach. I close my eyes, and the scents fill me.

The pandemic has taught us to pay closer attention to breaths, to realize they form the regulation of our very existence. The masks we wore because of COVID protected us from the possibility of taking in rich, new smells, creating new memory collections. Inside our masks, we were reminded of our own breaths and the preciousness of each inhalation.

"I can't breathe."

The idea that an invisible contagion or a deliberate swipe of injustice forced upon someone because of racist hate could eliminate anyone at any time was ubiquitous, foreboding. COVID retaught us that breath forms our present and our presence, and they inform how we can cope with what is put before us. The uncertainties of COVID taught so many to reassign certainty to the mindfulness that we urgently need in each moment just to maintain and continue.

The past few years are blocks of time; within them are scents we learned, scents we cannot or choose not to erase. They are bundled into treasure chests within us that we can decide to open.

The memory of a newly born child who smells like the ocean air is deep within me. It mixes with feelings of hope and possibility, like the sensation you get standing in a completely empty field shifting in your smallness, grazed by infinity. It is a confirmation of newness, of a moment yet to be touched by the waterfall of experiences to come. No matter what yesterdays have transpired, this is the joyous smell of unknown tomorrows. Together breathing into the future.

May 2022

AFTERWORD

WHEN I WAS A TEENAGER, THERE WAS A STORE IN MALLS
called 5-7-9 because those were the sizes of the inexpensive,
trendy clothing it carried—jeans, tube tops, jackets, sweaters,
prom dresses with tulle and sequins, bathing suits the size of
headbands. Every price tag ended in .99, and every item was
fashionably obsolete by the next season, if not the next washing. Wasteful, disposable.

The retail stores were sold off in 1999 by the parent company, and a few still exist; I imagine the chain's disappearance
is in part due to a consciousness—and conscience—about mass-
produced clothes churned out in factories where people are
treated poorly and what they mass produce damages the planet
with their cheap fashion that is unwise and unsustainable and
mangles the landfills.

Also perhaps the original target audience is now around
my age, and many of us are in more conservative outfits sized
in double digits. Thanks to the pandemic, the way many people like me approach clothing is more about comfort and
planet-friendly fabrics, giving way to a style dubbed "Coastal
Grandmother," regardless of where you live and whether you
indeed have grandchildren.

Looking at anything—including fast fashion—in such
a tightly finite definition feels out of touch, inappropriate,

exclusionary, and inapplicable to twenty-first-century times. The impermanence feels like predetermined obsolescence.

What COVID taught me—and maybe more—is that much of life can be defined as haltingly minimizing and incomplete. Like outfits from 5-7-9.

Trying to write about life during this time also feels incomplete, like writing a eulogy for a complicated person who was at once destructive and instructive. The choice of words matters, condensing enormity into an edible cultural slice.

Attempting to discern some meaning from this confusing scoop of time, I find writing is a way of dissecting the body of truth. It is how I discovered wading pools of moments that were grief-filled, but also alternately sharp, bright escapes that were illuminating, offering up a realignment of choices, intention, and a refreshed way to be, or at least a new approach. My sincere friendships brightened. I became decisive more quickly in my partnering and de-partnering choices. I worked harder to have meaningful stretches of intense work projects: signing on to missions I believed in, lending my energy to work that was about more than money and time.

I think about death differently now; yes, in part because of COVID but also because of the pervasiveness of random violence around me in the world, my personal loss, and what I see as my own proximity to death. I imagine many do. It is a view not devoid of faith or purpose, but a distinction that death is here with us, beside us, and before us—it has been all along. Some are not afraid of death at all. Faith can be a partner and respite in that acknowledgment. I try never to devolve into the plaguing, unanswerable question of "Why me?" Because there is no logic in that explanation.

I may be inexcusably obvious, as many viewed death this way all along. I now see death as randomly imminent, possible without a moment's notice, not something you can plan for or expect to happen when you are reminded by probability that soon it will be your time. So it is best to live in the moment, aiming not to do something you will regret. There may be no space for an apology. Yes, you can plan for the future—it would be foolhardy not to—but expecting everything to happen as you envision ignores reality. No one predicted or planned for a pandemic that would change the world.

There is now.

As a cancer survivor (now twice, following a new diagnosis in the summer of 2023), my fear of dying had been very specific. The breast cancer I had in 2006 that was treated and eradicated, returned in a new spot as a new type after almost seventeen years.

It was my annual ritual every October to go in for an annual mammogram. Each year I worried this was the year when they will find a mass?

In the summer of 2023, bothered by shooting breast pain that mimicked the scar tissue expansion from my 2006 lumpectomy, I advised my general physician at my annual wellness check of my concerns and she found it palpably. Two days later I was in the radiologist's office terrified. The seven-centimeter trio of triple negative masses he did not find on a mammogram but in an ultrasound. Chemo, surgery, more chemo and radiation have me cancer-free again. Second chances. I am extraordinarily grateful.

What I learned is the cancer had been invisible until then, hidden, just as COVID was and is invisible in the air it contaminates, on the surfaces it affects, in the breaths that spread its contagion. One more mortal element out of my control. Out of anyone's control.

Listen to your body. Listen to your instincts. Listen to your breath.

What I am discovering is that view of mortality gives way not just to despair and surrender, but also to the urge to be present, to fill the moments and days thoughtfully. The resilience required to open each day with positive anticipation and the promise to be someone who lives truthfully, honestly, and intentionally. Living for good. Doing what may be seen as good for myself, my family, circle of friends, work colleagues, neighbors, communities, and for those whom I mentor and train to share their ideas with the world.

This is the time we have. This is all the time we have. It is urgent to use it wisely.

For me and possibly for many others, this intense focus on what is finite manifests from the daily COVID death tolls from your zip code and all around the world that were available to ingest along with sips of morning coffee—fat-free cream, no sugar—and the updates about the parallel pandemic of social injustice with death tolls of mass shootings and random street violence forming the background bass of daily living. This was followed by the gruesome daily visuals of an unprovoked war in Ukraine, earthquakes, the war in Gaza, weather calamities, social injustice, hate crimes and brutal crimes against humanity.

Death was there all along, but I was busy looking the other way or closing my eyes in fear.

The death of my brother Paul convinces me to be careful with every breath, not only for myself or some imagined and contrived declaration of purpose, but for the well-being of everyone around me. I must be careful with the life I have been granted and enhance the world around me, not subtract from it. I want to be more like him, always gesturing toward the hopeful; I realize I may never be.

The death of my dear friend Lisa scorches me with a conviction of the scarcity of all we are granted and that we are all adrift unless we create anchors in each other.

Trying to assign meaning to objects, talismans, memories, and beliefs is one way to fill up a life. Working to be an asset—not a liability—to family, community, and the wider world is another. Underscoring each day with measurable acts of compassion—as well as humor—as Paul did, is also a promise I make to myself.

The brief stay in the ICU forces an acute awareness of my body as a temporary vessel for a life, a shipping container placed here now and transported elsewhere without notice. It also shines blaring headlights on the way the world assigns a staggeringly cruel hierarchy to the value of lives.

Oddly, there comes with that a vibrant newness to this unimagined post-COVID or forever-COVID life, where and when you realize you do not need a permission slip to rearrange the furniture and your place in the world. The recurring reminders of an end date make the possibilities of the present feel fresh, more clearly visible, wiped clean after a storm.

* * *

HINDSIGHT SHOWS THAT COVERAGE OF THE PANDEMIC WAS at times inadequate and dismissive. Kendra Pierre-Louis outlined those failures in *Nieman Reports* in 2023. "In the process, we've failed at our field's core tenets—to hold power to account and to follow the evidence. Our failures here could last a generation. As reporters, it's our responsibility to accurately represent the needs of diverse perspectives and avoid an ableist bias that diminishes the real and lasting health concerns not only of those who are keenly at risk but those who are cautious about repeatedly catching a virus that scientists are still grappling to understand."

How each of us has endured and observed the pandemic over the last few years is fodder for research, likely for generations; the stories we tell about this particular time we have spent are worth sharing, preserving and validating, even if just to garner a modicum of hope, a glimpse into other perspectives, a chance for true recovery.

The milestone of one million deaths globally was reached in early 2022, only two years after the Dallas mayor declared the city in a state of emergency over five cases of COVID.

One million is a mighty number. Each one of those million individuals who perished had a story, dreams, regrets, and accomplishments, as well as someone or many someones whose lives they affected, who hold some aspect of their existence capsulized in a memory.

For context, one million is roughly the population of San Jose, California. It is less than the population of Dallas, more than the population of Austin. A million people live in Cologne, Germany. A million dollars will get you a Jaguar C-X75 Supercar.

Madam C. J. Walker, born Sarah Breedlove in 1867, was the first Black millionaire female entrepreneur in the United States, making her fortune in hair care products. In 1903, opera singer Enrico Caruso was the first person to sell one million record albums. Rita Moreno was the first Latina actress to win an Oscar for her role in the 1961 film *West Side Story*; the album of the movie soundtrack sold more than one million records.

One million is how many followers Ashton Kutcher earned in 2004, the first person to do so. Taylor Swift sold one million records in 2020 for her album *Folklore*. Justin Bieber logged in a million Instagram followers in 2021. James Patterson was the first author to sell more than one million ebooks.

Pew Research Center research shows the #BlackLivesMatter hashtag went from 1 million shares on May 25, 2020, when George Floyd was murdered, to more than 8.8 million shares three days later. The hashtag #StopAsianHate was the most retweeted in 2021, with more than one million retweets, most of them retweeted from a tweet by the Korean pop group BTS.

One million hours adds up to about fifteen years, less than a lifetime for those who are lucky to grow old. Putting the measurement of one million into context is dizzying.

In a virtual talk she gave for The OpEd Project in May 2023, journalist, author, entrepreneur, and creator of the podcast *Our Body Politic* Farai Chideya spoke about the need to discover and honor truth, particularly in an era of "both side-isms" and alternative facts on issues from slavery to elections and social justice: "I have this formula for what truth is: facts plus time plus perspective. To understand the scope of a global enterprise, it takes time. Sometimes you just need time to reveal the truth."

ON AN EARLY MONDAY MORNING IN MAY 2022, THE VILLAGE'S Forestry Division planted a chinquapin oak tree on the parkway in front of my house. It is narrow and lean, perhaps fifteen feet high, its lower trunk wrapped in black coiled plastic that resembles a tightly wound slinky. The tree is meant to replace the hundred-foot elm tree that died the previous fall; efficient workers cut down, dismantled, and hauled away the leafless, gray tree over a stretch of four hours. Without the benevolent shade of that enormous elm, my house is warmer, unprotected from the western-facing sun.

The Parkway Reforestation Program placed in my mail slot a typewritten list of what I need to do to care for my new tree: how often I should water and optimal "tree care practices." I will oblige.

A handful of blocks from my house, the church bells of Grace Lutheran Church ring on the hour: clear, familiar, soothing. The predictable melody is a calming chorus, reminding me of the chimes from the grandfather clock in our house growing up, the one my brothers helped my mother wind after my father passed. It was the clock in the hallway chiming every fifteen minutes as my mother waited up for me to be sure I returned home safe.

The sound is finite, reliable, and rhythmic, one clear tone for each hour to declare the time that has passed, to announce the time still ahead before the next toll rings. It has been ringing for decades, filling the airwaves with a refrain, a wordless song that is soothing and affirming. It is a song of hope I need, a reassuring cadence aligned to the heartbeats of all those who can listen. There will always be another chiming melody; whether I am here or not. I am grateful for every note.

January 2024

ACKNOWLEDGMENTS

MY SONS—WELDON, BRENDAN, AND COLIN—ARE SINCERE inspirations, and I am grateful for their support. They remind me what is genuinely important to hold dear. I forever love them for the men they have become and the ways they fill my heart and life always.

My siblings—Mary Pat (and her husband Ken), Maureen, Bill, and Madeleine (and her husband Mike)—are always present for me for whatever I may need, even if it's just to dance a little. We are closer after the loss of our dear brother Paul.

My writing group allies—Arlene Malinowski, Pamela Todd, Veronica Chapa, and Teresa Puente—keep me honest in my writing and push me to try even harder to improve, aiming for excellence in every sentence. My journalism support system—Susy Schultz, Katherine Lanpher, Deborah Douglas, and Amy Guth—are keen eyes and ears on all my queries and questions about work. I miss my beautiful, funny, brilliant friend Alicia "Lisa" Shepard, who helped me not only with my writing but with my life. I mourn her absence.

Thanks to Katie Orenstein for founding an organization that allows me to do work that I love, be a part of a mission I honor, and interact with colleagues at The OpEd Project I respect and admire—Angela Wright, Mary C. Curtis, Zeba Khan, Amanda

Crawford, Stephanie Drenka, Heidi Stevens, Njeri Mathis Rutledge, and Princella Talley.

I am remarkably lucky to call Dana Halsted my lifelong forever friend, as she so patiently warms every aspect of my life. My close friends Sue Schmidt, Lisa Lauren, Sarah White, Swati Saxena, Rebecca Dunkel, Amanda Rybka D'Anca, Lorraine Iannello, Jennefer Witter, Diane Frisch, Julie Shelgren, Deborah Hill, Carmela Corsini, and Linda Berger fill my existence with their love, honesty, and laughter. My artist friends Sherry Shanahan and Ann Marie Stephenson turn weekends into colorful excursions.

I am grateful to my editor, Marisa Emily Siegel, at Northwestern University Press, for her insights on framing the positioning of these essays and directing me with grace and precision. I know I am blessed to be able to publish my ideas and to have editorial and marketing teams dedicated to the book's success.

I welcome comments or questions at micheleweldon.com or by mail:

P.O. Box 5721
River Forest, Illinois 60305

I look forward to hearing from you.

CREDITS

Chapter 2, "Children," is adapted from Michele Weldon, "COVID-19 has made me rethink much of my life—including my parenting style," in *NBC Think*, August 30, 2020, https://www.nbcnews.com/think/opinion/covid-19-has-made-me-rethink-much-my-life-including-ncna1238289. Reprinted with permission.

Chapter 4, "Old Ladies," is adapted from Michele Weldon, "I Can't Forget Those Silver Haired Ladies on the Silver Screen," *USA Today*, December 23, 2020, https://www.usatoday.com/story/opinion/voices/2020/12/23/women-media-movies-film-age-hollywood-column/3961904001/. Reprinted with permission.

Chapter 14, "Shame," is adapted from Michele Weldon, "No Shame on You: Is Humiliation Gendered?" *Ms. Magazine*, March 21, 2021, https://msmagazine.com/2021/03/20/no-shame-on-you-is-humiliation-gendered/. Reprinted with permission.

Chapter 19, "Nicknames," is adapted from Michele Weldon, "My family has used nicknames to express love," *NBC Think*, March 13, 2021, https://www.nbcnews.com/think/opinion/my-family-has-always-used-nicknames-express-love-even-silly-ncna1259361. Reprinted with permission.

Chapter 22, "Soup," is adapted from Michele Weldon, "Not About the Soup: A Sister's Recipe for Her Brother's Last Days," *Next Avenue*, October 28, 2021, https://www.nextavenue.org/sisters-recipe-for-brothers-last-days/. Reprinted with permission.